D1462472

Microcosm

*Structural, Psychological and
Religious Evolution in Groups*

Microcosm

Structural, Psychological and Religious
Evolution in Groups

PHILIP E. SLATER

John Wiley & Sons, Inc.   **New York · London · Sydney**

Library of Congress Catalog Card Number: 66–16131
Printed in the United States of America

ISBN 0 471 79646 8

To Dori Appel Slater

Preface

This book grew out of a decade devoted to learning and helping students to learn about interpersonal relationships and group processes. It began as a paper, first written many years ago after a particularly exciting and illuminating group, then put aside for two years, revised, and put aside again. As the years went by, I accumulated a large collection of notes, tapes, transcripts, and anecdotes; some of these were related to the paper, although the transcribed examples were originally destined for a more general book to be used in teaching group process —one which would provide typical illustrations of the handling of various group problems.

When I finally came to revise the paper for publication, I discovered it had outgrown its original boundaries, and each attempt to clarify the ideas suggested by the material seemed to lead to further expansion. The process is by no means ended, and the present volume in its final form must be viewed as a very preliminary exploration, full of unanswered questions and ambiguities. My hope is that it will, nonetheless, be of use to the ever growing number of people in academic, medical, and industrial settings who are concerned with teaching and learning about groups and that the general sociologist will also find it helpful.

The book lends itself to subdivision to some degree. The more complex theoretical sections are in the later chapters, and for those primarily interested in obtaining a clinical grasp of group issues Part One can form a more or less self-contained unit. I say this with some regret, since Part Two contains most of what I feel to be the important ideas in the book. I can point out with less hesitancy, however, that Chapter 3 is written primarily for those with psychological (particularly psychoanalytic) interests and can be omitted without much loss by the more general reader.

I owe a large and complex debt to the many people who helped me construct this volume. My gratitude goes first to the students who participated in groups with me over the past decade and shared the struggles which this entailed. Nor do I mean by this to offer a condescending nod for their having unwittingly provided me with raw material for interpretations. I learned from the perceptions and insights of my students as much as from their spontaneous behavior and fantasy products.

Among my colleagues, my most overwhelming debt is to Theodore Mills. In all questions pertaining to Freud's primal horde theory and the relation between aggression and identification, I have merely expounded, elaborated, or distorted his ideas. For the rest, at every stage of the way I have been incalculably obligated to him for ideas and suggestions offered during our many conversations about groups, specific and general. Indeed, there is scarcely any thought in the entire work that I can say is not partly his, although he of course bears no responsibility for the way in which it is presented.

I would also like to acknowledge an earlier debt to Robert F. Bales, who was my chief mentor in my efforts to learn how to observe and understand groups, both in the laboratory and more "clinical" settings; and to Hugh Cabot, who introduced me to the gratifications and tribulations of teaching with groups of this kind.

This book had its genesis in the years 1958 to 1961 in a course at Harvard which is now called "Social Relations 120: Analysis of Interpersonal Behavior." It was in the staff meetings of this course that some of the ideas herein were first discussed and challenged. The staff was and is headed by Robert F. Bales, and during this period included at various times Warren G. Bennis, Richard D. Mann, Theodore M. Mills and Charles P. Whitlock. Their role in stimulating and clarifying these ideas was a profound one.

Examples from their own groups were generously contributed, in the form of tapes, transcripts, notes, and verbal reports, by Robert F. Bales, Warren G. Bennis, Richard D. Mann, Matthew B. Miles, Theodore M. Mills, and Charles P. Whitlock. The final version of the manuscript also owes much to the detailed and helpful criticisms of Theodore M. Mills, Robert A. Gordon, Richard M. Jones, Robert N. Bellah, and Dori A. Slater.

For permission to reproduce quotations from published works, grateful acknowledgment is made to the following: to Warren G. Bennis, Herbert A. Shepard, and Tavistock publications for "A Theory of Group Development"; to the Smith Ely Jelliffe Trust for *The Myth of the Birth of the Hero;* to H. Ezriel and the British Journal of Medical Psychology for "A Psycho-analytic Approach to Group Treatment"; to the Bollingen Foundation for *The Origins and History of Consciousness* (Bollingen Series XLVII) and *The Great Mother* (Bollingen Series XLII); to S. G. Phillips, Inc., for *The New Golden Bough* (copyright 1959); to the Cambridge University Press for *Prolegomena to the Study of Greek Religion;* to the Josiah Macy, Jr. Foundation for *Group Processes;* to Routledge and Kegan Paul, Ltd., and The Free Press of Glencoe for *The Moral Judgment of the Child;* to Routledge and Kegan Paul, Ltd., and W. W. Norton for *Totem and Taboo;* to The Free Press of Glencoe for *Elementary Forms of the Religious Life;* to the International Journal of Psychoanalysis for "The Scapegoat Motif in Society and its Manifestations in a Therapeutic Group"; to the William Alanson White Psychiatric Foundation for "Symbiotic Identification in Schizophrenia"; to the American-Scanadinavian Foundation for *The Prose Edda;* to the Journal Press for "The Need to Know and the Fear of Knowing"; to the International Universities Press, Inc. for *Patterns of Mothering;* to Charles C Thomas Publishing Company for *An Application of Psychoanalysis to Education;* to Alfred A. Knopf, Inc. for *Moses and Monotheism;* to the Merrill-Palmer Quarterly for "Defenses Against 'Depressive Anxiety' in Groups"; to Paul Hamlyn, Ltd. for the *Larousse Encyclopedia of Mythology;* to the Psychoanalytic Quarterly for *Thalassa;* to Basic Books, Inc. for *New Directions in Psychoanalysis;* to the Hogarth Press, Ltd. and W. W. Norton, Inc. for *New Introductory Lectures on Psychoanalysis;* to the Clarendon Press, Oxford, for *The Babylonian Epic of Creation;* to Robert N. Bellah and the American Sociological Association for "Religious Evolution"; to Yonina Talmon and the American Sociological Association for "Mate Selection in Collective Settlements"; and to Willis Kingsley Wing for *The Greek Myths* (copyright 1955 by International Authors).

The transcribing of many of the materials used as illustrations was made possible by a grant from the Clark Fund, administered by the Harvard Foundation for Advanced Study and Research, while Brandeis University underwrote expenses attendant on the preparation of the manuscript itself. I would also like to thank Mrs. Elinor Stang Lund for her help in preparing the manuscript, and Philip Kraft for making the index.

Philip E. Slater

Waltham, Massachusetts, March 1966

Contents

Microcosm

Structural, Psychological and
Religious Evolution in Groups

Introduction

One of the advantages most frequently claimed for the study of small groups is the opportunity it provides for examination of elementary societal phenomena in microcosmic form. This virtue pertains particularly to groups which last for some length of time and generate some degree of emotional involvement in the participants. Training and therapy groups fall under this heading and may profitably be studied not only because of the involvement they arouse but also because the norms of such groups support the removal of certain inhibitions which characterize formal task groups and informal social groups in everyday life.[1] While such norms do not eliminate the surface structures which are found in all natural groups, they succeed in making underlying feelings more conspicuous.

The ruminations which follow are based on observations of groups of this kind. They are not organized deductively. They do not demonstrate the applicability of a theory, nor do they advance a new one. They do not impose a very severe logic on the data, nor do they yet cling very rigorously to these data. They are more in the nature of a protracted interpretation—an attempt to order a variety of phenomena which are curious, interesting, and not fully understood.

My goal in committing these thoughts to paper, however, was only in part one of relieving the mental pressure of accumulated impressions.

---

[1] This is not to say that training and therapy groups are necessarily more "uninhibited" in the popular sense of "acting out" more, but rather that the strange eruptions, bizarre ideological alignments, and startling scapegoatings that sometimes occur in all groups are normally left unanalyzed. I have always been impressed with the wealth of anecdotes which can be elicited from the average person who encounters for the first time the notion that groups can be studied and analyzed, and with the length of time that these mysteries can be carried on an individual's "books" without any attempt at solution.

1

It has always disturbed me that many questions of legitimate scientific concern tend to exist in a kind of academic preconscious, where they are discussed orally and informally but seldom reach print, and hence are never objects of careful empirical examination. The purpose of this book is to widen the range and increase the depth of small group analysis—to suggest neglected avenues of exploration. As such it will of necessity be irritating to those looking for a more satisfactory ordering of existing concepts.

Part I deals with some of the vicissitudes of the group's orientation to its formal leader, pointing out certain parallels with the rituals and belief systems of larger social entities and speculating about the possible principles underlying these variegated social phenomena.

Part II is an attempt to generalize and extend these observations —to approach a more abstract conceptualization of these issues in group formation and development. The member-leader phenomena are placed in the larger context of changes in the nature of group bonds, and these are in turn related to existing paradigms of religious and mythological evolution. Fluctuations in the awareness of individual and group boundaries are seen as the factor common to all of these systems.

Since the viewpoint I have taken in this volume is a somewhat detached sociological one, it is perhaps necessary to point out here that the individual members of the groups described below have goals of their own which provide the motive force for much of what takes place and which are only obliquely related to the phenomena I describe.[2] Whatever unconscious fantasies and neurotic needs are present when a member enters a group of this kind, he is also striving for personal insight and knowledge of group processes, and it is these goals which presumably carry him through the difficult and frustrating events which lie ahead of him.

The illustrations which are included throughout the volume should be treated precisely as the term itself implies. They are word-pictures describing some of the phenomena which stimulated the ideas presented. As documentation they suffer from various kinds of contamination and are quite inadequate, but they should serve to give the reader a more concrete grasp of the empirical setting. For a more detailed discussion of problems associated with the examples the reader is referred to Appendix II.

Our inquiry begins with a phenomenon which is familiar to many group leaders and which I have rather dramatically called the "revolt."

[2] See Appendix I.

The term is used variously to refer to a specific event—the "ganging up" of group members in some sort of hostile attack on the assigned group leader—and to a process—the group members' growing independence of, yet identification with, the leader. As will later become clear, one might argue that every interaction between leader and member represents this process microscopically, but for the moment let us concentrate our attention on the more explicit macroscopic event, which is easily described and exhibits more visible symbols. A modal description of such an event is provided for us by Bennis and Shepard (1956):

A group member may openly express the opinion that the trainer's presence and comments are holding the group back, suggest that "as an experiment" the trainer leave the group "to see how things go without him." When the trainer is thus directly challenged, the whole atmosphere of the meeting changes. There is a sudden increase in alertness and tension. Previously, there had been much acting out of the wish that the trainer were absent, but at the same time a conviction that he was the *raison d'être* of the group's existence—that it would fall apart without him. Previously, absence of the trainer would have constituted desertion, or defeat, fulfilment of the members' worst fears as to their own inadequacy or the trainer's. But now leaving the group can have a different meaning. General agreement that the trainer should leave is rarely achieved. However, after a little further discussion it becomes clear that he is at liberty to leave, with the understanding that he wishes to be a member of the group, and will return if and when the group is willing to accept him. . . .

An interesting parallel, which throws light on the order of events in group development, is given in Freud's discussion of the myth of the primal horde. In his version:

"These many individuals eventually banded themselves together, killed [the father], and cut him in pieces. . . . They then formed the totemistic community of brothers all with equal rights and united by the totem prohibitions which were to preserve and to expiate the memory of the murder. . . ."

The event is always marked in group history as "a turning point," "the time we became a group," "when I first got involved," etc. The mounting tension, followed by sometimes uproarious euphoria, cannot be entirely explained by the surface events. It may be that the revolt represents a realization of important fantasies individuals hold in all organizations, that the emotions involved are undercurrents wherever rebellious and submissive tendencies toward existing authorities must be controlled.

(Bennis and Shepard, 1956, pp. 424–425)

As we shall see, the correspondences between the group revolt and Freud's primal horde myth are quite elaborate, suggesting the possibility that the latter reflects a systematic process rather than an historical event.[3] Before examining the revolt itself, however, we will explore the conditions and responses which normally precede it. In so doing we are not attempting to ascertain the general stages of group development, a feat which has already been skillfully performed by Bennis and Shepard (1956), Mills (1964b), and Mann (1965). The group revolt is part of a cycle which repeats itself and which takes a variety of simultaneous forms. It is focussed on the leader-member relationship and on issues associated both with the formation of groups and with their termination. It is rooted in the initial trauma created by the leader's refusal to assume a traditional, active, directive role in the group, and thus springs from a sense of deprivation and an intense ambivalence about the freedom so suddenly thrust upon the group members.

[3] My views on this matter derive from Theodore Mills, who sees the primal horde story as a metaphorical condensation of a slow and complex social-structural development, one of Freud's infrequent lapses into the kind of intellectual slothfulness discussed in Appendix II. See "A Sociological Interpretation of Freud's *Group Psychology and the Analysis of the Ego*" (1959). Mills' approach seems to me an advance over the view taken earlier by Lévi-Strauss, that the myth merely represents "l'expression permanente d'un désir de désordre, ou plutôt de contreordre" (1949, p. 610).

PART ONE

The Evolution of Independence

CHAPTER I

Deification as an Antidote to Deprivation

A commonplace occurrence in training and therapy groups is the metaphorical or derisive reference to the leader as some sort of deity. This typically arises very early in the life of the group, although it may continue in some form for a considerable period.

I.[4] Ezriel quotes the following exchange from the opening minutes of the first session of a therapy group:

F2: . . . I am inclined to agree with Dr. Ezriel. There is a slight resentment against him. I feel you [Ezriel] should have been talking to us for a little longer.

F4: I think we all agree that we have been rather left in the lurch, in the open.

M2: It may arise from the fact that Dr. Ezriel sits there and says nothing. As if we were all gathered in front of an altar.

(Ezriel, 1950, p. 65)

Note the rapid shift here from feelings of abandonment, to hostility toward the one who abandons, to deification of this abandoning one. Note also the direct relationship between the leader's silence and the religious metaphor. It is this passivity which perhaps makes "Buddha" a particularly favored designation for the leader.

The anxiety generated by the leader's passive role is acute, even in sophisticated groups where it is anticipated. Some members may have been in similar groups before, or may have undergone psychoanalysis or a comparable experience. Yet the knowledge gained in such situations fades before the fantasies aroused by a new group leader, especially when he first appears in the garb of one of those archetypal

[4] See Appendix II for a discussion of the sources and significance of examples in this volume.

autocrats, the doctor or the teacher. His violation of these fantasies is experienced as abandonment, and produces feelings of helplessness and bewilderment.

IIc. A student reported to an observer, "I feel like a mosquito trying to bite an iron ball."

IId. A student reported: "During the first several discussions I was filled with anxiety. A half hour before class my stomach would get tight and when class was over I felt very relaxed and relieved."

IIe. A member of this group said, after several meetings, that he experienced a feeling of emotional starvation every time he entered the room where the group was held. A second member reported a dream in which the group leader gave him an exam with three questions. He answered the first but had difficulty reading the second, and before he could make it out, the examination was over.[5] A few meetings later, a third member reported a dream in which he waved his arms and castigated the group for not doing its job, but when they asked him what he wanted to say he couldn't think of anything. A fourth reported a dream in which he came to the group meeting and the room was empty.

IIf. In an early meeting of another group several members reported coming to the session "empty," i.e., with "nothing particular" on their minds. They suggested holding the session out of doors, and when this movement lost impetus, began a discussion of nursery schools, of observing children through one-way mirrors, and of the difficulty of managing interaction in a group of twelve people. Several people were eating during this discussion and food was mentioned a good deal. The first meeting of this group had begun with a ten minute silence.

In a later chapter we will deal in more detail with oral manifestations in groups, but the following illustration is noteworthy in its fusion of hunger and deification.

XII. One woman had brought some chocolate, which she diffidently invited her . . . neighbor . . . to share. One man was eating a sandwich. A graduate in philosophy, who had in earlier sessions told the group he had no belief in God, and no religion, sat silent, as indeed he often did, until one of the women with a touch of acerbity in her tone, remarked that he had asked no questions. He replied, "I do not need to talk because I know that I only have to come here long enough and all my questions will be answered without my having to do anything."

I then said that I had become a kind of group deity; that the

---

[5] Among other things this is a rather beautiful representation of conscious, preconscious, and unconscious material. The first is understood, the second can scarcely be made out, and the third is utterly unavailable.

questions were directed to me as one who knew the answers without need to resort to work . . . and that the philosopher's reply indicated a disbelief in the efficacy of prayer but seemed otherwise to belie earlier statements he had made about his disbelief in God. . . . By the time I had finished speaking I felt I had committed some kind of gaffe. . . . In me a conviction began to harden that I had been guilty of blasphemy in a group of true believers.

(Bion, 1957, p. 445. Cf. also 1949b, pp. 299–300)

This process of loss and deification is described most dramatically by Bennis (1961) in a paper on "depressive anxiety" in groups. Of particular relevance to deification is the following exchange which occurred in a group whose leader was actually absent for several meetings.

III. During a skittish part of that meeting the group talked about "a sort of spontaneous fountain that will bring forth and all we have to do is sit and drink."

"I think you are referring to the rock pile."

"I think the 'rock pile' is interesting since rocks were the original god figures when people used to worship gods all the time."

"This is too deep."

" 'Rock of Ages, Rock of my Fathers.' "

(Bennis, 1961, p. 11)

Here the feeling of oral deprivation is combined with the fantasy of nurturant abundance, and a supernatural solidity and permanence is substituted for realistic loss and uncertainty. The concept of the stone deity is an ambivalent fusion, for although stone is on the one hand reliable and everlasting, unlike the elusive and forsaking leader, it is also ungiving and comfortless, just as he is, and epitomizes the loneliness and desolation the members feel in response to his lack of nurturance.

The "rock pile" response is more than a sophisticated metaphor, however, and goes to the root of all religious phenomena. It is found even at the animal level, considerably developed among primates but observable in the simplest of herd animals. Thus Brody (1956) gives the following account, drawn from Guthrie-Smith, of the behavior of baby lambs when the mother dies:

The orphaned one then stands for long intervals by the mother's body, bleating, cold, hungry. When compelled to nibble at the grass, she does not venture far, and if perchance shepherds pass near she runs to the spot where the mother lies. She continues to do so for days and weeks, always camping by the store of wool and bones at night, even when they have sunk putrefied into the ground. *Eventually the feelings originally called forth by the ewe appear to be transferred to the prominent object near which the ewe died. This "foster mother rock" then is put in the role of parent, protector and companion* (Italics mine).

(Brody, 1956, p. 95) [6]

This process is vital to an understanding of primeval religion (i.e., those forms of which modern primitive religions are highly elaborated offshoots). It bears a relatively transparent relationship, for example, to such later phenomena as ancestor worship, totemism, and the early worship of trees in Europe and stones, stone piles, or stone pillars in the Eastern Mediterranean countries. In the latter cases it is often explicit that the landmark denotes either a grave or at least the dwelling of an ancestral spirit. Neumann argues that stones "are among the oldest symbols of the Great Mother Goddess, from Cybele and the stone of Pessinus . . . to the Islamic Kaaba and the stone of the temple in Jerusalem, not to mention the *omphaloi,* the navel stones, which we find in so many parts of the world" (Neumann, 1955, p. 260).

The importance of permanence in this worship of stones is underlined by the Tsimshian myth of Stone and Elderberry Bush, who quarrel as to who will give birth first. Txämsem assists Elderberry Bush: "For that reason people do not live many years. . . . If Stone had given birth first to her child, it would not be so" (Boas, 1916, p. 62).

Jane Harrison also emphasizes the concept of permanence in early religions. She quotes Pausanias' statement that "in the olden time all the Greeks worshipped unwrought stones instead of images" and points out that the Herm was both tomb and boundary marker (a survival of which she finds in the fact that the Russian word *tchur* means both boundary and grandfather). "Into that pillar the mourner outpours, 'projects' all his sorrow for the dead protector, all his passionate hope that the ghost will protect him still." She suggests that the use of the Herm as an oracle simply extends the practice of going to the living elders for advice (Harrison, 1924, pp. 5–10).

But it is the combination of permanence and silence or motionlessness which gives the stone its religious utility and poignance. The dreaded aloneness and the fantasy devised to forfend it are fused in this symbol, for although indifferent, the stone nonetheless endureth forever.

[6] Compare the use of stone in connection with burials in our own society. For a fascinating fictional rendering of this process see Gloag (1963). Readers familiar with this novel will appreciate its relevance to many of the phenomena discussed here.

To thee, O Lord, I call; my rock, be not deaf to me, lest, if thou be silent to me, I become like those who go down to the pit.

(Psalms 28:1)

Be thou to me a rock of refuge.

(Psalms 71:3)

Totemism reflects a translation of this basic idea of "not-alone-ness" into the more symbolic and sophisticated terms of relatedness to a species, partly because of the greater salience of these kinds of objects in the environments of totemistic cultures.

That the relationship is more basic than these specific connections is argued most vigorously by Freud, who sees all religious manifestations as an effort to recapture the blissful dependency of childhood.

When a human being has himself grown up, he knows, to be sure, that he is in possession of greater strength, but his insight into the perils of life has also grown greater, and he rightly concludes that fundamentally he still remains just as helpless and unprotected as he was in his childhood, that faced by the world he is still a child. Even now, therefore, he cannot do without the protection which he enjoyed as a child. But he has long since recognized, too, that his father is a being of narrowly restricted power, and not equipped with every excellence. He therefore harks back to the mnemic image of the father whom in his childhood he so greatly overvalued. He exalts the image into a deity and makes it into something contemporary and real. The effective strength of this mnemic image and the persistence of his need for protection jointly sustain his belief in God.
(Freud, 1933, p. 163) [7]

In much of Western religion the key factor in this process is (in psychoanalytic terms) the transfer of many ego functions to the superego. One need not be strong, or intelligent, or able, or realistic—one need only be good. The world is transformed from an uncertain, chaotic, and indifferent environment in which the pathways to success, happiness, or even survival are unknown and unpredictable to one which is ordered, controlled, and planned, with simple rules (either ethical or ritual) of behavior which all can follow.[8]

In most nonwestern religions this "good behavior" approach is absent or far less marked, but the substitution of order for chaos, pre-

[7] Piaget seems to hold a similar view (1932, p. 88). We need not, of course, include Freud's patriarchal bias in our acceptance of this basic idea.

[8] We might therefore be justified in positing a "morality principle" intermediate to the pleasure and reality principles. Parental love induces the child to adopt the latter. Fear of losing this love causes regression to the morality principle. Absence of such love causes inability to abandon the pleasure principle. The aesthetic stance is a primitive form of this morality principle.

scription for ambiguity, and deity for isolation is present wherever the separateness of man from his environment is clearly perceived.[9]

From this viewpoint the oft heard accusation that the training group situation is an "artificial" one is not only absurd but ironic, for in fact it is a rather precise analogue of life itself. What differentiates training groups from "natural" task groups is their mortality, their confusion, and their leadership structure. Most groups formed to accomplish some purpose are potentially immortal, have a more or less clear goal or at least a plan of action or an agenda, and a clearly defined leadership. Training groups are born knowing they must die; they do not know, aside from some ill-formulated notions about self-understanding, growth, and knowledge of group processes, why they are there or what they are going to do; and struggle perpetually with the fact that the object whom they fantasy to be powerful and omniscient in fact does nothing, fails to protect them or tell them what to do, and hardly seems to be there at all. Is this unlifelike? Is the most persistent theme of the training group situation, the plaintive, "what are we supposed to be doing; what is the purpose and meaning of it all?" a query that is never heard outside of the esoteric confines of an unnatural "laboratory" setting? On the contrary, it issues from the central dilemma of life itself—that which human beings have always been most unable to face, taking refuge instead in collective fantasies of a planned and preordained universe, or in the artificial imperatives of a daily routine and personal or institutional obligation.

Training groups have similar difficulty in accepting the idea of an unprogrammed existence. They react with dread to the realization that nothing will happen unless they make it happen—that they are literally being left to their own devices, that there are no rules, no plan, no restraints, no explicit goals.[10] They, too, construct myths which serve to

[9] I am indebted to a student, William Bauer, for developing the connection between this line of thought and Huizinga's analysis of the pleasure derived from play. For play, religion, and indeed all of culture may be seen as an attempt to create an improved little world, ordered and manageable, intellectually imaginable, with fixed rules and a finite set of outcomes, as an escape from and an insulation against the accidental, uncertain, infinite, chaotic, ambiguous, and inexorably indifferent and insensitive character of nature. Choice seems to frighten humans, and when religious fantasies decay men employ clocks and other machines to regulate their movements.

[10] This is, of course, a highly exaggerated picture of the freedom of the situation. It is surprising how many requirements, explicitly stated goals, and structural limits can be added to the setting without altering in the slightest this feeling about it or perception of it.

deny the frightening responsibility and aloneness which this state of affairs confers upon them. These myths and individual fantasies, furthermore, tend to confirm Fromm's thesis that even a sadomasochistic relationship in which one is used, abused, and exploited is often preferred to a state of "moral aloneness" (Fromm, 1942), for they are often sinister and macabre in the extreme.

The most common, the most pervasive, the most elaborated of these myths is the notion that the entire group experience is some kind of complicated scientific experiment. This takes many forms—sometimes it is seen as a stress experiment, sometimes as a stealthy personality test, or more often simply as a laboratory study of group development —but all varieties have two themes in common: (1) that the goal of the group leader is acquisitive and inquisitive rather than didactic or therapeutic, and (2) that the situation is not under the members' control—that they are helpless pawns in an unknown and unknowable game. Every occurrence is seen as a calculated experimental intervention. A visitor is a "plant," a leader's illness is a "test," objects left behind, chairs disarranged by previous occupants of the room, external noises, disturbances, or intrusions are all "gimmicks" to "see how we would react." These interpretations are thus comparable to religious visions and other paranoid "insights."

Often conjoined with the experiment myth, but sometimes occurring independently, is the myth of Inevitable Evolution or Universal Utility: the idea that everything taking place in the group, no matter how trivial, frivolous, tedious, and repetitive it may seem, is an essential and anticipated aspect of the group's development. This myth is equivalent to religious explanations of "evil." Since group leaders usually perceive more order and meaning in the interaction than do other members, they contribute heavily to the formation of this myth.

IIb. It was the fourth meeting, and Monty was expressing some discomfort with the lack of "niches" and "limits" in the course. John agreed, saying, ". . . actually, we're—guinea pigs, kind of. We're the experiment, where we think we're discussing the situation and deciding it, and actually we're all revealing to ourselves our psychological makeup and so on and so forth, and we're putting ourselves on display, whereas in other courses it's exactly the reverse. I mean it's kind of like a science fiction story, where we think we're in control of everything and actually we're looking up to something." Monty then quoted a joke told in another course about conditioning experiments: ". . . every time the rat presses a bar the man drops in—the experimenter drops in a piece of food, and the rat goes over and presses this bar when he's hungry, and when he's filled he stops, and the man says, 'look how well I have this rat trained,' and then you look at the rat and the rat says, 'well, look how well I have *him* trained. Every time I push the bar he drops food in'" (laughter).

Note the conjunction of the religious theme ("looking up to something") and the theme of oral plenty, both arising from the anxiety produced by the lack of structure in the group situation. John effectively denies that the members are free to make what they want of the group ("we *think* we're in control . . ."). Yet in the joke about the rat we can see the first seeds of the idea (later to blossom) that they might one day turn the tables on this "experimenter."

IIg. A difficult session a few weeks after the group began was characterized by depression, inaudibility, and long silences. Unhappiness was expressed over the absence of rules of order, which serve, it was said, to keep people from getting "cut up." Experiences in tutoring children were described. It was remarked that in a similar course at another university tape recorders were used to help "make sense" out of the interaction. Someone then told of an experiment in which tape recordings of the remarks of psychotic patients were edited in such a way as to "make sense," following which they were played back to the patient. A little later Debby described a movie, *The Fly*, in which a mad scientist attempted to recompose the scattered atoms of a cat. (See this volume, pp. 207–208.) There were fantasies of observing the group from the ceiling, with the notion that perhaps more could be seen from there, or from some vantage point outside of it. Penny then confessed that a recent change in her own seating position had been a premeditated attempt to prove a theory of the group leader's about which she had read.

Three weeks later, during a difficult period surrounding the writing of a term paper, there was a long discussion of a "chance music" concert, "happenings," and other "planned-random" experiences.

Here we have examples both of obliquely stated experiment myths and of the myth of universal meaning. The desire for protection and the feeling of abandonment are reflected in the "rules of order" discussion. The regressed feeling of helplessness appears in the association to the tutoring of children. The dependent stance is beautifully depicted in the blissful passivity of the fantasy of the experimenter who "makes sense" out of psychotic utterances and feeds them back. Yet the experiment myth backfires because their helplessness makes them totally dependent on a possibly incompetent authority, who may not be able to "make sense" out of it at all and hence may leave them utterly atomized and psychotic—fragmenting not only the collectivity but individual egos. (See this volume, pp. 207 ff.) Occasionally we see a striving towards active initiative, primarily through identification with the group leader; that is, by finding some detached viewpoint similar to the leader's from which to view the proceedings. Yet along with this exaggerated magical respect for the leader's interpretive skills goes a comparable doubt about his competence (the "mad scientist"), which must be exorcised by devices such as Penny's. In the "chance music" discussion we find the same ambivalence: a desire to remove the group from authoritarian direction combined with a desire to have meaning and significance somehow emerge spontaneously and effortlessly from the proceedings without any activity, initiative, or interpretation on the part of the members.

IIb. At the end of this group members were asked on an exam to cite any group myths that had emerged during the course of the year, and to interpret their function for the group. While a great variety of "myths," fantasies, beliefs, and truths were offered in response to this question, the experiment myth was the overwhelming favorite (this was also true in three other groups, with different leaders, who took the same exam). It also seemed to have the greatest potency, for several of those who volunteered it as a myth and explained most brilliantly its motivational sources, also confessed that they still believed in it. The following are actual quotes from the responses to the exam question, consisting first of the various versions of the myths, then of some of the interpretations offered:

"This course was a large scale experiment."

"He was using us for his books as a live experiment." [11]

". . . the idea, to which I still cling, that the course was a proving ground for the young science of human relations, and that the members of the class were white rats."

"The course was an experiment in anxiety, similar to the conflicting Pavlov reflex experiments designed to make cats or white mice neurotic."

"The Department was selecting each individual's utterance from each

[11] It might be expected that knowledge of actual scientific interest in the group, such as is exhibited by this book, would increase the frequency of such fantasies, but the contrary seems to be the case. Groups conducted in laboratory observation rooms, knowing they are being observed, recorded, categorized, subjected to regular questionnaires and interviews, seem far less inclined to interpret events in this manner than those run under normal circumstances. Authorship of books on groups is often attributed to those who have written none, as part of the general tendency to aggrandize the group leader. The reader should perhaps be assured, however, that at the time this exam was given the present book was not contemplated nor was the significance of the experiment myth recognized. It was only because of a university regulation that exam books be kept a year that these data were still available when their significance was appreciated.

session and was making a composite picture of each person, lifting his utterances out of context and splicing them on one after the other."

"It helped counteract our desire not to be too helpful to one another, because we were competing for grades and the favor of the authority figure. . . ."

". . . it would . . . suggest that there were ends we weren't being told . . . responsibility is taken from the group and placed in the hands of a directing authority. . . . The fact that it remains in my mind indicates that it is not yet cleared up. . . . It is an expression of a desire for a stronger authority, for outright direction."

"Fearing the knowledge of Dr. Slater we often said we believed we were being used as an experiment, thus invalidating the possible experiment."

". . . I think it is a truthful one. . . . It provides justification for Dr. S.'s avoidance of the position of leadership and guidance that we were so accustomed to in other courses. Dr. S. must be silent for some reason. . . . It could justify Dr. S.'s strange role."

". . . an aetiological myth, providing a reason for the existence of the class, where none seemed to exist—*it seemed better to think that there was a purpose, however hostile, behind the class than to remain in a group without any limits*" (italics mine).

IIf. The day before a meeting at which the group leader was to be absent, the group discussed teaching machines, Skinner boxes, and self-teaching physics books, and the alleged ill effects of such devices on the learning and mental health of the young. When this complaint was interpreted by the group leader, they launched into a full-fledged exposition of the experiment myth, complete with white rats and all.

Some weeks later a member remarked on an examination: "that the group felt the presence of a mother was evidenced in its most pronounced fantasy, i.e., the idea that the group was an experiment controlled from above."

The experiment myth is thus a religious one. It states, "We are not alone. All of this is part of a master plan which will only be revealed to us at the end. God is testing us, but if we are good and brave and true all will be well." It says that what seems like an uncontrolled and frightening chaos to ignorant mortals is really an orderly game. It is thus identical with the notion of a universe created by a quasi-omniscient deity, either as a testing-ground to separate sheep from goats or for some other abstruse purpose.[12]

[12] The survival and hardy persistence of Judaism results in part from the timely introduction of an experiment myth. In biblical times warlike tribes who lost battles assigned the cause to the impotence of their god-of-battles. If conquered

This is not the place to engage in a comparative study of religions, because although I think that most religions (see Chapter V for the exceptions), both primitive and modern, can be shown to contain aspects of the experiment myth, such a task is beyond the scope of this work. For the moment I shall merely present as an example of a limiting case an unusual religious myth in which we can observe a kind of "return of the repressed." In this myth much of the sense of isolation, abandonment, and uncertainty against which religion is directed is retained, although an explanation for it is provided. It thus holds more firmly to that piece of reality which it seeks to overcome than perhaps any other religious myth in the world, and although it comes from a primitive society, it has a strangely modern, Kafka-like ring to it: [13]

> Once upon a time *Ndriananahary* (God) sent down to earth his son Ataokoloinona . . . to look into everything and advise on the possibility of creating living beings. . . . But, they say, it was so insufferably hot everywhere that Ataokoloinona could not live there, and plunged into the depths of the earth to find a little coolness. He never appeared again.
>
> Ndriananahary waited a long time for his son to return. Extremely uneasy . . . he sent servants to look for Ataokoloinona. They were men,

they assumed the enemy god to be more powerful and shifted some of their allegiance. The people of Israel, however, concluded that their god was not impotent but angry and bent on punishing them. This enabled them still to retain their belief in his omnipotence and to preserve their group identity intact.

[13] It need hardly be pointed out that a number of modern plays reflect the kinds of concerns we have been discussing in this section, e.g., Beckett's *Waiting for Godot* (which I have more than once heard used as a self-characterization by groups) and Pinter's *The Dumbwaiter*. Perhaps another expression of the same issue is the popularity in American films and television dramas of what I have called the "democratic pathos": the opposition of a strong, efficient, despotic, attractive, but villainous figure to either a young and powerless hero or an older, bumbling, kindly figure, with the villain being overcome only at the last moment by essentially implausible means. The villain may be a cattle baron, a captain of industry, a crime lord, a Hollywood producer, or, as in the film *Seven Days in May* (which epitomizes the theme), a military leader, but the essential conflict is the same. It is the American catharsis for ambivalence about democracy: the attractive tyrant is rejected in the end for the ineffectual, easy-going father who holds the proper values. Normally, these two images are kept sharply apart (cf. Wolfenstein and Leites, 1950), but one could easily detect a tendency toward fusion in the public image of the late President Kennedy, who while maintaining the value emphasis, nonetheless communicated certain qualities of toughness, efficiency, and invincibility that seemed to tap the more latent fantasy. This fusion may have contributed some of the intensity which characterized the grief reaction to his sudden death.

who came down to earth, and each of them went a different way to try
to find the missing person. But all their searching was fruitless. . . .

Seeing the uselessness of their efforts, men from time to time sent
one of their number to inform Ndriananahary of the failure of their
search, and to ask for fresh instructions.

Numbers of them were thus despatched to the Creator, but unluckily
not one returned to earth. They are the Dead. To this day messengers
are still sent to Heaven since Ataokoloinona has not yet been found, and
no reply from Ndriananahary has yet reached the earth, where the first
men settled down and have multiplied. They don't know what to do—
should they go on looking or should they give up? Alas, not one of the
messengers has returned to give us information on this point. And yet we
still keep sending them, and the unsuccessful search continues.

(Fauconnet, 1959, pp. 480–481)

Whereas in macrocosmic mythmaking it is the perpetual silence of
deities which must somehow be explained (or denied), in the training
group it is the more immediate and concrete silence of the group
leader. For it is this silence which activates the entire process. As soon
as the members begin fully to realize that they have no one to lean on
but each other, religious themes begin to creep into the discussion, and
tend to recur whenever the members feel particularly abandoned and
unprotected. Usually the remarks are highly tinged with sarcasm, that
traditional measuring-rod of the gap between fantasy and reality. The
group leader may be referred to as "the great stone face" (see the
previous discussion about the "rock pile"), a "brooding inscrutable
deity," a "metaphysical entity," or "The Impersonal Objective Being,"
and his interpretive function sardonically labelled "the Delphic Oracle"
or "Zeus hurling thunderbolts."

IIc. During a prolonged period of great tension and confusion several
group members one morning greeted the group leader as he entered with
a blow-by-blow narration of his preliminary rituals: ". . . now he takes
off his coat, now he starts the tape recorder, adjusts his chair . . ." etc.,
etc., concluding, as he seated himself, with the remark, ". . . and now
God's in his Heaven and all's right with the world."

Here the hostile ridicule masks an intense yearning for order and
control—a palpable pleasure was taken in this one bit of regularity
(however functionless) in the situation. There is a particularly delicious
irony in the closing remark, since all knew that although the leader's
act of settling himself in his chair might in other situations signal the
group's "coming to order," what seemed to them like utter chaos was

about to ensue, and that "God in his Heaven" would simply look on with interest.

XI. During the first meeting of a group of adolescent females with a male leader, the members reacted to the lack of structure with some anxiety. They asked the leader what he wanted of them, and when he declined to provide an agenda they decided to discuss dreams, one member wondering if the leader would "psychoanalyze" them and report his conclusions at the end of the year. Another suggested he would help them do it themselves. After some further discussion of what their "assignment" was and another vain effort to obtain direction from the leader, there were several complaints that they "weren't getting any-where." A discussion of dreams (it is entirely possible that the members knew this was a topic in which the leader had a special interest and competence) then began, but very rapidly led to the topic of religion, and whether beliefs in reincarnation or spiritualism were incompatible with a belief in God.

Toward the end of the year the question of religion again came up, again following a discussion of the leader's refusal to help. One member suggested that "maybe we're fighting for Mr. J. to give the answers to prove that we don't have any answers ourselves, but we really do!" After some discussion of the possibility of punishing the leader with a "silence strike," one girl argued that "maybe we don't want to be members of a mass; just female blobs. Maybe we want to be us; individuals; ourselves." To which another member replied, "A person can be himself and still be a part of something else. It's like being one with God." There ensued a long discussion of free will and determinism.

(Jones, 1960, pp. 31–33, 72–73)

These two religious discussions are analogous, since both involve conflict over dependency needs. The first is aroused by the initial shock of lack of structure, while the second appears when the members are taking tentative steps toward actively accepting independence.

The following example, although it contains no explicit religious references, is rather typical in its ambivalence about the freedom afforded by the leader's passive role.

IVc. In the fourth meeting of the group one girl made the following summary statement, directed to the group leader: "In the three days we've been together in the group I think everybody's loosened up a little bit, and intentionally you've deliberately—you haven't said anything at first—I think it's hard for people to—when they do speak—you start out with an artificial—or with a very academic approach and we don't know where we're going and we don't know exactly what we're trying to get at in this case—and you won't answer anything, so—we've got to do everything on our own—and just looking around at how we've come to do anything—certain people have come out, more or less leaders of the group, you've seen people—instead of addressing you, addressing members of the group in particular, raising their hands to that person, and other people at first afraid to say anything, and one by one I think almost everyone has contributed a little bit, and as we continue the group has developed a structure on its own, and I think it's almost your intention that we should be able to work on our own, so that perhaps some day if you didn't even come to class the discussion ought to run—with its own directions, and we could continue to think on our own so that perhaps (laughter) when we've left the context of the class we should be able to do the same as we've done in here on our own."

(T. M. Mills, transcript)

On one level this statement is a reasonable summary not only of what takes place in the early meetings of groups, but also of some of the explicit goals of group leaders. At the same time we detect in it a rather plaintive note ("it's hard," "you won't answer," "we've got to do everything on our own") and mixed with group pride a touch of anxious and pious resentment ("certain people have come out," "instead of addressing you"), capped with a stubborn faith ("I think it's almost your intention"). This mixture of total acceptance of the leader's wisdom and resentment of his inactivity is fused in the remarks about the group's growing independence, as if to say, "I am a faithful believer, but look what's happening here: other people are taking over. I hope you know what you're doing." This aspect of her complex statement is reminiscent of a less ambivalent voice from the distant past:

Arise, O Lord! Let not man prevail.

(*Psalms 9:19*)

Why dost thou stand afar off, O Lord?
Why dost thou hide thyself in times of trouble?

(*Psalms 10:1–2*)

Rouse thyself! Why sleepest thou, O Lord?
Awake! Do not cast us off forever!
Why dost thou hide Thy face?
Why dost thou forget our affliction and oppression?

(*Psalms 44:23–4*)

. . . their tongue struts through the earth.
Therefore the people turn and praise them.

(*Psalms 73:9–10*)

Thy foes have roared in the midst of thy holy place;
they set up their own signs for signs.

(Psalms 74:4)

Put not your trust in princes.

(Psalms 146:3)

Be still before the Lord, and wait patiently for him;
fret not yourself over him who prospers in his way.

(Psalms 37:7)

How great are thy works, O Lord!
Thy thoughts are very deep!
The dull man cannot know,
the stupid cannot understand.

(Psalms 92:5–6)

In groups, as in life, the ambiguity of the situation creates uncertainty about the relative efficacy of conformity to the imagined authoritarianism of a silent figurehead or active striving toward the successes of the world. Mixed with pious acceptance of his wishes, we find doubt as to whether he prefers docile submission or "those who help themselves."

IIe. In the first three weeks of this group, in which the group leader was generally referred to rather casually as "God," the members were very concerned with how they were doing, and how this compared with the leader's expectations. One member had the fantasy that each person was receiving a tiny grade for every remark made. Another suggested that they were really like a primal group starting from scratch, and would have to develop their own god, cosmogony, polity, etc., after the manner of *Lord of the Flies* (Golding, 1955). This led to some discussion of the group leader, after which they concluded that if they had come in at the beginning and he had not been there at all, they would still have required (*a*) an unknown, and (*b*) an authority, and would have fantasied a hidden tape recorder or one-way mirror, or that one of their number was really a spy.

In this fantasy they are simply describing in a more extreme form what has actually taken place.

Let us now summarize this early phase. We have suggested that the problems posed by death, loss, abandonment, and isolation generate religious ideas and sentiments. Dead parents become *Manes;* a dead leader becomes a hero or a god.[14] An attitude of reverence develops out

---

[14] If honored through a sufficient number of generations by a sufficiently prolific family, an ancestor may even become a god, somewhat after the fashion of a winner in a pyramid club (cf. Fustel de Coulanges, 1956, pp. 35–36).

of dependent longings and the removal of the real object. Similarly, in training groups the passive role played by the leader is experienced as a death or loss, and reverent fantasies are produced by precisely the same two factors: (1) the withdrawal of authoritarian direction, which aggravates dependency needs, and (2) the minimization of personality cues through silence, which like physical absence facilitates transference responses. Frightened by the freedom and responsibility given to them, afraid that the shadowy and passive figure cannot fulfill their childlike longing, they begin to mold from early parental images a fantasy of an omniscient and omnipotent protector, who one day will step forward and lead them out of their labyrinthine confusion or give them the key or the secret formula which will reveal the master design behind the apparent disorder and chaos. The anarchic nature of the discussions will be shown to be an essential part of this larger predetermined order, which will all be understood at the "latter day," when the group comes to an end. The "experiment" myth is the most concrete version of this belief—a perfect example of a religious cosmogony in microcosm. We are reminded of Bacon's remark regarding Solomon: ". . . for so he saith expressly, 'The glory of God is to conceal a thing, but the glory of the King is to find it out'; as if, according to the innocent play of children, the Divine Majesty took delight to hide His works, to the end to have them found out; and as if kings could not obtain a greater honour than to be God's playfellows in that game . . ." (quoted in McLuhan, 1962, p. 190).

Before considering the revolt itself let us examine a group in which the experiment myth, had it arisen, would have been unusually veridical, since the group was explicitly formed as part of a social psychological experiment. Volunteers were paid for their participation in the group and in addition to the group sessions were interviewed and tested individually for several hours. The group exemplifies rather clearly the transition from passivity and deification to a more active definition of their own role in the proceedings. (See this volume, p. 127, for a fuller description of part of this process.)

XIII. The group met four times. During the first session the discussion turned briefly to the observers behind a one-way mirror and to the group leader, of whom it was remarked that "every once in a while he interjects—sort of like God." A little later George argued that "it would defeat the purpose if we analyzed what we were saying. That's their job. We're just supposed to talk." But Patty objected that "this is supposed to be for us, too. It's not just for them." Toward the end of the session the question of luncheon arrangements arose (there was to be an afternoon session also), since Patty, who was wearing a cast, did not want to go a long distance. Henry joked about intravenous feeding, and little pellets provided by the experimenters. A few minutes later George "wondered about the significance of J. B." (the group leader). The connection with MacLeish's play was quickly made, and Henry suggested that he was "having his dialogue with the devil and god," and Jane that he was "like a god or something." A little later they discussed "testimonies," which they quickly associated to the "brainwashing" techniques of the Chinese, noting that the groups used there also had a leader.

The second and third sessions brought more expanded definitions of the role of the members, beginning as defiant expressions of flight, such as a suggestion in the second session that "we can all put our heads down on the desk and go to sleep if we want to," and a fantasy of all leaving and going to the beach in the third. (See this volume, p. 127.) But more and more they became interested in becoming closer to one another and learning about group process.

During the fourth and last meeting, when considerable attention was being paid to thoughts of separation and fantasies of reunion, the issue of what each person would take with them arose. Patty made the following statements: ". . . I know all of you, and . . . you mean something to me, that you didn't mean two Saturdays ago. But more than that we've made a thing here. See, we've made it. It wasn't here and now it's here, and we did it, and that's—and so, the trouble is, we have a responsibility to this thing we've made and I don't know whether this responsibility ends after we walk out of the door at five o'clock. . . ."

Later, amidst talk of whether they and the experimenters had learned anything she said: "But you're still treating it like it was, like what it was to begin with. You're saying, 'Here is an experiment, and you will participate and gain a lot for yourself.' But we made something more than that—more than what it was at the beginning, you see."

(R. D. Mann, transcript)

This is a reasonably definitive statement of what the revolt signifies.

CHAPTER II

The Attack on the Leader

The revolt against the leader represents the decay of the original religious fantasy. In real life the god never appears, so that the fantasy of his ultimate power and protection can be preserved indefinitely. In the training group the fantasied protector is present and visible, as well as increasingly human and fallible. The myth of the omniscient protector is thus constantly confronted with an annoying reality. This might be called the Problem of Chronic Epiphany. The living personage not only fails to protect, or solve, or give, but on the few occasions when he does speak often seems irrelevant, gauche, or schizoid.

Faced with these facts, the group member is forced back to one of two positions. He must believe either that the group leader is not omniscient but in fact incompetent or that he is indeed omniscient and is simply withholding his knowledge and guidance out of stubborn perversity. The latter view may seem self-contradictory, but it is a less shattering admission than the former and is of course reinforced whenever the group leader says anything clever or cryptic.

When this point is reached, the anger aroused by the leader's primordial deprivation of the group can be released. What is particularly compelling about the attack which follows, however, is the variety of fantasy themes associated with it: themes of group murder, of cannibalism, of orgy. Sometimes all of these appear together, sometimes one or two at a time, depending on the major area of tension existing in a specific group at a specific time. Let us therefore consider several of these themes separately, noting, however, the points of overlap.

A. The Theme of Group Murder

This notion appears in two forms. First, it appears in vague and ominous prophecies concerning the fate of the leader which sometimes

24

occur early in the life of the group. Second, it appears in the group's *post hoc* definition of the group revolt. What in prospect is presented as a polite and rational motion to conduct an experimental meeting without the leader is subsequently referred to as "the day we threw him out" or "the day we killed authority."

IIe. After the group had met for several weeks one member, Henry, suggested at the beginning of a session that he thought the group leader would "end up getting killed." He then proceeded to take a highly interpretive role for the remainder of the hour, using many of the leader's most characteristic speech mannerisms. The group members began to court Sandra, the most silent and inactive member, expressing their resentment and fear toward her but also their desire for her participation. At this point Henry said, "It almost sounds as if we were recruiting for something," and the discussion began to center around the desire for an external danger to focus their feelings of inadequacy and helplessness.

A week later Jim observed that he and other members often sat with hands clasped in a manner which resembled the leader's. It was then suggested that the function of this mannerism was to "hide a smirk." Amid much hilarity, resentment was expressed at the compulsiveness with which his title was always used in referring to him, and it was alternatively suggested that he be called solely by his last or solely by his first name. When one girl made reference to his dimpled smile, guilt set in over "knocking him off his pedestal." Paul, who was sitting twisting a scarf, was then asked jokingly if he was "getting ready to kill the king."

A week later the group was engaged in a discussion of the Twist. When asked what had stimulated the desire to dance, Laura replied, "we want to dance around in a circle with you in the middle—on a stake."

Two weeks later the group indulged in the pleasant fantasy (it was now mid-December) of having a picnic in May. First it was suggested that they eat ham—in part a sardonic reference to the killing of the "pig" in *Lord of the Flies* (an inexhaustible fountain of metaphorical references for this group). Then they gleefully decided to have a drunken party without the group leader, in the middle of which they would call him up defiantly to tell him he was being excluded. The group very quickly backed off from these fantasies, however, and expressed guilt over them.

IXb. In a short-term intensive training group the group leader was called away one day after a few meetings had been held. During his absence the group members, young business executives, set fire to his name card (each participant had such a card in front of him on the table).

(W. G. Bennis, personal communication)

Themes of deification, murder, guilt, and expiation are intermingled in the following example.

IVa. The history of this group was a rather involved one. At midyear the group changed leaders and at the same time lost one of its most active members, around whom much of the interaction of the first half-year had centered. The group had been prepared for the change in leaders, which was done in response to contingencies of academic scheduling rather than experimental curiosity, and there were occasional substitutions in both terms to ease the transition.

It was during the third week of the second term. The group had been discussing the biblical story of Joseph and his brothers during the previous session, with particular attention to the significance of the dreams, the rather passive role played by Jacob in the activities of his sons, and parallels between the story and the group. They had also made a self-conscious effort to change their usual seats, and to depart from their usual custom of using last names. The leader entered to find an empty chair standing in the center of the space around which the members were seated. There was some discussion about a paper which was being assigned, references to the former group leader, and then to some of their readings on groups—particularly the Bennis and Shepard paper on group development. There followed a long argument about differences between training and therapy groups and exactly where their own group fit in. Comparisons between the two leaders were made, and an attempt to outline their respective roles in relation to Redl's "Group Emotion and Leadership" (1942). Having suggested that their former leader was a "patriarchal sovereign" they wondered if that meant that he was outside the group. One member argued that "there was always the possibility that he would speak up and become a member of the group. Although we—we ignored him pretty much and he—ah—didn't say anything that was—he was always present physically and there was always the kind of overhanging possibility that he would speak forth and enlighten us and lead us in the right direction—even though we didn't depend upon him to do it." Another maintained that although the present leader had never been a member, the former leader had seemed so on two occasions, which were then recalled. The leaders were then compared on the frequency and intensity with which they laughed or smiled. One member mentioned having met the former leader at a concert recently, and remarked that "he looked younger and happier outside the classroom." Another member's suggestion that the present leader was "holding himself back" from laughing elicited the remark that "at times you feel as if you're conducting this at the foot of Mount Rushmore." This in turn was followed by a query as to whether the group would continue spontaneously with neither leader present. Some thought it would fall apart with "no one up there," particularly in the absence of their departed member. There was some discussion of how many would come, and of how many were absent at the present session, following which the leader wondered if those present would "erect a monument in the square, for those people who are not there."

There followed a long discussion of the missing member and whether he had left because the group had hurt him. This was interrupted by an argument over the distinction between "central person" and "leader," and how these terms should be applied to the three persons in question. Again the group leader was said to be both a member and not a member of the group, and again the effect of his hypothetical absence was discussed, this time briefly. The leader's apparent unwillingness to use his formal authority to override an interruption was for the second time mentioned, as were his metaphorical comments. The discussion then returned to the missing member.

The next session found two chairs in the square, which were referred to jocularly as "*two* monuments for the dead." There was some early discussion about retaining their new seats, and when the group leader remarked that a constant seating pattern was helpful in learning names, there was some brief talk about name changes. When this was interpreted a little later by the group leader, they again began to discuss whether or not the group would differ in his absence. One member suggested it wouldn't work now but perhaps in April, while another felt the group was no longer a group. This led to a prolonged discussion of the relevance of readings and cases, some members expressing a decreasing interest in them. One member cited: "For instance, this thing on totem and taboo— is I think a little hard to relate to our group. Maybe we shouldn't relate it to our group. Maybe we should relate our group to it or—(laughter) or not, not try to relate it to anything, but it's hard to get the connection, and hence it was hard to get interested in it." Reminiscences of past cases led to recall of the leader's first appearance in the group during the Fall Term, and one of his interpretations was mentioned as having "stuck" in the speaker's mind. A long discussion of the different effects of the two group leaders, and the role of peer leaders, followed. One girl then introduced a series of stories about radio stations which experienced mass defections of personnel and one suicide upon achieving financial solvency.

(R. F. Bales and T. M. Mills, transcript)

Note the "Mount Rushmore" remark, reminiscent of the "rock pile" and similar references; and the gloomy predictions offered at the end about the consequences of independence.

IIa. In this group the revolt was precipitous. The only hint of its advent occurred in an early session when one student remarked that the family in a case they were discussing reminded him of a "benevolent dictatorship," in which the father was "not too steady in his dictatorship and knows that they could put him out at any time, but right now they're happy with him." During the two sessions preceding the revolt the group seemed peaceful and industrious as they discussed a case dealing with a conflict between a girl and her mother over a memento of the girl's deceased father. The group leader was struck, however, by the group's preoccupation with the theme of guilt over death-wishes, which was given exaggerated emphasis relative to its tangential importance in the case.

The next session began with a discussion of the tape recorder and their concern over self-revelation. There was some fear expressed of the consequences of introspection, culminating in a denial of their ability to interpret their own behavior as a group, and an assertion that only the group leader could make such interpretations. At this point the suggestion was made that the group try, as an experiment, to operate sometime without the group leader. Immediately the activity level quickened and there was a great deal of excitement, laughter, and hostile joking. The more dependent students protested that all would disintegrate, while others concerned themselves with whether or not a new leader would emerge, and, if so, who it would be. Someone asked what the topic of discussion would be, and it was agreed that, although a case would be safest, it would most likely be the absent group leader. While elaborating on this point, one student, who had shown great preoccupation with obtaining the group leader's approval, and who had been playing a role which has been aptly called the "doctor's assistant" (Frank, et al., 1952), argued that such a topic would be more interesting than discussing a member of the group, such as himself, and was met with the suggestion that he, too, might profitably leave. The question of timing now came up. One member looked at his watch and then remarked pointedly to the group leader that there were still ten minutes left and "what are we waiting for?" Another objected, however, that the group wanted to get rid of the leader for a full hour and not just ten minutes. This was agreed, but when it came to deciding which hour, the more diffident voices began to make themselves heard, and a decision was not reached until several sessions later—perhaps not accidently after some term papers had been graded. After they had finally asked the leader to depart and he had done so, they settled into an orderly discussion (which was tape-recorded) of some assigned case material. Only twice was this interrupted to comment on the immediate situation, and then it was to observe discontentedly the lack of disagreement or even intellectual interchange. Everyone was "just patting everyone else on the back." One student later remarked semi-seriously that they all felt "guilty for having murdered our father." Amidst the ensuing laughter a girl rather earnestly remarked that "we haven't really murdered him because we can bring him back whenever we want." More laughter followed, and then an abrupt return to the case discussion. They wondered how the boy in the case had been able to improve despite lack of change in his parents' pathogenic behavior, and decided it was due to relationships with peers, especially siblings.

Note that although these comments were made in a facetious context, although the entire situation had been initially defined as an "experiment" [15] in the most polite manner possible, and although the group leader had departed of his own volition, the group was actually behaving in an expiatory fashion. Having rid themselves of their oppressor they were unable to celebrate their freedom, but instead embraced an assigned task, like "good children," and presented the leader with the tape recording. The final relinquishing of dependence is only presaged by their concluding remarks about the case.

IIa. The sessions following their solo flight, furthermore, were in part devoted to attempts to absolve themselves of responsibility for the event. They argued that the revolt was provoked, that the leader "gave us the idea way back at the beginning," and that "I heard that this happens every year." [16] Finally, opposition to psychodynamic interpretations of social relations, intense prior to the revolt, ceased dramatically at this point.

The following example shows how the theme of group murder of the leader is tied to the development of group solidarity. It may also be helpful for those concerned about the problem of contamination, which is raised in Appendix II, since there is an unusual amount of discussion of relevant theoretical materials.

IVd. A large all-male group met once a week as part of an academic course emphasizing case discussion as well as group self-analysis and assigned readings. For the first four meetings cases were assigned and

[15] As Bennis and Shepard point out, the expulsion of the leader is almost always raised in these terms. The experienced group leader who hears the words, "some day, just as an experiment, why don't we try . . ." knows long before the sentence is completed what it will be, no matter whether the tone of voice be angry, deferential, excited, or rational and disinterested. He knows it in part by the little twinge of fear that his autonomic nervous system sends him—a pale analogue of the terror that Frazer's sacred king must have experienced when one of his subjects remarked on his waning vigor. The use of the word "experiment" is interesting in view of the experiment myth described above; it expresses the desire to turn the tables on the "experimenter" and to free themselves from their dependence on him. It is the first step in the relinquishing of the experiment myth itself by translating it from a passive to an active experience. (See the discussion of the "repetition compulsion" below.)

[16] In fact, postmortems of revolt build-ups generally show a series of unconscious maneuvers on the part of the leader to ward off the event. The rumor of its annual occurrence is an interesting myth, since consummated expulsions are rare (to my knowledge there were none in the several years preceding this one). Its origin is perhaps suggested by the statement that the leader "gave us the idea way back at the beginning." The revolt is indeed tied directly to the early frustration of dependency needs by the leader, and the *fantasy* of revolt may be universal.

discussed. For the fifth meeting, however, there was no assigned content. One member opened the meeting by asking how they should spend their time, and it was suggested that the general "work question" of the group, i.e., the relative emphasis to be placed on case analysis versus self-analysis, be the agenda for the day. One member read a quotation from "our illustrious teacher," another said that "the group hasn't nearly decided, or it hasn't been decided *for* the group by Mr. Mills or those who are running the course exactly *what* we're supposed to be doing," and wondered how to devise a work scheme which would satisfy the "various needs we have." One thought they might be lectured to, another objected that they were "going along pretty well." There was a silence, followed by a discussion of the sundry problems usually raised by groups contemplating self-analysis (e.g., self-consciousness, the feeling that constant introspection will deprive them of "subject matter for analysis," the difficulty in observing while participating, etc.). One member suggested the assigned materials had been used as a way of avoiding their problems, and that their absence in this meeting was a "trauma"—that they had been "cast adrift." There was more argument about case analysis as opposed to self-analysis, but a member's question as to whether the individuals in the two camps showed any behavioral differences was met with silence.

One member now pointed out that there were more than these two alternatives open to them: they could all leave, meet another time, go to a concert. "We're just thrown in here; nobody said a damn thing what we have to do. We can do anything we want to." To this the objection was made that they had a goal of learning something about groups, and another member mentioned the final exam. This produced general laughter, much discussion, and a little scorn. Some said the exam gave the group its only reality, relating it to the rest of their lives, while their opponents called them "chicken," said the exam was unrelated to the group, and maintained that talking about it made it sound as if the group was being run by someone else and not themselves.

A member now told of a course at Harvard some friends were taking in which there was no instructor in the room at all (a good example of distortion in rumor), and the group just devoted themselves to "big brotherhood." Another commented on how subtle the group had become, in the absence of "orders," at trying to discern any "underlying hints" of what the group leader might want them to do. Still another argued against strong opposition that the group leader *was* directing them—that he had "brought us up sharply" once when they had wandered from the case material and that he himself had "felt very good" when the leader did this. A suggestion that this perception be checked by asking the group leader about it was interrupted by another member who argued that if the group leader weren't there, they would all go home, that there was a "certain symbol in him just sitting there," that he was like the conch in

Lord of the Flies in providing a sense of continuity, and that he didn't have to say much. Although perhaps at some future date they "could do without him," at present, they decided, he was a cohesive force keeping them together and in the room. One member then said the discussion reminded him of his Sunday School class in Junior High: "there was an acknowledgement that a god exists who will judge us in the last judgment, but who only speaks in certain enigmatic phrases and questions, and cannot be asked directly. Then discussion arose as to what we should do, therefore, and how we should satisfy him in the last judgment." He pointed out the importance that had been assigned to the final exam. They now began discussing the extent to which they felt they were being judged, and the fact that the group leader had all the tapes was mentioned. Finally they asked the group leader if they would be graded on their performance in meetings. He responded by pointing out that they were all "tape recorders" and referred them to his structuring remarks on the first day.

There now ensued a prolonged discussion about group goals. It was suggested by various members that a group failure was their own loss but not with regard to grades; that while they were not being judged in their discussion, if they learned nothing from it they would indeed fail individually at the end; that they could do anything they wanted—meet here with the group leader or go somewhere else—so long as they learned from the group; and that they were engaged in a "random search" trying to "hit the right combination." One member wondered how much resentment was produced by the "lack of feedback," and asked if they were mindless creatures incapable of providing for themselves, like those in *1984* and *Brave New World*. Another said he resented "being used as a research animal to be run through the Interaction Laboratory maze every Tuesday." Another said he didn't resent it if there was a "purpose in his not telling us the purpose," and suggested that "we are looking for a Christ to interpret the word to us, and our resentment is against the false prophets who take up our time speaking and don't get us any closer to it" (cf. this volume, pp. 19–21). Another countered with the suggestion that they take a book like *Totem and Taboo* (which was on the reading list) and study it together, deciding what it meant for the group and giving this collective version on the exam. This was seconded with the argument that the group had to develop its own rationality: "You can't just expect the tablets to be brought down the hill by Mr. Mills and thrown at you. You probably couldn't even read them."

The question as to whether the group was progressing "in the way the father wants" led to the conclusion that if it was not, he could in any case use it for research purposes with another group, and they should concern themselves with pleasing themselves and being "better than any other group." One member said that if they could make a go of it them-selves and get rid of the leader their self-sufficiency and the consequent reduction of anxiety would in itself signify progress. Another asked how this was to be done. There was laughter and someone suggested having a "totem meal." Another member then read aloud, from a paper by the group leader, a passage describing the "executive system" of a group, placing particular emphasis on the group's awareness of itself. They argued over whether their group did have an executive system, then over whether referring to this idea of the leader's was "leaning on him"—some saying that the idea should be treated on its merits, others saying the group should make a complete break, utilizing only its own ideas. It was noted that they kept hoping for direction, and they discussed models of organizing themselves, particularly the idea of ad hoc leadership, which one member said was how they were now operating. They wondered whether if the group leader were "in the group" things would go better, and observed that his comments were often followed by a silence, as if he were a "prophet." One member suggested giving him paper and telling him to write during the meeting, but this was pronounced unfeasible. Another declared himself unable to ignore his presence.

A member now suggested that there was a time in every group when its relation to the "alleged instructor" had to be altered by the group itself. This was first seen as an either-or situation: the "king" must "either be guillotined or not" (although someone suggested he could just leave the country)—the "benign gray eminence" must either be accepted into the group or rejected. They argued as to whether the group leader knew the direction in which the group was going, and referred to his book (Mills, 1964b). Some said that this situation was new and that the leader was in the same boat as the group, trying to figure out what direction the group would take. The "guinea pig" complaint was again voiced, but several claimed no resentment about it, one arguing that "if the boat was sinking" the leader would say something, and another finding reassurance in the idea that an experimenter wouldn't get mad at his rats "if they run the wrong way."

One member suggested taking a segment of interaction in the group and analyzing it. They briefly discussed (primarily in terms of participation rates) some notes taken by a member on an earlier meeting, but soon abandoned this when one of them said they were mired in detail. They then discussed the tactics of self-scrutiny for some time; e.g., criteria of validity, how to use concepts, etc.

A member now began to argue that the group leader should be taken into the group. Amid much laughter he announced there was "hope for him" and that he was "ready to go to work on him." He pictured the leader as a "little prince with tears in his eyes," wanting to be a member. Several members urged the speaker to "go up there and befriend him," "pat him on the back," "go ahead, go ahead." When he demurred, saying the *group* had to do it, they offered to follow him one by one. Over much ridicule and interruption he asserted that the leader's desire to be a member was prevented by the reverent, "word of God" attitude taken toward his utterances, and that if he could "get blasted" for his opinions he would join the group. The leader asked if he was saying that the person who wanted to move the group ahead must sacrifice himself. When this received little response they remarked that they had rejected the leader again, and should have "blasted him." One member now said, "let him go, I think he's gonna say something else," which produced raucous laughter and hooting. Amid mock protests that the leader's confidence was being destroyed, that he would be reduced to tears by this display, one member said, "Hey, somebody push the 'on' button."

After a bit they became serious about the desire to make the leader a group member, suggesting that first they had to "cut him down." It was objected that "you can't attack a question," but this met the retort that "you can attack his right to say it." It was then argued that it would be necessary to take away the leader's judging and grading power, which prevented him from being "one of us." They asked the leader if he would be willing to give up this prerogative, to which the leader replied by asking the relevance of this question to the person who spoke first each day. After a brief discussion of this they returned to the group leader, one member suggesting amid laughter that if he was just another group member he should be called "Millsie." The leader's comment was then revived and they recalled that he had started the first meeting and wondered why they always "stomped on" his successors in this role. Discussion of tactics for future group operation—in particular the question of what they should discuss next time—was interspersed with interpretations of this tendency to "stomp on" initiators. One member expressed satisfaction with what they had achieved in the meeting. Another tried to tie the "first speaker" question to *Totem and Taboo,* but was interrupted. They agreed that anyone who took the group leader's role got "stomped on" and then argued about whether to read and discuss Fromm's *Escape from Freedom, Totem and Taboo,* or some other book in the next session. A vote between the first two was taken, with the Freud a heavy favorite, and other suggestions were discarded. They talked more about leaving the leader alone, "cutting him out," and the tactics of "running the group ourselves." One member made a comment at the end that they had decided to "replace Mr. Mills with Mr. Freud," but another added the qualification that it was only for the next session.

The next session opened with one member having pre-empted the group leader's usual chair, and another having brought a bottle of cherry brandy. No comment was made about either of these events at first, save that one member remarked (rather prophetically) to the group leader: "Mr. Khrushchev, he has your chair." For a time they avoided their agenda, joking about whether there was anything relating to incest in the group, and about the avoidance itself. One member finally said that

if they didn't "do what we decided last week, it will be a bad president—
uh—precedent." They began to discuss *Totem and Taboo,* deciding that
the sections on ambivalence toward the king were most "relevant" and
"applicable," especially the idea of isolating dangerous persons with a
"taboo wall," and the material dealing with "what authority can and cannot
do, and what the group can do to authority." A member asked if they
were talking about the group leader and upon receiving an affirmative
answer asked, "why don't you *name* it?" One member said that their
situation was the reverse of the primitive case, in that "we want to touch
him but he won't touch us." Another denied any hostility toward the group
leader, saying he felt like a rat that had been "shoved in a cage," and was
objectively interested in seeing where he would go, where the food pellet
was. Another quoted a passage from *Totem and Taboo* saying that the
king who would not "preserve" them had to make room for one who
would. They then discussed the problems of the "brother horde"—especially
with regard to solidarity and management of both adaptive and integrative
requirements.

Someone now pointed out the two changes that had taken place in
their own setting, and another asked the brandy owner to pass it around.
They began to question the chair usurper at length, first about his motives.
Was he just "copying the book," trying to change an "aimless situation,"
providing a diversion, or a "new spark of life," or something "deeper"?
One felt that since they "had set up some kind of democratic government"
the previous week and "completely displaced" the group leader, it was
"only fitting and proper that you guys are up at the helm." Another asked
the usurper what his "outlook" was, "now that you're at the top looking
down instead of at the bottom looking up?" Someone pointed out that
the table was level and they joked about torturing and killing the group
leader. It now turned out that the chair usurpation and the brandy were
separate "plots" by two different parties with different aims, working
somewhat at cross-purposes. While the chair usurper was rather taciturn,
the brandy group let it be known that they had also planned to rearrange
the seating—somewhat differently, however—with the aim of making the
group leader more of a member. When they offered him "a drink, sir?"
the group leader wondered aloud what it was he was drinking. Amid
raucous laughter they joked about there being two bottles, but the brandy
owner very seriously assured him that they were all drinking from the
same bottle and that it was "just cherry brandy."

When the leader asked what the significance of it was, various
members pointed out that it was "red like blood," mentioned "Communion—the body and blood" (an identification to which they frequently
returned in subsequent discussions of this session), and suggested a desire
to "have the teacher violate taboos," to make him "no longer separate,
taboo," to "break with the past."

But the members of the brandy clique itself were vociferous in

denying any hostile or hidden significance to their act. They said it was
"purely social," for "friendship." They rejected the notion that the leader's
participation in drinking in class made him less distant or broke an academic
taboo. Amid laughter it was suggested that because of the special nature
of the class they could do a flamenco dance on the table and it "wouldn't
be unusual." One said he did it "as an outbreak of a very meaningful
philosophical system," that he considered himself a subject in a social
experiment designed by the group leader, that as a good student he
wanted to contribute to the validity of the experiment by eliminating
limitations and restrictions on his behavior, so that, like "rats in a cage,"
he could move about naturally and go where he felt like "within certain
limitations."

They then argued whether drinking interfered with the goals of the
group and whether the leader, by accepting a drink or by not stopping
them from leading themselves, had accepted a new role in the group.
They argued whether they were progressing, decided they had "polarized
themselves into a group at the expense of the instructor," and noted the
close correspondence of all this with Freud's theories. They wondered
if they felt guilt, and questioned each other. They wondered about the
leader's present status: could he be "functional" now? Could his suggestions be accepted? Was he really "down"? Who was the leader? Was
Totem and Taboo the new leader—a totem which kept the group from
disintegrating? One member observed that they were a group only in
this room, that "we die when we walk out that door." The chair usurper
was asked to read a passage from Redl, describing an outburst of rebellious
yelling toward a teacher, as proof that the brandy drinkers had performed
an "initiatory act" of rebellion, which they again denied. One member
noted that the leader was ignored because they were still oriented
toward the end of the table. They decided that the tense joking earlier
indicated how "emotionally charged" the situation was, although no
one seemed to feel any conscious guilt. One member said he felt better
when the group leader took the drink (at no time did the leader
in fact drink the cherry brandy), that it brought him down to their
level. Another said that by doing this he had taken the guilt on himself.
Still another argued that the leader "could take charge again" at any
moment, but he was sharply rebuked: "we decided he is *not* going
to come down the mountain and explain everything. We have to create
our own tablets. When you bring this up you show you're still dependent on the guy and don't want the group to function independently
of him." When it was objected that the group leader "still has an
assignment to give us," one member suggested doing a group paper.
Another said that the leader would have the power even if he were
absent, but that it was his presence which created ambivalence. When
the group leader asked if they meant they couldn't escape the power of
learning, they interpreted this as meaning they were rejecting learning

when they rejected him. One member objected that they were merely rejecting a passive learning model for an active one.

A member now stated that whereas at the beginning of the meeting he had thought of the leader as a nonentity, he had "suddenly just reversed completely," feeling that they could try to get along without him, but that he was "like a god" and could change things at will, regardless of what they did. Another agreed that he was "not dethroned" because of his external power. A dissident from this view was egged on to say he would refuse to write a paper if it were imposed and then was reminded amid laughter that his statement was on tape. Others took up the theme, saying the group leader seemed more "implacable" and "intractable" than before he was tested, that they hadn't deposed him but just engaged in "passive attacks" which were "ridiculous," "ineffective," and so forth, to satisfy a need for independence, but that grades and exams were the "final law," a "god-given divine power to do these things to us as long as he's alive and we're connected to him" (unlike their friends outside, who were not thus "inextricably bound"). One member wondered if they could make him give them the grades they wanted, another whether these things would affect them if the leader weren't in the room. Several people took up this theme, suggesting that they hold the rest of the meeting without him, "separating church and state" and relegating the group leader to the status of an "outside god." But then they wondered how to do it: "We can't throw him out." Amid much hubbub it was suggested that they could request him to leave, and one member observed that while this was obviously the most efficient approach, the three or four times the issue had been brought up in the group, it had been phrased in terms of the *members* leaving. A member asked what the purpose would be in "kicking him out," and was told that it would test a hypothesis. Another wondered if something wouldn't be lost by taking away what held the group together. One announced that if the group moved he would go back to his room.

They then considered the fact that the leader would have the tapes and could listen and judge, that their independent existence was a "game," since the leader had the power. Against this it was argued that the goals of the group did not involve the grade, and this led to a prolonged discussion of the relative importance of individual achievement and group learning, of exams and group discussion. They also argued over whether the group leader could be relegated to the role of an external god who would "wreak his wrath" occasionally but could otherwise be ignored, or whether they had to relate to him somehow in order to learn. They then discussed bridging the gap between group discussion and formal course content. Interspersed with this they began to comment more on their own roles—especially those of the chair usurper and the principal brandy drinker, both of whom they accused of talking less, and the former of talking like the group leader.

There now ensued a long discussion of the sources of authority. They wondered, for example, if it would inhere in any 35-to-40 year old person, even if he had no power to grade. Satisfaction was expressed with the way they had used *Totem and Taboo* throughout the meeting in relation to their own situation, rather than merely engaging in pedantic summaries, and one member noted they had created a common vocabulary. At the same time increasing dissatisfaction with the primitive society analogue was expressed. One member who had not attended the previous meeting said that the entire discussion today sounded like a rationalization for whatever had happened last time. (At one point the group leader attempted to interpret but was overridden.) Another said they alternated between trying to get down to work and trying to depose the group leader, but never succeeded at either, so that the tension still remained.

Just before the end of the session they tried to decide what to do the next time, with several conversations going at once much of the time. One suggested reading the group leader's book, another a case the leader was just distributing which was to be used as the basis for a paper due a month hence. The group leader's mention of *Lord of the Flies* (which had previously been assigned) was rejected, and his question as to whether discussing something and going through it were confused in their minds was treated with scorn. After some difficulty they decided to read a paper by Redl and discuss the problem of cooperation vs. competition in group learning.

The next session opened with a member suggesting that the group could be better structured by doing a group paper, which would generate more meaningful commitment, and the entire two hours were spent discussing the pros, cons, forms, and tactics of such a move. Some wanted to utilize their numbers to do a large research project on something outside the group, saying that they "had enough people here so we could really get together and do something potent." Others wanted to study the group itself. A few wanted to do an individual paper, and one thought they should "consult with 'God' to see if it's reasonable." They wondered whether the paper would produce cohesion or vice versa. Some wanted to "learn as a group" for the first time—to be a "producer instead of a consumer." One objected to the "communistic" quality of these plans, but when a poll was taken to see who "wanted to be a group," there were few dissenters. Although at first there were many elaborate fantasies about doing an "external" group research project, they began increasingly to talk of analyzing their own group, with particular emphasis on "studying conflict." They talked of "writing a paper about a group writing a paper," of splitting the group into observers and participants, of accepting a group grade, of how to participate and observe simultaneously. The group leader restated his original remarks the first day about the tapes being available to be listened to, and this was interpreted as reinforcement. They continued to discuss various approaches although showing increasing favor for the idea of having subgroups of observers write papers analyzing each meeting and reporting at the next.

At the next meeting one member read a summary and analysis of a five-minute segment from the fifth meeting (see above). The individuals involved were then questioned at length by the other members, as was the analyst, whose interpretations were accepted with great interest and curiosity. He expressed surprise that he was not "being stomped on" as he would have been "two weeks ago," but others pointed out that the incident was now far in the past. This was quickly altered, however, as a member pointed out that a role analyzed in the paper had just been re-enacted by its incumbent in talking about it. They continued talking about roles, leadership, solidarity, and self-awareness for the rest of the meeting.

(T. M. Mills, tape recording)

The detail presented in this example may help to place the rather typical symbolic utterances in better perspective than is possible in our more abbreviated cases. Despite the necessary condensation to which the discussion has been subjected, it also enables us to get a clearer picture of the peculiar crablike character of group locomotion. The participants move from one group issue to another and then back again, from jocular symbolism to serious worry and back again—always seeming to say the same things about the same dilemmas, and fighting the same battles with each other. But although any ten-minute segment resembles every other one in this respect, they nonetheless move steadily toward greater and greater independence, achieve consensus repeatedly, show increasing realism about their situation, and continually deepen their insight and understanding about what is going on. Gains are reinvested, and insight into several separate issues is broadened into insights that encompass the interrelationship of these issues. The former condition is exemplified early in the discussion when we find two opposing camps, one adopting a "counterdependent" stance (Bennis and Shepard, 1956) which accepts the group's autonomy but only at the price of denying that the situation has any relevance for their lives outside the group; the other accepting the reality of authority, grades, and exams, but denying the group's autonomy with regard to the conduct of its meetings. When the first group calls the second "chicken," it is projecting its own fear of even mentioning the exam (which threatens its brittle facade of independence). Only gradually is the idea of behavioral autonomy combined with recognition of their own desires for knowledge and the ultimate institutional reality of tests of this knowledge. The theme of group murder in part expresses the wish to reduce this complexity into one of its simpler components.

Perhaps even more important, however, is the fact that the group suddenly finds itself even more dramatically "on its own" than in previous sessions, "cast adrift" as one puts it. We see the usual religious images in particular richness, and one member even fantasies a superior force beyond the group leader ("those who are running the course"). When a totally leaderless group is considered, an even more compelling authority is fantasied in the ambiguous image "big brotherhood."

The insight of some members that they have replaced the leader with a bible seems to be confirmed by the slip made at the opening of the second session, when "president" is substituted for "precedent." The slip serves to remind us of an unconscious equation which is perhaps universal, for note that when we express fear that a given act will "establish a precedent" we are using language appropriate to the investiture of an individual with power, and the fear expressed is the fear of this power. There is no logical basis for assuming that any act once performed will tend automatically to reproduce itself, but the loathing for choice which characterizes human beings impels us to treat precedent as a person to whose authority we can submit, thus removing most situations from the realm of the problematic. Substituting the rule of law for the rule of man is thus only a partial process, for while we have changed effigies, the emotional responses and attitudes remain much the same.

Also of interest in this example is the lack of correlation between verbalizing or acting out a symbolic fantasy and having insight into it. While the usurpers are seen by others as possibly merely "copying" *Totem and Taboo,* so elaborate are the parallels which can be drawn between their behavior and the book, they themselves tend vehemently to reject these analogues and offer simpler explanations for their behavior. Meanwhile the principal exponent of the experiment myth continually denies feeling resentment about it, although he describes it in almost brutal terms.

The two groups of "plotters" in the second meeting reflect the poles of the group's ambivalence toward the leader, and the two "solutions" most typically offered to resolve this ambivalence. Although the gestures are stagey, manipulative, and sometimes facetious and disingenuous, they typically proceed from a serious conviction that such a "dramatic" maneuver will "get the group out of its rut" and disappointment is clearly visible when this fails to happen. In this example the recognition that ambivalence tends to survive the efforts to resolve it is explicitly verbalized.

IIc. About a month after this group began, a member reported the following dream:

"I had a dream about [the group]. Everybody in the room was dancing around on the tables. At the end of the room was an open casket. We danced around it, waving whirligigs and setting off firecrackers, but no voice came from the casket."

Here bloody celebration and desperate solicitation are fused. The sense of deprivation, passively experienced, is combined with an actively achieved triumph.

In some sense the revolt may be viewed simply as a kind of repetition-compulsion, identical in most respects to Freud's example of the child who handled the problem of separation from his mother by throwing away objects and retrieving them: "At the outset he was in a *passive* situation—he was overpowered by the experience; but, by repeating it, unpleasurable though it was, as a game, he took on an *active* part" (Freud, 1950, p. 15). Whereas the child suffers a real though temporary loss, the group experiences the permanent loss of a fantasy object, a guiding and protective authority. "Game" is simply translated into "experiment," but it is played with the original figure rather than a substitute object. The transformation of abandonment into expulsion also has a vindictive quality, as Freud suggested with respect to the child: "'All right, then, go away! I don't need you. I'm sending you away myself.'" In making this passive-to-active transition, "they abreact the strength of the impression and, as one might put it, make themselves master of the situation."

Mary Renault, in her fictional account of the Cretan bull-dancers, provides another example of the process just described. A group of enslaved dancers, led by Theseus, let loose a bull of their own accord and practice with it: "We were captives and slaves whose comings and goings were our own no longer. . . . But now we had gone to the bull in our own time, as if we were free, and it freed our hearts. Never again did we feel like helpless victims . . ." (Renault, 1958, p. 241).

IId. The revolt in this group—sudden, though mild—occurred early in November. During the preceding session there had been a rather harsh battle between Ed and Jack, ostensibly over the degree of self-revelation appropriate to their discussions (Ed taking the affirmative position), and the question of how to deal with aggression in the group was now voiced. Ed observed that those individuals were attacked who in any way tended to act as replacements for the group leader. David suggested that the purpose was to push back into the group anyone who seemed to rise above it. Andy argued that aggression always built up when the group got into "lower levels." David suggested that weakness in a leader brought it about. He and Ted discussed types of leadership, and with Andy arrived at the conclusion that a peer leader was accepted so long as he merely expressed a "temporary principle," but was rejected when he tried to generalize this leadership. Ed then asked the group leader if "we could try something on Wednesday," and meet without him. The group leader asked what the "general feeling" about this was, and Andy asked, "Why do you want to get rid of him?" Ed protested:

"I don't want to get rid of him, actually. Actually this is something rational. Not something I—ah—sat bolt upright in bed and said 'let's get him out of there.' I was just thinking while driving along in the car what might give the group a little bit more latitude—more freedom." A little later he again objected that he didn't want to "bump him off."

Ted asked how the group was constrained. Ed pointed to their difficulties with aggression, and the way in which Ted himself had been severely scapegoated a week or two before. Because of the group leader's presence, he suggested, there was "still something left over of an authoritarian image." Andy opposed the move, but David said it might be an "interesting experiment." Jack suggested extensions of the idea, such as eliminating all the girls for a day, etc. He asked if Ed felt the group leader was "holding the group back." Ted pointed to Ed's earlier desire to get the group leader to "join the group." David again referred to the proposal as a "rational scientific experiment." Carol objected that since the group leader would listen to the tape anyway it would make no difference, but others began to express more interest, and someone even suggested "giving him a whole vacation" instead of just a day.

They now began to consider some of the effects, wondering how many members would come, what they might discuss, how the tape recorder would be handled, etc. Ed asked the group leader if he had "any objections, Sir," which the leader reflected, and then repeated the question to the other members, receiving no reply.

The fact that most members had changed their usual seats during the previous session was now brought up, and the group leader asked if there was a relationship between the two. Jack said no, since Ed was in the same seat and "he's the one who introduced this—ah—new—ah— theory. No one else had anything to do with it." Ken disagreed, saying that the group was "able to stand on its own feet because everyone's sitting at the table and unified." Shirley asked if it hadn't been Ed who also suggested the seat change, but Ted said scapegoating should be avoided, that Kirk had been sitting in the back "fomenting the dethroning of leaders" and he had wanted him at the table. They now decided to make room at the table for everyone sitting against the wall, and did so.

When they were all together, Andy said "I wonder what this need is, here—I mean we're really having a revolution here." Ed remarked a little later that after a "heated experience" and a subsequent lull, "now it seems as if everyone wants to join hands again and dance around the maypole."

Once again murder, dancing, and group unity are associated, with the addition of the symbol of the maypole. This image occurs often in these groups, usually in the context of revolt or separation. In one group it was a facetious term for the ceiling microphone used for tape recording. That it is a phallic symbol seems apparent, but this does not exhaust its meaning. It would be most correct to say it is totemic, for it represents at once the magical potency of the authority figure, which the group is attempting to wrest from him, and the resulting immortality of the group. This was particularly apparent in the case of the microphone, which was a realistic symbol both of the group leader's power and control and of the group's life-after-death on tape. Joking references to the microphone as a phallus have also been made, and on one occasion it aroused the fantasy of a corpse on the gallows, as we shall see. Through all of this runs the old Frazerian (as well as Christian) idea that a leader must die that the group may live; which is perhaps a way of inducing men to relinquish their desire for personal immortality in favor of group survival, and perhaps a more primitive kind of infantile sexual thinking regarding the loss of body fluids and the gain of biological continuity (cf. Weakland, 1956).

One point which should be emphasized before leaving this theme is the importance of some sense of unanimity, however spurious, in the development of a revolt. A common prelude to revolt is a kind of attack-and-rapprochement directed at members whose loyalty to the group rebellion is viewed as problematic, usually silent members and women. Since we shall deal in a later chapter with the issue of inter-sex solidarity in the revolt, only a few examples of recruiting will be given here.

IIe. About two weeks before the principal revolt a session began with a discussion about the film, *The Mark*. Some of the girls reported giggling together during the film over incidents and remarks which had reminded them of the group. It was agreed that despite these resemblances, however, the film psychotherapist was much warmer than the group leader. Some of the boys then began to argue that the film could only really be appreciated by males, since, for example, only a male knew what it was like to be hit in the testicles. The group leader asked after a bit if the boys were saying they didn't know whether or not they could take the girls hunting. This aroused considerable anger, and the group leader was attacked for making so many cryptic interpretations. Particular annoyance was expressed at his frequent use of metaphor in recent meetings, and most of the more active members admitted feeling angry. Paul was extremely qualified in his statement, however, and Jim claimed that his feeling was not anger but anxiety. The collective hostility appeared nevertheless to be fast building up, and the group leader began to feel that a revolt was evolving, but the members seemed unable to achieve any resolution of their feelings. They talked of throwing things at the leader, raged at his coldness and distance, wondered if he was deliberately teasing them, and whether he knew what he was doing at all. Jim and Paul played a somewhat palliative role during this attack, but the girls were unanimous in their anger. Edna then asked Frank, the group's most consistently silent member, why he looked so angry. Frank then revealed an intense desire for the group to attack the leader' (he did not say how), and said that they had "missed golden opportunities" for two sessions in a row. He accused Jim and Paul of glossing over everything, whereupon Jim levelled a general attack on the silent members, and there was an interlude in which everyone seemed to be snapping at everyone else. The group leader suggested that perhaps they felt that so long as each one was accusing someone else of being Joseph they could all be Joseph (in reference to the biblical story, which they had been discussing in recent sessions). There was a kind of collective snarl in response to this, and Laura angrily walked out of the room. They returned to attacking the three silent members, who defended themselves a little before the session ended.

Frank did not attend the next session, nor did Laura return. The discussion nevertheless returned to the silent members, with whom Nancy, a moderately inactive member, now identified herself, explaining her bewilderment at the complexity of the multilevel communication in which the group seemed to engage. They discussed this for a time, and the group leader suggested that they didn't feel able to trust one another unless they were attacking the beast for the same reason. They agreed and continued, with great involvement, to attack the silent ones. The group leader asked if they regarded the latter as company stooges, and they discussed this possibility briefly. Lorna wondered if their hostility to the silent members was displaced from the group leader. During all of this the silent ones had been silent, and the active members became increasingly aware of, and amused by, their own transparent unwillingness to let the silent ones talk. This awareness did not influence their behavior, however, and they continued to express their fear, guilt, and distrust. Finally Peggy, a silent member, let loose a barrage of contemptuous criticism of the active members, and they pursued her, rather ambivalently but very earnestly, for the rest of the session, alternately asking about her feelings, remonstrating with her, and defending their own position.

This was, in fact, a turning point for Peggy, who, although she was quite variable in her output, essentially ceased to be a silent member from this meeting on, and became to other members a symbol of "progress" in the group, reporting personality changes and criticizing the group whenever it "regressed" to patterns which had existed before she became "a part of" the group.

This sequence shows the continuing preoccupation with group unity, and the inability of the members to deal with their anger at the leader until it is clear that their feelings are shared. The first doubt arises over the coquettish stance adopted by the girls vis-à-vis the group leader, and the ominous theme reflected in the film they had seen, in which a little boy who is rather too successful in his Oedipal strivings grows up with a great fear of mature women and turns to molesting little girls. The statement that only males could appreciate the film reflects (in addition to putting down the girls for their seductiveness) a similar fear that if they attack the leader (like the little boy, who hit his father in the testicles), they will not be adequate to match the sexuality of the girls, who outnumber them. (We will encounter this theme again in Chapter III). This problem is not resolved in the sessions presented, but the members do make headway in recruiting the silent ones, who, like the girls, turn out to be more militant rebels than their accusers. The problem with silent members is essentially solved the moment they speak at any length and engage in interaction. No matter how venomous or devastating their assault may be, it always seems to fall short of the active ones' fantasies about their potential destructiveness and malevolence. The silent ones, on the other hand, are so certain of rejection if they speak their thoughts that the continued interest of the other members in their diatribes is exhilarating.

The importance of the recruitment process lies not so much in the addition of members to the revolutionary party as in the achievement of an explicit recognition of a common orientation, however ambivalent, toward the leader as a group problem. Usually both sides of the ambivalence must be expressed and shared before any collective action can take place. There must be some feeling that both dependent and resentful feelings toward the leader are widespread in the group. As the members become more aware of the generality of one feeling, the other can be more freely voiced. There is a back and forth movement, extending the recognition and expression of both feelings in everwidening circles until a sufficient bulk of the group (a kind of emotional quorum) is included to enable it to act.

Our next example again shows recruiting in the context of revolt. In this case the attack is more immediate, although somewhat abortive. The success of the recruiting effort seems to outweigh the normally overwhelming damping effect of small numbers.

IIb. It was the day after Thanksgiving and only about half of the group was present. There was some desire expressed to hear the tapes made of previous sessions, to get an idea of the progress of the group through the year, and to see how much people changed. There was some feeling that because of their small numbers they would be "conspicuous" on tape. They then began to focus rather negatively on the silent members, although giving the latter very little opportunity to change their role. One did respond, however, and was encouraged and reassured by Barry. (He in fact remained active throughout the rest of the year.) Vic then wondered if the group leader made a difference to the discussion, although claiming that he himself never looked toward that end of the room. Barry mentioned the search for approval through grades. Joe then suggested an "interesting experiment" to see how important the approval issue was, namely, separating authority from its symbol (there was a desk at the head of the room near where the group leader sat) by having the group leader sit at the back of the room. Some said this would be upsetting, but a majority felt it would not. They joked about where people's eyes would go, and who would want to sit in front of him. Barry suggested they try it at their next meeting without telling the absentees, to see where they would sit. The group leader commented that perhaps this was a way of seeking revenge against the absentees, who weren't "sticking their necks out and getting them chopped off" (a phrase used earlier by Vic in relation to the silent members). Barry argued that the best discussion they had had was when the group leader had been ill and only a few had come. The group leader reflected that numbers were thus not important when he was not present. Bob noted that everyone had "brightened up" at the experiment idea but couldn't see any reason for not telling the others. Barry objected that it would no longer be an experiment. Eric suggested that the leader do it someday without telling anyone, then all would be surprised. Vic felt there were other things more important than seating patterns, and so the argument continued, becoming increasingly hypothetical as it did. Madeline said that by participating the group leader would lose the "power of authority," since he wouldn't be able to analyze, and "look through" everyone. She likened the situation to a kindergarten. Bob wondered what would happen if the leader said he wouldn't be there and simply plugged in the tape recorder. Madeline said someone would unplug it. Vic said the recorder was a symbol of authority also. They speculated on possible effects of the leader's absence and concluded that the simple friendliness desired by many would still not occur.

In the course of wondering whether people would change seats, and someone assume leadership, Vic remarked that one day when there were no seats where he usually sat, he had had to take a seat at the end, where "you feel closer to the authority, and in a little bit more important position—all eyes are on you." He compared this with his normal seat at the opposite end where "you have a whole lot of people around you."

The last comment expresses succinctly the nature of the conflict between leader-oriented and peer-oriented behavior: the difficulty of relinquishing the purely reflected glory of a dependent relation to the leader for an anonymous although secure role with an autonomous group of peers. We will return to this issue in Chapter IV. Conversely, the actual or threatened loss of members acts as a strongly inhibiting force with regard to revolt. The following example illustrates this effect.

IIg. Two weeks after the group's inception hostility toward the group leader began to be expressed more openly. The members joked about his apartness and said it was like not being there at all. At one point it was suggested that not only the leader but also the rectangular table around which they sat constituted a common possession. The group leader then asked what the function of the table might be, and they argued about whether it united them or kept them apart. Lucy maintained that in therapy groups the table was usually round. Debbie joked about all joining hands, and they wondered where the group leader would sit with a round table. Some suggested under it, others that he might be suspended from the ceiling, or that he sit revolving in the center of the table. When the ceiling was mentioned Penny looked up at it bemusedly and commented that the indentations looked like a lot of coffins. They ended with a discussion of the effects of seating position, expressing some feeling that talk was overly concentrated among those who sat directly opposite the group leader, and they talked of changing for the next session in such a way as to distribute these members more evenly.

The group leader entered the next session to find Art sitting in his chair. When he took another one along the side of the table, Art expressed dismay at the lack of response to the gesture, and hence its "meaninglessness." Elizabeth talked about dropping the course, and general concern about the group getting smaller was expressed (several members came in late). Debbie asked about the desirability of bringing visitors to the group, and there was some agreement that this would provide a substitute which would prevent the constant talk about the group leader and "fill up the hole in the table."

With the exception of an isolated remark by Julie about a week later, expressing a desire to "throw out" the group leader—a remark which was ignored by the other members—no further attacks on the group leader occurred until mid-December, in the next-to-last session before vacation. All members were present, as well as two visitors whom various members had invited. When the group leader ignored a question some anger was evinced by several members, and a discussion of his role began (see this volume, p. 116), during which the group leader was referred to scornfully as "it" and "that." The build-up dwindled quickly when Penny mentioned, "apropos of nothing," that Elizabeth would be leaving the group at the end of the term, since she was dropping out of school.

The second session after vacation began with a comparison between the group and Golding's novel, *Lord of the Flies.* This led to discussion of the "etiquette" of the group situation—what kinds of behavior would really be "out of bounds." They wondered how they would react if someone sat on the floor. They pointed out that in *Lord of the Flies* the behavior of the group had no consequences outside of the island on which they were located, but that this was not true of them (the imminence of exams was never mentioned in this discussion, although it had been the principal focus of the previous session). They talked of equality, of people operating within fixed roles, and of who might be leaders in the group (under a hypothetical condition which was never specified).

In the next session they began talking of the lack of frankness in the group, and whether this would be remedied if they were simply sitting together in a nearby snack bar. The group leader asked if they were saying that authority inhibited such frankness, and they agreed that it did. Some members then began arguing that hostility in the group was too intense to permit a critical attack on anyone, since it would be too destructive. The group leader pointed out that if the intensity of hostility inhibited frankness and if meeting alone in the snack bar might allow frankness, one might infer that the hostility was in some way associated with the group leader—that perhaps displacement of hostile feelings toward him onto other group members created an "overload" which was constraining. The reaction to this interpretation was mixed, with the negative view prevailing. Sylvia suggested the group leader was self-centered to assume they were preoccupied with him, and they wondered how much of his behavior was role-determined and how much a function of his own personality. Upon Elizabeth's reminder, however, Sylvia admitted having a dream in which she and the group leader were talking together privately. Stuart suggested that it was easier to attack the group leader than each other since he did not respond, and they turned to other attacks that had been made upon individual members, discussing these for most of the session.

During the next session Neil expressed annoyance at their constant talk of fantasies of a "one-to-one relationship" with the group leader. Margo said hers had diminished. Elizabeth asked the males whether they also had such fantasies. Paul said that he did. Neil spoke of going to talk with the group leader in his office, and was immediately accused of having achieved the very fantasy he was criticizing, especially inasmuch as he had not mentioned the visit to the group, but had "cherished" it to himself.

The next session began with a discussion of the university administration, and how "submission" on the part of students was achieved "seductively" by these authorities. Penny said she felt more positively disposed toward authority lately because of a wave of stranglings in the local area. Lucy said it was difficult to rebel against a permissive authority, especially when its values had been internalized. They then talked of child-rearing techniques, particularly punishment methods, and drifted into a discussion of the leader's impersonal style. The group leader asked what it was to which they were afraid he would respond punitively. They continued to talk of his role, and Sylvia noted that in "The Gray Book" (Stock and Thelen, 1958, which some of them had been reading, and which had become a kind of bible) it had been mentioned that styles of group leadership varied a great deal. Neil remarked that personality determined selection of style, and they again talked for some time on the relation between personality and role. They wondered whether the group leader's role had changed at all, if it would in the future, and whether, if so, this would be whimsical, manipulative, or "part of the role." The group leader remarked that they were omitting themselves from this equation, and wondered in response to what conditions a change on his part might occur. This was taken as a criticism that "nothing was happening" in the group, inspiring some resentment. Elizabeth then said that the discussion in the previous session had made her realize how much the coming examination was "getting in the way." They then moved again to the question of "etiquette" in the group, consequences of group behavior extending beyond the bounds of the group, whether the group leader would be influenced by his personal feelings, etc. They asked who was a recognized leader in the group. Margo suggested that Debbie was, whereupon Julie argued that Margo was and the discussion quickly came to a halt. The group leader remarked that all of these issues seemed to revolve around a hypothetical but unstated change in the physical or attitudinal nature of the group and wondered what this was. There was no response to this except that Lucy suggested that the discussion of leaders might be a consideration of "doing without" the group leader. Penny then started discussing the exam, and her preference for impersonality in academic situations. Julie objected that in this course they were not allowed to separate person and task.

At the end of the first term Elizabeth left school. During the second and third sessions of the second term a visitor was brought by one of the silent members. At the beginning of the second session Debbie said she felt the group was simply involved in the "same old games," and told a story of a child therapist who terminated a patient because of a similar repetitiveness. The third session began with a reconsideration of this issue and some expression of annoyance at the reappearance of the visitor. There was a long discussion of whether the group could be called a "game" or whether it was "real," and how one should define "game." Much of the content resembled the earlier "etiquette" and "person vs. role" discussions, Julie for example remarking that since grades were given in the course and since one's later career was dependent upon such grades, the group was very "real" indeed. The group leader then asked what the concrete issue was around which this rather abstract discussion seemed to be revolving. After some hesitation and visible anxiety (nail-biting and the like), they turned upon the visitor, calling him an intruder, and talked of "kicking him out." When someone suggested that they might really be talking of expelling the group leader this was quickly passed over with the comment that this also would be a good idea, whereupon they returned to the visitor and talked of taking a vote. The visitor in the meantime, looking hurt and a little frightened, accused them of "playing a game" about something "very meaningful" to him. This seemed to undermine the manic, gleeful, and rather aggressive mood that had preceded this response, and they turned to a rather abstract discussion of group involvement. Toward the end of the session the group leader interpreted a later conversation (see this volume, p. 90) as reflecting a feeling that he was keeping them apart. Penny said "good!" in a loud stage whisper, and when questioned by other members, refused to give any reasons for her response. The group seemed to become tense, joked about the increasing number of silent members and a fantasy that the group would end with all members silent and the leader talking.

The next session Penny announced that she was leaving the group and made formal arrangements to do so. Two sessions later she changed her mind and returned. These sessions and the two following were devoted primarily to Penny's role in the group and the various subgroup formations which her departure had brought into focus. The next scheduled meeting did not take place—the group leader being snowbound and the other members disbanding as this became apparent. The session following this was concerned with the reasons why no meeting had taken place. It gradually became clear that most of the members had at one time or another, either individually or collectively, come to the room, and rather quickly found some pretext for not staying. They quickly exposed their own and each other's rationalizations, and jovially flagellated themselves for seeming to require authoritarian sanction in order to meet. Neil and Sylvia then commented on their feeling of inertia about the group—that it never moved by itself or seemed to retain what was gained from the previous session, that they always felt surprise that they had to work to "crank it up" anew each time. Neil said, "every day we start with the same emptiness and have to fill it up." A little later Penny brought up the Bennis and Shepard paper (1956) mentioned above, which she had just read, as had Neil.[17] They talked of what stage they were in and of their "failure" with regard to the lost meeting. No one suggested expulsion of the leader, although Art proposed planning a meeting on a day when he would not be around. In response to a question, Dorothy, who had not come to the lost meeting, said bluntly that she would not have come anyway had she known the group leader wasn't there. Neil said, "You don't love us," and Dorothy replied, "that's right."

Two sessions later they began to discuss the Bennis and Shepard paper, particularly the section dealing with expulsion of the leader. They talked about the visitor they had attacked three weeks earlier, and whether the hostility toward him was really displaced from the leader. (Some wanted the visitor to return so they could expel him.) Art's plan for a "clandestine" meeting was mentioned again, Neil hoped for another snowstorm, while Julie wanted to walk out in the middle of the session, primarily to avoid the group leader's end-of-the-hour interpretation, which had become somewhat ritualized. No one suggested asking the leader to leave. Penny said she was afraid of hurting the group leader's feelings, while Paul felt any move toward doing without the leader would be a silly ritual. Five or ten minutes before the end of the hour Dorothy got up and walked out, and the other members discussed her and her hostility and alienation for the remaining minutes.

Although the *work* of revolt—recognition of dependency, greater frankness and consciousness of motives, greater group solidarity, and increased ability to function without the leader—is progressing throughout this series, every overt attack on the leader is immediately enervated by an actual or threatened withdrawal by some group member. The series includes all attacks made on the leader during the period, but the sense of "build-up and fizzle" is not adequately conveyed, since the example does not show the several sessions of slow and undramatic work toward group integration that preceded each of these attacks.

Several other facets of this series deserve brief mention. Once again we find a close association between changing seats and attacking the leader. More unique to this group, in its frequency, is the use of visitors as a device for handling ambivalence about revolt. On the one hand, visitors act as simple replacements at times of real or threatened member loss, and ward off the feeling of panic caused by the spectre of gradual group disintegration. On the other hand, this device reinforces the effect of member withdrawal in diluting attacks on the leader, since it introduces an unknown into the group and makes its solidarity problematic. In this group, as in others with which

[17] See Appendix II.

I am familiar, visitors were introduced into the group by members who would initially have been classified as "dependent counterpersonals," members who hoped for a special relationship with the leader, wanted him to "take charge" more, and who feared too great an intimacy with other members.

Another unusual aspect of this group is the frequent preoccupation with spatial position, particularly vertical (it recurs in a later session not included in the series): sitting above, on, under the table, or just on the floor. This reflects their intense concern with the issue of "spontaneous" action as opposed to "detached" observation, their fear of impulse, and their desire to achieve personal change through some magic formula.

The chronicity of the "etiquette" and "person-role" issues in this group is also unusual. It reaches its climax in the discussion of whether the group is a "game" or "real." The group here is confronting a sophisticated dilemma: if they consider the group leader simply as playing a role, their attack upon him will be in some sense meaningless and ritual in nature, although safe and without harmful consequences; if, on the other hand, they view his behavior as a function of his personality, then attacking him becomes dangerous and fraught with serious consequences, but thereby meaningful and courageous. We will return to this issue in our discussion of the "Sacred King" theme.

Vb. Toward the end of the year one of the males in the group suggested asking the group leader to leave. In the discussion which followed there were some mild objections that it "wouldn't make any difference," since they "tend to forget he's here." One girl thought he should stay away at least a week if "anything really definite" were going to happen. Most members nevertheless seemed willing to "go along" with the suggestion. One boy then asked why this had been brought up, and another said, "Well, I don't know. You think this is—that everybody is kind of mad at Dr. Bales or what?" Ray, who had suggested the move, said he was just curious. The problem then arose as to whether the group leader should be allowed to sit in the observation room, behind the one-way mirrors, where there were graduate student observers, and it was agreed that he should not. One member now asked, "Why do you want to throw him out?" Again, curiosity was advanced as the reason. A girl now noted that, "This isn't the first time it's been brought up by any means."

MALE: No, but this is the first time instead of going around the table asking what everyone thinks of it and would he mind leaving and if everyone is in agreement then we'll do this; this is the first time we've had any decisive action, and I just wonder why—what happened in the last session?

MALE: There has been nothing special about our recent sessions. I think Ray's experiment is still valid.

There was comment at various points about Ray's "assumption of leadership" with regard to this question. One boy, who was reminded by one of the girls that he had always been opposed to having the leader leave, said, "No, not now. Just thinking about that when I questioned Ray—perhaps I should have told you that I've been thinking the same thing myself, lately, that I was wondering if anyone else had—that I could feel this idea mounting in the last number of sessions and I was wondering why—" and later, ". . . I want him to go but I keep thinking, so what if he does, what's going to happen to us?"

A girl remarked that she didn't "consciously feel mad" at the group leader now although she had at first, to which one of the males replied that "he's already dead." Although he dodged a question as to what he had meant by this the idea appeared again later, when two of the girls were discussing the notion that the group leader had inhibited the emergence of a peer leader and one suggested that Ray had made a "bid" for such leadership in recommending the expulsion. Ray denied any such motivation, whereupon one of the girls suggested he was trying to "make the group guilty and responsible for his death rather than take the responsibility on yourself." Ray said he didn't "consider this his death, actually, maybe it is his death, I don't know."

The objection was now made that the act was like a child running away from home through resentment of authority. They questioned that the leader's absence would make them "any more individuated," and argued that "if we're really going to be people who can separate themselves and become individuals we should be able to do so with Dr. Bales still here." This was dismissed as mere faintheartedness. One of the girls then asked the group leader if his feelings weren't "a little hurt by all this," and after some attempt to deflect this question as irrelevant, he responded to a solid feminine phalanx by admitting that it was "an odd feeling"—to the dismay of one boy who "never thought you'd take it that way."

The majority now concentrated its attention on the two members who seemed to object to the expulsion. One, Shirley, said it would serve no purpose and would make her feel guilty. They objected that she had been "very aggressive" toward the group leader, and had reacted to an earlier, unsolicited absence of the group leader as paternal abandonment, thus demonstrating that the expulsion would "make a difference." The male objector argued that it would simply be a diversion, but one girl opposed him on the grounds that "if Dr. Bales isn't the cause of it, who is?" And later, "he makes me so mad that I would like to throw something at him. You say something in a joking way and he—I have a feeling that he can see into all my motives."

They now confronted the problem of how to let the leader know when to return, since there was some feeling that an absence of more than one session would be desirable. This resolved, someone realized that the group leader had not yet indicated whether in fact he would leave. Ray refused to be the one to ask, on the grounds that the responsibility should be shared. All announced together their willingness to do so, and one of the girls asked if the group leader would leave for the next session, to which he agreed.

During the first of the two sessions in which they met alone they decided to discuss—after a period of preliminary frolicking (see this volume, pp. 118–119)—some previously distributed excerpts from *The Golden Bough,* including the opening and closing passages concerning the Sacred Grove of Diana at Aricia, the quotation from the *Aeneid,* and the material on Dionysus from Book IV. Early in the conversation one boy asked, with regard to the struggle for the priesthood, "I don't see why anyone would want to kill him, frankly. . . . who would want to be head-priest?" In reply one girl asked, "Who wants to be leader?" Later it was suggested that Aeneas' visiting of his dead father with the golden bough was a "symbolic killing" and a "triumphal visit," since "his father is out of the way and he is coming down with the branch in his hand." Another girl said, "I had the impression that his father would tell him something." A boy referred to the incident as "lording it over his father," a girl as "getting strength to go on, and getting authorization and permission and help . . . from the father-figure, the authority—" at which point the relevance to the immediate situation became manifest and amid laughter one of the girls asked where the golden bough was.

They now began gradually to shift to Dionysus, sibling rivalry, and the similarities between the Dionysian and Christian traditions with regard to the killing, eating, and annual resurrection of the god. One girl pointed out that in Christianity the eternal cycle of killing and retribution, exemplified by the priest at Nemi who kills the former priest to win the post and is killed when he himself can no longer defend it, is brought to an end, since the murder is forgiven. Another objected that "that's the worst retribution there could be as far as I'm concerned." They then discussed to what extent the sacrifice rituals were an expiation of guilt. One boy suggested that since gods and animals were at one time identified, the sacrifice fused appeasement and hostility towards the god. "The people feel inferior to the gods." They then began a long discussion of orgies and "guilt-ridden" religious sects, following which they returned to the priest at Nemi, asking, "What would compel a person to want to be King of the Wood?" Guilt and homicidal tendencies were suggested, then they wondered if there might be other rewards attendant upon the position. Diana, as the "virgin mother" was mentioned briefly, and someone asked if they were going to invite the group leader to return next time. They now expressed gratification at their performance, suggesting that they "did better without him," "worked a little harder," "made a lot of progress," and finally agreed to spend another session alone.

(R. F. Bales, transcript)

This example illustrates most of the usual themes which occur in a group revolt. Particularly striking is the consistency with which the two contrary definitions of the event are juxtaposed: the rational, experimental curiosity and desire to test their level of independence on the one hand; and on the other, anger and revenge, fantasies of murder, guilt, and expiation. What is one moment discussed as if it were a respectful request is at another referred to as "throwing him out." This is typical, and both definitions of the situation are accurate and genuinely felt.

Note also the references to past consideration of the question, and the sense of the idea "mounting" in the group over time. In no other situation can the difference between an individual and a collective impulse be so closely observed. The suggestion may be made countless times in countless forms, and the members may even take a poll, as was reported here, but until some point of readiness is reached it is not heard, or not felt, or not relevant, or purely academic, until suddenly it is mentioned and essentially agreed on without any discussion at all. Prior to this point a single verbalized dissent will scotch it, while after it is reached several vocal dissenters will be unable to offset the illusion of unanimity. The sense of mounting readiness is, of course, the growth of group solidarity and independence. This is the true revolt, the expulsion being merely a ritual expression, testing, and consolidation of it. The phrase "he's already dead" expresses this fact that independence and secularization of the leader have already been achieved.

The use of the word "experiment" and the argument over responsibility are by now familiar to us, as are the anxieties over what is going to happen, and the veridical feeling that the group leader's presence inhibits the emergence of a peer leader. Also interesting is the notion (stated negatively) that the expulsion of the leader might be related in some way to establishing separate identities, a problem we will encounter again in Chapter V.

Since the group had *already* met once without the leader, the "curiosity" explanation for the move is not entirely rational, yet one should not for this reason regard it altogether as a mask for a hostile act. One of the aims of the revolt is the achievement of the collective act of expulsion itself. The curiosity over their performance is not a curiosity over "how we will make out alone" (which they already know), but rather a curiosity over their ability to perform after having of their own volition committed themselves to the expulsion. This curiosity contains both a magical hope that having so acted they will miraculously become united and productive, and a superstitious fear that having acted independently and aggressively they will promptly disintegrate ("what's going to happen to us?").

The discussion of *The Golden Bough* echoes these concerns, focusing primarily on questions of guilt and the motivation for succession. A specific preoccupation is legitimation: how to derive one's peer leadership from the authority of the departed group leader. The fantasy that Aeneas' father "would tell him something" (aside from being correct) expresses not only a dependent wish for the absent leader, but also a wish for his certification of a replacement, for a "golden bough." The basic dilemma of succession is always that the peer leader should be the group leader's victorious slayer, yet guiltless, and also imbued with his *mana*.

Themes of cannibalistic incorporation, to which we shall return in a later section, and of putting an end to the cycle of replacement, a notion prominent in Freud's primal horde theory, are also apparent. The amusing idea that hostility toward the gods derives from feeling inferior to them underlines the desire to acquire the group leader's interpretive skills.

B. The Theme of Autotomy

Closely related to the theme of group murder is the theme of autotomy: the separation of a part of an organism from the whole in the service of tension reduction ("if thine eye offend thee, pluck it out"). The group leader is a source of irritation and anxiety to the group and his removal is sought simply to preserve the group from being overwhelmed with disturbing and disruptive tension.[18] At one

[18] Many suicides, especially those of psychopaths, may usefully be viewed as a kind of autotomy carried to its logical extreme. It is precisely those types of individuals to whom the guilt or turning-against-the-self model seems least applicable who are most notoriously unable to tolerate any kind of tension state, pleasurable or unpleasurable, for any length of time without motor discharge. Just as all people seek refuge from the day's stimuli in sleep, so the psychopath seeks refuge from overpowering internal stimuli (usually intense dependency needs, which he is least adept at managing) in prolonged sleep. A lethal quantity of sleeping pills is less an instrumental means of permanently ending one's life than

level many of the events in the group can be regarded as alternative approaches to dealing with a chronic irritant. "Confronted with a person who is not under its control and persists in upsetting the proceedings," [19] the group members can either try to make the leader one of them or get rid of him altogether. Typically both are attempted before the group achieves enough stability and tolerance for ambiguity to accept the group leader's "half-in-half-out" relation to the group.

Now although in very primitive organisms autotomy may be used to refer to a general disintegration, in more advanced species one usually has in mind the extrusion of a specialized organ. In such a case one must always examine the possibility that the autotomy and the prior specialization are not merely coincidental—that in fact the development of a specialized organ is in the service of ridding the organism of that which the specialized organ represents. Thus Ferenczi argues that the efficiency of the organs of the body is increased "when it becomes possible continuously to turn aside sexual excitations from them and to store these up in a special reservoir from which they are periodically tapped. If there were no such separation of pleasure activities, the eye would be absorbed in erotic looking, the mouth would be exclusively utilized as an oral-erotic instrument, instead of being employed in necessary self-preservative activities," and so on. "By ridding the organism of sexual cravings and concentrating these in the genital, the level of efficiency of the organism is definitely raised" (Ferenczi, 1928, p. 16). He sees genital discharge as a kind of vestigial autotomy.

All of this has considerable relevance for groups, whatever its validity as a "bioanalytic" generalization, and we shall return later to the question of "genital specialization" at the group level. For the present let us simply note that groups have a pronounced tendency to select specific individuals to represent or even act out particular emotional constellations in which all group members actually share. Students of family interaction have been most sensitive to this phenomenon in recent years (cf. Bell and Vogel, 1960, pp. 382 ff., 573 ff., 595 ff.). Any affect which threatens to disorganize the group is the

it is an index of the amount of tension one is experiencing. If one pill cures a little tension, fifty pills cures a lot of tension. To say that a psychopath wishes to die is to attribute to him the very foresight which he by definition lacks. He wishes he were dead only in the sense that a seasick voyager wishes it, but he acts to relieve his distress without regard for the consequences.

[19] For some of these thoughts on alternative approaches to the "irritant" I am indebted to one of my students, Evan R. Wolarsky.

best candidate for such a resolution, and if the affect is too intense, specialization will be followed by a more complete form of autotomy. Just as the family extrudes the sick member into the mental hospital, so the group extrudes its leader, loaded with the collected hostility of all the members. It is, of course, only a temporary solution, since new tensions will accumulate. The sick family member must then be brought back into the family, and the leader back into the group.

In the training group situation anger is the most disorganizing affect, and what we are discussing is therefore the mechanism of scapegoating. The Greek townspeople who loaded their *pharmacos* with the sins of the community and then killed him or drove him out were practicing autotomy as surely as does the lizard. When it is the group leader who serves this purpose, however, the term is somewhat misleading, since there is little displacement involved; the leader actually arouses much of the hostile affect which is directed toward him. It is he who deprives, confuses, disrupts, and makes demands on the group, and hence an attack on him has very different consequences than an attack on some hapless substitute.[20]

Paradoxically, the expulsion of the leader is often delayed by group members on the grounds that the leader controls the hostility in the group, and that if he were not present some horrendous free-for-all would ensue. "He keeps us from killing each other" is a phrase often heard in this connection, although it is sometimes countered by the skeptical retort that, on the contrary, the leader would sit placidly by amidst the bloodiest carnage.

IIe. During such a discussion, some weeks prior to a revolt, the group leader was compared to the naval officer in *Lord of the Flies*, who arrives at the last moment in time to prevent the death of the hero, but unwittingly, and not before much bloodshed has already occurred. He is extremely detached from the action, and does not take the struggles of the boys very seriously.

This comparison fuses nicely the opposing views of the group leader's ability or readiness to control the group's hostility.

During the same discussion, however, reference was made to the group leader "looking down from the mountaintop." In view of the contiguous reference to *Lord of the Flies*, perhaps this signifies more than his detachment, for in Golding's novel the only resident of the "moun-

---

[20] Particularly with regard to the identification which tends to follow such an attack (see Section D below), a point stressed by Theodore Mills.

taintop" is the rotting corpse which becomes the receptacle for the boys' overwhelming terror at their own uncontrollable savagery. We have several ideas combined here: (1) that the group leader will directly protect individuals from each other's malevolence, (2) that he will not, (3) that aggression arises out of abandonment (being "left on an island" without "adults"), and (4) that the leader *indirectly* manages aggression by permitting himself to be killed.

Further confusion is added by the observation that when a group *does* expel the leader and meets alone, there is not the least sign that such a thing as intermember hostility exists. The subject matter chosen is usually noncontroversial, and disagreement is studiously avoided. They may even make some mechanical arrangement that avoids any interaction beyond the exchange of information (cf. IId of this volume, p. 118). Does this avoidance of hostility signify its presence or its absence? We cannot tell more than that it is typically well controlled, although at some cost, and that relationships among group members do seem subsequently to be closer and more intimate.

One cannot avoid the impression, however, that expression of aggression toward the group leader relieves the members of a great burden and facilitates their relationships with one another.[21] The belief that through his presence the leader directly controls aggression is unrealistic and reflects the desire of the members to seek support from him rather than from each other. Since he is the cause of much of their anger, it requires substantial self-deception to see him as a benign protector, and at some point their vicious attacks on each other begin to seem misdirected. Seeing the leader as one who involuntarily can provide the solution to the problem of hostility control, however, is a realistic though not ideal approach. By periodically discharging their aggression on the appropriate target their tender feelings toward one another are freed. They have in this way established a specialized organ, in Ferenczi's terms, to achieve the discharge of one kind of tension.

It may be objected here that actual autotomy and this partial, symbolic, chronic autotomy are mutually exclusive. If the specialized organ is sloughed off it can no longer protect the rest of the organism from the bother of having to manage this type of tension.[22] But the

[21] Theodore Mills is the original exponent of this theorem.

[22] At the biological level this would seem to be problematic. If the entire genital apparatus of an individual were removed, would the other organs of the body become "re-eroticised"? Studies of castrated animals might throw partial

"autotomy" of the group leader is after all temporary. What the act of expulsion does (among many other things) is to demonstrate that the group leader *can* serve this function, and that therefore the members may as well abandon the hope that he will perform other, antithetical functions, which, indeed, they are capable of performing themselves.

Freud felt this need for a specialized object of hostility was essential to group formation and development: "Men clearly do not find it easy to do without satisfaction of this tendency to aggression that is in them. . . . It is always possible to unite considerable numbers of men in love towards one another, so long as there are still some remaining as objects for aggressive manifestations" (Freud, 1953, pp. 90–91). The fundamental message of *Totem and Taboo* is that civilization is only possible by discharging hostility onto a scapegoat, a point which is also implicit in Frazer, and, indeed, in Christianity. This view has found modern support in the work of ethologists like Lorenz, who relates intraspecific aggression directly to the ability to form personal bonds and shows how these bonds are formed in part by the diversion of mutual antagonism onto a third object (Lorenz, 1959).

If this relationship holds for geese and other animals, how much more intense must be the dependence of humans on such an object. Humans are among the most aggressive of all species—killing not merely for food or defense but for pleasure and sport and out of irritability and ambition.[23] This should be especially obvious today, when it becomes increasingly difficult to disguise from ourselves our secret collusion in mass destruction.[24] Many species have failed because

light on this question, which really concerns the extent to which this specialization is permanent and irreversible. In the human group it is not problematic at all; reversibility and substitutability are startlingly rapid in most cases. Observers are often impressed at the extent to which an individual's personality can seem to change when confronted with an empty role for which he is the nearest substitute. Yet recent studies of relearning in brain-damaged individuals have shown that specialization in the human brain is also more reversible than previously imagined.

[23] Man's sexuality is also unique in its chronicity and intensity. Thus he is not only the most dependent but also the most sexual and aggressive of all living things. It is hardly surprising that he should have such difficulties with impulse control.

[24] In part because we are caught in a vicious circle. The more we feel helpless and impotent in the face of this complex danger the more angry and destructive we become. But the more we begin to feel destructive the more receptive we are to a cataclysmic upheaval which will bring release from this tension and frustration and anger. And the more we wish this the more helpless we feel, since we are now fighting ourselves—part of us has joined the "war party." This feeling

changing conditions made some hypertrophied trait maladaptive, and man seems destined for a similar fate. Until now his aggressiveness has served him well, partly because of its more or less successful control through the slipshod mechanism to which Freud and Lorenz refer, and now that it has become increasingly superfluous and pernicious, there seems to be no way of modifying it in time. An understanding of the scapegoating mechanism, then (if we may use a specific term to refer to a more general phenomenon), becomes increasingly important as it becomes decreasingly available.

C. The Theme of Cannibalism

One day the brothers . . . came together, killed and devoured their father and so made an end of the patriarchal horde. United, they had the courage to do and succeeded in doing what would have been impossible for them individually. . . . Cannibal savages as they were, it goes without saying that they devoured their victim. . . . The violent primal father had doubtless been the feared and envied model of each one of the company of brothers: and in the act of devouring him they accomplished their identification with him, and each one acquired a portion of his strength. The totem meal . . . would thus be a repetition and a commemoration of this memorable and criminal deed, which was the beginning of so many things. . . .

(Freud, 1950b, pp. 141–142)

It will be recalled that the watershed of the revolt is the frustration of dependency needs by the group leader. He supplies not only the motive force for the revolt but also the means, since his nonresponsiveness forces them to talk about him rather than to him and thereby draws them together.

Since deprivation is thus the keynote of the attack on the leader, we should not be surprised to find such attacks often accompanied by oral manifestations of one kind or another, usually a group feast. The basis of this trend is best illustrated by a discussion in Group IIe, occurring in a meeting about three weeks before Christmas, when, amid much hilarity, the members decided that they should collectively apply to *The New York Times* as a candidate for the year's "100 Neediest Cases." Bion also notes the importance of the feeling of being starved (1949b, p. 296).

of impotence breeds more destructive urges, and so on, until war is the only solution to our tension.

IIf. It was the last meeting of the fall term and the discussion was extremely lethargic. The members became aware that they were waiting for the group leader to make an interpretation about their desultory conversation which would "get them going." They now considered the possibility that perhaps he would say nothing for the entire hour. They tried to interpret their own interaction but decided rather apathetically that all their interpretations were "meaningless." They then began to exchange examples of "meaningless" facts, particularly those used as "fillers" in newspaper columns. Danny reported one saying that the bean surplus in the United States would feed the entire population for an extended period. Helen quoted one which stated the average number of licks in an ice cream cone. Aaron raised the mathematical problem of how many facets there were to a pear.

IIb. It was shortly before Christmas vacation, and papers had been returned after the previous session. Despite many indications of anger over what were felt to be low grades there seemed to be great reluctance to discuss this in the group setting, and a long silence resulted when the group leader pointed out the contrast. Eve then remarked that she was "affected by a sense of—of inappropriateness of—of my reaction to— to my paper when I got it back." Roger described the reaction of several of them as "exaggerated. We sort of blew until the first black inky cloud passed and then we went our own separate ways, perhaps felt a little better for having exploded to someone who could understand what we meant." Gordon mentioned their preoccupation with who got what grade, and when others said this was typical of all courses, Eve disagreed: "*We* stood around like buzzards outside the door and as everyone came down the steps we pounced on them."

There followed a long series of complaints about the leader's role ("he just sits there"), his treatment of the papers ("too many comments," "too few," etc.), their lack of preparation or "model" for the papers, their feeling of betrayal ("we hoped we had been moving toward what you wanted"), and some suspicion that the supposedly low grades had been given for some ulterior purpose. In the midst of this Brad, who was the most consistent of all the group members in protesting the lack of structure, said, "You have expressed the fact that we have not learned what you wanted us to learn and yet you will not *tell* us what we are trying to learn." A little later Madeline remarked, "You've got the golden key to the little box of A's and we can't have it." Vic wondered if after all their problems weren't their own, but John clouded this polarization by suggesting that the group leader must have a reason for "running the course in this way." Gordon and Roger then expressed openly their feeling of "intense competition" with other group members for the leader's approval. Eve said it was easy in group meetings to ignore the leader, but that writing a paper put her "at a complete loss." Joe said what if the leader were evaluating each comment, but others also protested their unselfconsciousness in the group setting. Roger then wondered if the grades would affect the structure of the group in the coming term.

This session is particularly interesting since it shows not only the sense of deprivation and the competition it generates, but also the approach to a solution. Through direct *expression* of the invidious impulses, the members achieve unity, and through similar expression of dependency needs, a step toward independence is taken. Once such feelings are shared they seem to lose their potency, perhaps because the act of sharing them in itself expresses a commitment to other group members and a relinquishing of the fantasy of a private and secret relationship with the leader.

IIg. About a month after the group began there was a period in which dependency needs seemed very acute. A session immediately following one in which experiment myths were verbalized (see this volume, p. 14) began with comments about the Passover custom of leaving an empty chair at the table and a glass of wine for Elijah—wondering if the custom should be inaugurated in the group. Later on in the session Julie said that up to now she had been able to maintain a veneer of responsibility but today she felt childish and wanted someone else to do things. Neil had the fantasy of an entire society in which everyone simply lay down.

The next session was the day after Hallowe'en, and Penny passed out "Sugar Daddys" to everyone in the group, joking about the "totem" on the back of the wrapper. They then talked of how much personal revelation took place in meetings outside the "class," and a few of their personal feelings toward one another were now exchanged. At the end of the hour, in response to an interpretation by the group leader concerning expressions of dependency, Margo told about a fantasy of having the entire group play "Trick or Treat" on the group leader. She and Julie then exchanged reports of feelings of jealousy and gratification about particularizing comments of the leader.

It is indeed an unusual group which does not at some point or another bring in food and pass it around, usually with great satisfaction and high spirits. At times this seems merely to express a dim beginning awareness that the group must "feed" itself. At other times it is clearly associated with aggression against the leader, and has the air of a kind of symbolic cannibalistic revenge on him for his failure to gratify their needs. Finally, one often finds signs that the act of eating expresses a desire to incorporate desired attributes of the leader, such as his knowledge and ability to interpret group behavior.

This notion that desirable attributes can be acquired by devouring their possessor is of course a familiar one:

> The Bushmen will not give their children a jackal's heart to eat, lest it should make them timid like the jackal; but they give them a leopard's heart to make them correspondingly brave. British Central Africa aspirants after courage consume the flesh and especially the hearts of lions, while lecherous persons eat the testicles of goats. . . . To restore the aged Aeson to youth, the witch Medea infused into his veins a decoction of the liver of the long-lived deer and the head of a crow that had outlived nine human generations. . . . and when Sigurd killed the dragon Fafnir and tasted his heart's blood he thereby acquired a knowledge of the language of birds. . . . Again, the flesh and blood of *dead men* are commonly eaten and drunk to inspire bravery, wisdom, or other qualities for which those men were remarkable. . . .
>
> It is now easy to see why a savage should desire to partake of the flesh of an animal or man whom he regards as divine. By eating the body of the god he shares in the god's attributes and powers. . . . Thus the drinking of wine in the rites of a vine-god like Dionysus is not an act of revelry, it is a solemn sacrament.
>
> (Frazer, 1959, pp. 464, 466)

As usual, it is impossible to find examples which express a single idea in isolation, but those which follow can be grouped roughly according to their relative emphasis on the three aforementioned themes of self-feeding, revenge, and identification.

Group members often express their feeling of deprivation by remarking that the group has a "father" but no "mother" (unless the group leader is a female). Sometimes there is banter about constructing or importing one, or assigning the role to any faintly nurturant or mature female in the group, but occasionally someone will appear with his or her mother in tow to "sit in" on the group. In one group (VIb), the oral quality of the latter maneuver was intensified by the fact that the boy who brought his mother to the group also distributed some jelly beans which she had given him.

IIf. After they had been meeting for about seven weeks, the group leader entered one day with a pile of graded papers to return to the members. When asked if they would be handed out at the end of the hour he nodded. No move was made to obtain them any sooner, although it was their first grade of any kind in the course and they were clearly anxious to see how well they had performed. Before long, the discussion drifted into the question of the meaningfulness of their sessions. They asked each other whether they thought they were "taking anything away" from the group, and while many claimed they were, and said that they missed the group when they were absent, they also felt that they were somehow "trivializing" everything they discussed, and wondered if perhaps all of their interaction wasn't a "distraction." This led to some talk of cognitive processes and someone mentioned the old saw about telling someone "don't think about 'hippopotamus.'" Many of them had never heard it and they were enormously intrigued with the notion, trying it out and weaving facetious comments around it. The group leader then suggested that perhaps the image pleased them because a hippopotamus was so large that if they all took some there would still be some left. This seemed to tickle them but they paid little attention to it and began talking about each other's love affairs, complaining finally that they still hid intimate details of their lives from each other. The group leader then suggested that it was hard for them to share with each other when they were so concerned with their papers, i.e., with competing for approval and rewards from him. He wondered if they were "too hungry" to share, a phrase which produced a wave of laughter followed by a series of efforts to get him to talk more. They then returned to the discussion. A few minutes before the end of the hour Helen announced she had to leave early to get to an exam across the campus, but said she did not want to leave without her paper. When the instructor made no response, Barbara reached over, seized the pile of papers, and passed them to Danny who distributed them.

At their next meeting they discussed this incident, which had delighted them, at some length. Danny brought an animal cracker shaped like a hippopotamus which they passed around the group but did not eat. The next session Aaron brought his mother. The following meeting occurred just prior to a vacation and only four members were present. Aaron was describing an affair with a fat woman whom he compared in size first to the table around which they were seated and then, quite ingenuously, to a hippopotamus. This aroused laughter but no interpretation. A week later the theme recurred, this time in the form of the fantasy that they should form 12 groups (there were 12 members), each consisting of a member, a hippopotamus, and the group leader.

By now the hippopotamus had become a group symbol of considerable salience, although it was always treated facetiously and no one ever ventured to interpret it. Barbara and Miriam reported seeing china or wooden hippopotami in shops, having the impulse to buy one and present it to the group, and refraining on the ground that it would be thought presumptuous. A week later someone brought in a bag of potato chips which they passed around to eat. It was suggested jokingly that they were "eating the hippopotamus" and that this was equivalent to "eating the group mother." Danny then remarked that they would "eat the group father later." A few days after this incident they were anticipating a meeting when the group leader was to be away. Although he had merely announced autocratically that "there would be no class" on the day in question, they now decided to meet without him. During the discussion Dora, who had been fiddling with a piece of paper, now suddenly announced that it was a hippopotamus, since it had an "eye" and was "clearly a mother." They then tried to remember how the symbol had first arisen, some even hypothesizing that it came from assigned reading. They wondered if they would be "eating the hippopotamus" on the day they were to meet alone, and began to analyze the symbol a little in terms of their efforts to "make a mother out of" the group leader. Someone then suggested that they would be killing the hippopotamus when they were alone.

It should be clear from this example that the hippopotamus was a complex symbol whose meaning centered around the dependency needs of the group members. It arose first out of their effort "not to think about" their papers, that is, their attempt to avoid lapsing into the competitive authority-oriented structure of the traditional classroom. But it also signified their wish for a less depriving, more nurturant leader, who would be something more than just an "eye." Finally, it stood for their aggressive strivings for collective independence, such as the seizing of the papers and the decision to meet alone. Thus it would seem to be of precisely the same order as the totem animals of primitive clans, which are also an attempt to gratify dependency needs through group solidarity based on common experience. It furthermore bears some resemblance to Freud's exposition in *Totem and Taboo:* the substitution of the totem animal for a paternal figure, the aggression against this figure, the taboo on eating the totem, and the ritual violation of that taboo. We shall discuss other parallels of this kind in a later section.

IIc. While food is always a symbol associated with any kind of deprivation, it occasionally happens that a specific deprivation gives rise to a specific symbolic sharing in which food (or tobacco, which sometimes serves the same purpose) plays no part. In this group one deprivation, although it was complex in its effect and meaning, was quite concrete: the two or three girls who had appeared in the first meetings of the group all dropped out—a misfortune from which the other members never seemed quite to recover. In the middle of one session a girl from a previous class entered and asked timidly if she could search for a purse she had left behind. One of the members immediately produced it, but

instead of giving it to her directly, it was passed from hand to hand around
the entire room in a deliberate, almost caressing fashion—much in the way
a peace-pipe is circulated in the standard Western. The hungry defiance,
resentment, and sensuality manifested by this gesture became apparent to
some of the group members before the purse reached its destination,
and there was much laughter. At the end of the hour someone asked
why the girl had had such an "electric effect" on the group.

VIc. This group had two formal leaders, a male and a female, and
after several weeks a discussion arose as to the desirability of expelling
both of them. During the session in which this took place the leaders
were explicitly ignored. Two meetings later the informal leader of the
expulsion party brought in cider and cupcakes for the group.

(R. D. Mann, personal communication)

Here is perhaps an expression of the feeling that the group member who seeks a position of leadership in the group must take on the
burden of relieving the group's sense of deprivation. He must say
to the other members, "See, I can provide more successfully than this
do-nothing." Bringing food is a simple symbolic mode of communicating this claim and is often done by active "counterdependent" members striving to fill the vacuum created by the group leader's behavior.
As in some of the examples which follow, it may be associated with
an aggressive attack on and replacement of the group leader, as well
as a seizing of what has been withheld.

VId. In a graduate seminar which was not being conducted as a
training group, but was rather a group engaged in *observing* a training
group led by the instructor, the latter entered one day to find his
customary chair usurped. The two students who had planned the coup
then proceeded to pass a box of raisins around the room.

(R. D. Mann, personal communication)

These scenes are somewhat reminiscent of the Aztec ritual of killing and eating the god Huitzilopochtli in effigy at the festival of the
winter solstice. This ceremony was called *teoqualo*, or "god is eaten."
An image of the god was "fashioned out of seeds of various sorts,
which were kneaded into a dough with the blood of children." A
priest, playing the part of Quetzalcoatl, threw a dart into the heart
of the image, which was cut out and given to the king to eat. "The
rest of the image was divided into minute pieces, of which every man
great and small, down to the male children in the cradle, received
one to eat." " 'And of this which they ate, it was said: "The god is
eaten." And of those who ate it, it was said: "They guard the god" ' "

(Frazer, 1959, pp. 455–6; Jung, 1958, p. 170). The Christian Eucharist is of the same order, and identically defined.

IIe. After a slow build-up of hostility over a two-month period, the group leader arrived one day to find the door to the room locked. Going around to a side door he entered, amid great uproar and hilarity, to find Paul and Jim seated in his normal place at the end of the table. There was a great deal of clowning by the two usurpers, largely in the form of parodistic interpretations uttered in a deep and pompous voice, to the great enjoyment of the other members. Paul then grabbed the group leader's folder, saying, "This is the conch" (referring to *Lord of the Flies*), and placed it in front of him. (Although he fingered the papers inside and peeked at the edges, he never opened it.) Jim then began an elaborate burlesque, calling Paul taboo and shrinking away from him. After a few minutes Laura entered late, and delighted at the scene before her, joined the two boys at the end of the table. At this there was some joking about the Trinity, and having concluded that Laura, being female, must represent the Magna Mater, the Holy Ghost obviously must be represented by the deposed group leader. This was followed by further banter to the effect that the group leader should be divided up into parts, with the various members of the triumvirate taking the id, ego, and superego, etc. At this point they noticed that Curt and Peggy, at the opposite end of the table, had been sharing a cigarette, and suggested it be passed around the group like a peace pipe, but nothing happened. Andrea then reported that during the morning she had seen some Easter eggs in a store and had had the impulse to buy them and give one to everyone in the group. Paul suggested some other food would be preferable, while Laura reported a similar impulse a few days earlier to bring some sherry.

At the beginning of the session there had been general agreement, after some discussion, that they would all collapse the moment the group leader said anything. Now, however, he asked whom they wanted to eat. Peggy replied, looking rather fixedly at him, that they already had, and this provoked another manic outburst. They joked about the primal horde and about its being spring and "all going to the seashore," and then began to talk about the anxiety they felt these comments revealed. This led to some questioning of the group members about whose loyalty and approval they felt most in doubt. Upon being reassured they began seriously to interpret a dream about the group and the group leader which Curt had reported at the beginning of the hour, treating the dream as if it were a group product. Most of the hour was devoted to this task, which included serious analysis of a wide range of problems in both leader-member and member-member relationships. The group leader felt great admiration for this performance (despite his earlier feelings of annoyance, anxiety and embarrassment at the raucous horseplay which he imagined to be reverberating throughout the building), and was unable to think of anything he might have added to it.

Here we observe an interesting shift from a symbolic sideshow to a more serious operation. Consider what has happened up to this point: they have attacked and "deposed" the group leader, "divided him up," "eaten" him, and pretended to be him. At a purely symbolic level they seem to have engaged in a "cannibalistic" attack, with the aim not only of destroying his power, but also of incorporating him: "They not merely hated and feared their father, but also honoured him as an example to follow; in fact, each son wanted to place himself in his father's position. The cannibalistic act thus becomes comprehensible as an attempt to assure one's identification with the father by incorporating a part of him" (Freud, 1958, p. 103). That this is more than a gesture, however, is suggested by the fact that it achieves its goal—that they *are* able to take over the leader's interpretive function and analyze both symbolic and concrete material without his help—an ability which had seemed to elude them in recent sessions. There is, of course, no change in their actual *capacity* to do this, which was present from the beginning and exhibited on many occasions. What changes is merely their willingness to *admit* that they are able to function quite well without the group leader. What the symbolic gestures seem to do is to help them give up the leader as an object of dependence (since they now have him inside). This process, however, is a protracted one:

IIe. In their next meeting the group was very subdued. In the beginning a cartoon brought in by Laura was passed around but the group leader ignored it when it was presented to him. This infuriated the members, who felt that the "revolt" had been meaningless since the leader still would not become "one of the group." There was extensive amnesia for the previous meeting, the events of which were not fully remembered by anyone until the end of the session, when they were able to piece it together from their recollected fragments.

The following session opened with the members passing around a box of crackerjack. Curt announced the discovery of a paper on groups written by the group leader, but most members expressed the feeling that reading it would be disturbing. Nancy then suggested as an experiment that they meet without the group leader some time during the following week, reporting that she had already discussed the idea with Andrea and Lorna; but there was little response, perhaps because there were several absentees. In arguing briefly for the plan she made the statement, "Maybe he'd be more really here if he were absent."

The rest of the meeting was replete with references to food.

Discussions of Purim and Passover led to a joke about "Goldiebear and the three lox." Suddenly they realized that no one could remember how the story of Goldilocks ended. After some speculation they realized that they were talking about the outcome of taking the group leader's chair. They then giggled a little about getting into his bed but quickly shifted back to the food theme via the porridge.

The next meeting was devoted to discussion of the several absentees, and at one point they had difficulty remembering whether the phrase "all present and accounted for," which Henry had used with regard to the absentees, typically occurred before or after a battle. In the following session, at which all members were present, they answered the question by finally deciding to expel the group leader, after some early bickering and a discussion of the incompleteness of their progress in dealing with him. The session had opened with the passing around of another cartoon, this time making no effort to include the group leader.

In the argument over expulsion some objected to the "unreality" of the maneuver, while others said that, on the contrary, it was a bit of reality-testing. Curt countered that it was "like taking Mommy out to dinner when Daddy's away," a mere Oedipal make-believe, but ultimately everyone supported the proposal and promised to come (as usual, however, not everyone did).

Note the oral focus recurring in Curt's simile, and the equation of group-as-a-whole with mother, a theme we shall encounter again.

In this rather lengthy example we see a continuing association between aggression against the group leader and the eating of food, in contexts that show a desire to take by force the nurturance which has been withheld from them, and to incorporate the power and knowledge that will enable them to be independent. Nancy's remark that the leader's expulsion would make him "more really here" suggests that one function of the revolt is to facilitate such incorporation.

VII. The T-group was approaching the usual crisis over control. I stopped at the mailboxes on the way to the group, and in mine was an enormous cigar, at least fifteen inches long. I brought it along, entered the room, and found the group assembled, and my chair, with name tag, put in the center of the table. Much hilarity. After retrieving the chair, and expressing the genuine vulnerability and embarrassment I felt, I asked the group what the cigar meant. They tried not to show pity at my stupidity, and did not answer directly, but one member did suggest brightly that we "cut it up into fifteen pieces, and each of us could smoke one."

(Matthew Miles, personal communication)

Here we find several themes concisely conjoined. The group invests the leader with superhuman potency, attacks him, and consumes him. The totemic symbol in which this potency resides is at once phallic and oral. They wish his power but they also wish to be fed. Placing his chair on the table does three things. At the reality level it deposes and humiliates him. At the symbolic level it exalts him to a kingly position. But finally, it also places him in a location which is normally appropriate for food. He will be cut into pieces and consumed.

Our two final examples deal with separation and are more particularly concerned with what will be taken away from the group and the experience by the individual members when they leave. It is well to remember that insofar as the group is a learning experience the entire process is one of incorporation, and since the group leader, rightly or wrongly, symbolizes the source of this learning, it is he who is in some sense seen as incorporated. (This is particularly true in academic settings, where knowledge is actively "fed" to students by instructors using traditional methods—often referred to by hostile critics as "spoonfeeding." When such "feeding" is denied them by the group leader the resultant process of learning in spite of him becomes a hostile taking of food from his very being.) Thus the revolt is only a symbol of the entire experience, and when we say that the final separation often recapitulates aspects of the revolt we are in part merely saying that separation recapitulates the entire group experience.

This in turn is partly due to the fact that, just as the most significant fact about life is the inevitability of death, so the most significant fact about a training group is that it has a fixed and limited lifespan and that everyone knows this at the start. The entire history of such groups can usefully be conceptualized as the evolution of ways of handling separation and dissolution. Even as the group gets underway the members are wondering if it is worthwhile getting involved, knowing it is all going to end one day, wondering how close they should get to each other, how to make something worthwhile out of the experience in the time available.

We should remember, too, that such groups begin, as well as end, with separation. They begin with the "loss" of the group leader—that is, of the fantasy of a helpful and protective authority—and end with the loss of everything. Part of the group life is spent trying to salvage something from the first loss, the remainder in trying to salvage something from the second.

VIa. Two feasts were held in this group, the first taking the form of a Christmas party promoted by two of the members. Cookies, coffee and doughnuts were served and each member, including the group leader, received somewhat symbolic gifts and hostile poems. Although it was perfectly clear which individuals had arranged the affair, some air of mystery seemed deliberately to be maintained. In the midst of this festive scene, as one member looked rather dubiously at his gift, his neighbor suggested, "If it moves, kill it; if it doesn't, eat it."

Several months later, when the group met for the last time, the group leader entered to find a paper figure with his name on it dangling from a hangman's noose which had been attached to the microphone cable in the center of the ceiling. The group members were munching rolls and sipping coffee, which had been brought in a large box. This they passed around the table, insisting that each newcomer partake as he entered the room. When the container was finally empty someone suggested that it was the group. For several sessions prior to this one, they had been talking about what they would take with them when the group dissolved.

(R. D. Mann, personal communication)

In the first feast, although the group is making an effort to "feed itself," no recognition is taken of the hostility toward the leader produced by their having to do so, and it is consequently diffused back upon the members themselves. In the meantime the spurious mystery can foster a fantasy of an unknown benefactor, which serves the same function as deification. In the second feast both the worshipful attitude and the hostility find their target.

Communal eating has always been an important way of expressing group solidarity in every culture and every age. That such meals often have an implicit or symbolic content has been stressed by many anthropologists, and of course by Freud in *Totem and Taboo*. The Christian Communion has always served as the most popular example of an explicit symbolic cannibalistic incorporation, but other examples abound. Many clubs and other organizations drink toasts to pictures of "our founder" on the wall, a ritual act highly similar to the incident just described,[25] and most group toasts have some cannibalistic overtones, in that the object of the toast is usually enjoying some good fortune in which the other participants would like to share. The accompanying speech enlarging upon this fortune or exaggerating the virtues of the recipient serves also to enhance the magical potency of what is consumed.[26] We shall give other examples of this phenomenon in the next section.

[25] I am indebted to a student, David Van Kleek, for this observation.

[26] The baseball ritual of passing the ball all around the infield after a successful infield play is based on a similar magical principle, i.e., sharing the *mana* of success among all participants so as to enhance their future performance.

In addition to the theme of oral incorporation, the last example illustrates the importance of fantasies of reproduction and continuation, as well as mechanisms of denial as the death of the group approaches.

IIe. It was the last day before a very late spring vacation. (After their return there would only be nine more meetings). Half of the group had already left for their homes, and those present were quite preoccupied with the absentees. This led to some reminiscing about the previous week, which had been spent revealing and discussing the sexual yearnings some of the members had for each other, and how much more relaxed one or two of them now felt after talking about it. The relation between "talking" and "reality" was then broached, and the group fell silent. Curt brought up the absentees again and Jim walked in, late. Everyone smiled, and the group leader suggested they had been trying to ward off the death of the group with fantasies of copulation. There was little direct reaction to this, but they now began sharing a whole series of fantasies they had had or were having about the meeting. Four admitted having had a fantasy during the morning that the group leader would not come. Several agreed that when Jim had entered they had thought all of the absentees were about to enter in a body. Two or three (it is difficult to count nods) shared a fantasy of semi-hallucinatory vividness that dim and partial shades of the absentees were actually present in their chairs.

Then began a discussion of separation. Almost all agreed that their image of the dissolution of the group involved the members disappearing one by one, leaving the individual in question alone. They decided that each member should take his chair with him, or a piece of the table, or a piece of the group leader's coat. They thought of coming back to watch the next group. They expressed great annoyance that the group leader would remain in the room and give the course to new people—"other people in *our* room!" They began to exchange accounts of how many people wanted to take it now, that it had become a great fad, but reminded themselves that the same had been true this year and yet in the end "only a few very brave people actually did." At ten minutes before the end of the hour Lorna said, "All I can think of is how I'll feel at ten minutes of two on the last day. I just can't imagine it somehow."

Note that when the first onslaught of the reality of imminent death occurs there is a kind of inverted recapitulation of the revolt. First they try in fantasy to recapture the moment of final triumph, when all of the members were present and the group leader was excluded. As the fact of many absentees erodes this fantasy they confront the reality of the many personal losses they will suffer when they part, and try to compensate for these losses by imagining what they will take away. First they think of each taking away what amounts to the role he has achieved in the group, but this seems not to suffice, and once again a fantasy of cannibalistic incorporation appears, this time in the form of the duodecimated coat. Finally they drift into the very Oedipal jealousy with which they began the year, and which prevented their collaboration for so long.

Yet the element of regression is not as marked as it might first appear. The recapitulation of the revolt is initially an attempt to *avoid* regression and dependency on the leader by recalling their strength and unity and independence. Second, the idea of taking away a piece of the group leader is in part simply an expression of their feeling of having learned something from their encounter with him. Third, this incorporation is at a somewhat more sublimated level than their food fantasies had been: we still, after all, take souvenirs from dead soldiers, and rip clothes and demand autographs from movie idols, in order to absorb their *mana*. But we no longer eat these objects of wonderment, and I believe that this transition from incorporating indispensable flesh to incorporating replaceable identity-receptacles is generally regarded as indicative of our achievement of a higher cultural level. Fourth, Oedipal jealousy no longer has any power to jeopardize the unity of the group—on the contrary, it activates feelings of exclusiveness and group pride.

IIe. When the last day actually came, food reappeared. Lorna entered with vermouth and potato chips and gave everyone a glass. All members were present. There were some joking references to the Christian Communion, tense pauses, and jokes about separating. Someone wanted to leave the door open and a glass for Elijah, and this was done. Feelings of numbness, anxiety, and disbelief were expressed. Then a discussion of the outside world began (10 of the 12 members were graduating), focussed around the question whether one could survive in a "dull, routinized life" unprotected by the "usual defenses." When the group leader asked whether needing repression in order to live was implied by needing it in order to die, they expressed concern that if they could not ascertain their own feelings at this moment they had not learned very much. Yet they felt quite unsure about this ability both for the present and the future. In the midst of this discussion, which was now centered around their images of their post-college lives, which they saw in terms of "routine jobs" and "living without change," Henry had great difficulty every time he tried to pronounce the words "leave" and "live," which he kept interchanging in a kind of stutter. These slips, a reference to Gibbon, and remarks about the global pessimism of many of the final course lectures they had heard, seemed to the group leader to express both anguish and urgency about leaving the group. He suggested that on the one hand they wished to abandon the group before it died, in order to avoid dying with it, but on the other hand they were afraid that in the process of decathecting the group they would leave all their insights behind. They then reiterated their confusion about how much insight they really had now, and whether it would really be of any value anyway in the "cold outside world" where "most people" had none. They picked up the image of the "dead group" and began exchanging Frazerian witticisms on this theme. Lorna suggested that the pieces of the corpse be scattered over the ground as fertility magic, and the hopeful note in this bit of whimsey stimulated brief hilarity. Edna pictured little groups springing up all over the land, or the nation being inundated with corn. Then they fell silent as the end of the hour approached. Henry, who had brought his camera, took some pictures.[27] Some of the members began to look expectantly at the group leader, who remarked that he had enjoyed working with them, finally drank his untouched glass of wine, and left. Laura gave a little shriek of frustration, revealing the hardiness of the now-it-can-be-told eschatology.

One is reminded of Theodore Mills' summary statement about group dissolution (which no one else has discussed so realistically and graphically): "Yearning for a benediction from some source, the group dies" (Mills, 1964b, p. 79).

D. The Theme of the Sacred King

Not all of the incorporation that we see in groups is purely symbolic, nor is it necessarily associated with oral manifestations. As time goes by the group members, with or without a concretized revolt experience, begin more and more to take unto themselves the interpretive skills of the group leader, together with the attitudes appropriate to such skills. The leader, increasingly divested of both his parental and oracular attributes, ends as little more than a sentimental souvenir of what is retrospectively distorted as having been a pleasurable group experience.

[27] Since Henry reported the experience as less rewarding than did the other members, this incident is congruent with Freud's developmental theory, which embraces the paradox that the more unpleasant and unsatisfying the years of childhood and the important relationships thereof, the more ferociously the individual will cling to them. Earlier in the meeting Henry had expressed the fear that in later years he would delude himself into thinking the group had been worthwhile. If his fear should prove correct, Festinger's theory of cognitive dissonance (Festinger, et al., 1956) could be invoked to account for the change (which is by no means uncommon).

Yet one cannot escape the feeling that this process seems to receive a boost every time the group overtly expresses collective hostility toward the group leader—that, in other words, identification tends to follow aggression. It could of course be argued that this is simply because all aggression is fundamentally an oral incorporation (an equation often made in psychoanalytic writing) and it is indeed difficult to find another way of interpreting the phenomenon, assuming it to have been correctly observed.

Fortunately we are not forced in this instance to rely on clinical observation. Two empirical studies have already been carried out which indicate that aggression and identification are related in the manner suggested.

The source of all interest in and concern with this problem is Theodore Mills, who first formulated the principle that aggression leads to identification with the object of the aggression, and who has conducted most of the research relevant to this issue. Mills found, for example, that male subjects who threw darts at a photograph subsequently described themselves in a manner more similar to their descriptions of the photograph. This was true with regard to undesirable as well as desirable characteristics, active as well as passive ones. The change in self-characterization was significantly greater than that of a control group (Mills, 1964a).

Similar results were obtained in an experiment by Ogilvie, a student of Mills. Ogilvie elaborated Mills' hypothesis somewhat, by arguing that all aggresssion is instrumental—that it is directed at a target as "a means of incorporating characteristics which the target has and the aggressor wants" (Ogilvie, 1961). This formulation is thus in keeping with Whiting's "status envy" hypothesis (Burton and Whiting, 1961). Ogilvie found not only that aggression was followed by identification (using previously determined behavioral cues), but that (a) despite the prestige of the target, identification virtually never occurred *without* a prior aggression, and that (b) there was a high negative correlation between the intensity of the aggression and the time interval before the first act of identification occurred.

As we have seen, the idea of identification through aggression is important in the primal horde myth and, indeed, in totemistic phenomena the world over. Cadmus the snake-slayer becomes a snake himself, and Apollo takes the name of the Delphic divinity when he conquers her oracle, just as a Marquesan warrior takes the name of the man he slays (Kardiner, 1939, pp. 149, 178). One becomes a hero by killing a brave man, a magician by killing a wizard, a divine being by wrestling with an angel (cf. Campbell, 1959, 217–19).[28] Perhaps the most bizarre ritual expression of the relation is found in our own society, where no major political figure ever campaigns for public office without donning the headdress of the much-aggressed-against Indian.

One explanation of the relationship is based on the concept of ambivalence. If we are simultaneously attracted and repelled by an object (whether person or nation), that is, if it is salient for us and arouses intense feelings, we can resolve this ambivalence by attacking the object, so that at one and the same time we express our repulsion and yet take unto ourselves the valued quality, possession, or attribute. Or the object may be not so much salient as simply alien, thus generating uncertainty as to how to respond. In any case, ambivalence is often handled by alternation, and identification through aggression seems to express this fact.[29]

Yet the specific nature of this ambivalence is of the greatest importance in determining the course of the identification. Mills lays considerable stress, for example, on the divergent effects of a group's attacking a leader or a "true" scapegoat (that is, one who is not himself perceived as possessing desired attributes to any marked extent). The former is essentially a dynamic process, since something is "added on" to the interaction, in the sense of group absorption of leader qual-

[28] This phenomenon is also found in the general historical tendency for conquerors to imitate and incorporate the characteristics of the conquered. Even when the conquered nation is culturally inferior, there is likely to be a certain amount of admiration, wonderment, and identification with it (cf. Harrison, 1957, p. 384).

[29] A few years ago I attempted to draw a distinction between two kinds of identification. One, which I called "personal identification," is based on love and admiration and seeks to achieve a closeness to the object through the incorporation of valued traits and attitudes. The other, which I called "positional identification," is based on hatred, envy, and fear and seeks to replace the object and assume his prerogatives (Slater, 1961c). For those interested in the relation between this distinction and the theory of identification through aggression, one or two words are necessary. In practice, these forms of identification are usually mixed, but even if they were to appear in pure form we should not assume that an attack on the object presupposes positional identification, since hostility is a part of all relationships. Rather, we can look to this distinction to tell us *what* is incorporated through the attack. Insofar as the attack is motivated by a desire for positional identification, the acquired traits will be surface mannerisms associated by the aggressor with the object's superior status, power position, or possessions. Insofar as the attack is motivated by a desire for personal identification, the acquired traits will be values and attitudes associated with the aggressor's admiration of the object and his desire to be like him and approved by him.

ities. The latter is static, since nothing is absorbed but undesired characteristics which must be projected anew onto the scapegoat.

It should be stressed, of course, that this is entirely a matter of perception. Whether these good or bad qualities actually reside in the object is unimportant as long as they are perceived as so residing. Their incorporation is a little more real, however, since this simply involves feeling, thinking, or behaving *like* the perceived object and can be achieved even if the perception is distorted. In the case of skills or capacities, of course, the incorporation is likely to be purely symbolic, but even here one can sometimes see startling increases in abilities of one kind or another following such identification. There is nothing magical in this—presumably the ability is latent but blocked by some emotional constellation or other. The aggression and identification process, by reshuffling this constellation, releases the ability and permits it to develop naturally.

A good example of the complexity of this process may be found in the orientation of the Southern white in America to the Negro. It is not merely metaphorical to say that the Negro is the South's 'totem,' because it is difficult to think of a distinctive aspect of Southern culture, real or imagined, which cannot be traced to the Negro (cf. Cash, 1941), a consequence, perhaps, of past aggressions against him. This raises a question as to the (unconsciously) intended and actual effects of lynchings, which are perhaps the best example to be found anywhere of primitive totem-killing. A Northern observer might feel that all the Southerner "absorbs" from this experience is the ignorance and slothfulness he attributes to the Negro, but clearly more than this is involved.

The real goal of this aggression seems to be the alleged sexual prowess of the Negro, an attribute whites have believed in and envied for centuries (this is conspicuous, for example, in the *Thousand Nights and a Night*). Normally the lynching is precipitated by an accusation that a Negro has raped a white woman, so that it takes place in the context of a challenge to the morbid Southern chimera of "feminine purity." Having created a fiction which throws everyone's sexual adequacy into question, the impotent white must borrow from the fantasied endless store of sexuality in the Negro. Only in this way can some of the more primitive aspects of the lynching ritual be explained. It is traditional, for example, for the corpse of the lynched Negro to be sexually mutilated, for the genitals to be divided among the participants as souvenirs, and for the party to be followed by a visit to a brothel.[30]

The technique of nonviolence depends for its success on the same mechanism. The attacker tends increasingly to identify with his non-retaliating victim. The characteristic absorbed in such a case might well be the ability to control hostile impulses—an ability which has always been notoriously deficient in the Southern white (cf. Cash, 1941, pp. 42–4, 73–4, 90, 118–121, 289).

But what does it mean to "borrow" or "take from" an object of aggression an intangible attribute? Can an essentially magical act produce emotional changes of any importance? Actually the process is not at all complicated. Let us suppose an individual is subject to two contradictory impulses which inhibit one another.[31] If one impulse can somehow be discharged, the other will be free to express itself also. Or suppose that an individual is conflicted about his sexual impulses. By attacking these impulses in another the ambivalent impasse is broken (the negative side having been expressed) and the impulses can be released.

We can observe this phenomenon in the frequency with which aggression and sexuality are alternated in fertility rites, wherein the fertility symbolism proper is usually preceded by a bloody sacrifice, a beating, a free-for-all, or a general orgy of vituperation (Harrison, 1957, pp. 101, 136). It is as if sexual expression (and hence fertility) were trapped by feelings of hostility, anxiety, or inadequacy between the

---

[30] Personal communication from Thomas Pettigrew. For variant practices and more detailed descriptions, see Miller and Dollard (1941, pp. 235–252), Pruden (1949), and Raper (1933).

[31] This is a phenomenon familiar to ethologists, who apply to one of its consequences the rather confusing (to psychologists) term "displacement activity." "Displacement activity happens if two mutually inhibiting motivations result in such a perfect equilibrium as to block each other completely. What happens then is that another movement, which is usually inhibited by both of them, becomes disinhibited because the other two neutralize each other.

"So, if a bird wants to attack and is afraid in more or less perfect equilibrium of these two motivations, he may start to preen or to scratch, or to perform other activities which are [usually] inhibited both by attack and by escape . . ." (Lorenz, 1959, p. 188).

In humans we might find, in place of "displacement activity," a neurotic symptom which expressed both motivations symbolically and simultaneously, but the principle is the same. If in some way or another the fighting motivation in the bird could be triggered off, it would subsequently fly away, just as lovers after a violent quarrel subsequently find themselves overwhelmed with tender and erotic feelings.

sexes and could only be released by some aggressive outburst. It is in this connection that we can perhaps best understand the fact that certain disturbed individuals must kill before copulating.

It may be, then, that identification through aggression is simply a special form of this more general tendency to resolve ambivalence through alternation, and the notion of "taking from" the other a metaphorical account of the process of using another person as a vehicle for rearranging the elements in one's own internal economy.

At the same time it seems clear that the subjective experience of the act of identification through aggression varies markedly according to the perceived value of the object. Although we may not ourselves observe any difference between groups who attack a valued or an unvalued object, there is no mistaking the sense of elated triumph in the former case and depressed futility in the latter. This seems to be associated not with a conscious, realistic perception of the object but with an unconscious, magical view.

In the case of the attack on the group leader, this distinction expresses itself in temporal form: that is, the earlier the attack comes in the history of the group the more satisfying it seems to be. Revolts occurring early in the group's history are permanently treasured as events inaugurating group strength and group life. Those taking place at mid-passage impart a feeling of group solidity along with a kind of disillusionment—a feeling that the revolt did not make as much difference as anticipated. Those that occur near the end are generally felt to have been sterile exercises or self-conscious rituals, despite the fact that the later the revolt the more considered, significant, and truly experimental it is in prospect.

The reason for this difference seems to lie in the gradual secularization of the group image of the leader over time. As has been pointed out, the initial view of him is highly suffused with an exaggerated and idealized parental image. But this fantasy of the group leader's omniscience is obviously doomed to decay. In the first place, it is based in considerable part on the feelings of abject dependence which are aroused by the initial lack of structure in the situation. The feeling calls forth the desire and also activates the world-view appropriate to the feeling when it was first experienced. Relative to the helpless child the parent *is* omnipotent, and whenever such helplessness is felt again, authority figures will tend to be viewed in the same way. But as the group members gain inner strength this perception will correspondingly wither.

In the second place, transference reactions bloom most richly in the absence of stimuli. As Franz Alexander has noted (1946), it is in the dark that we see ghosts, and it is easiest to attach an idealized parental image to the group leader when he is unknown. In everyday situations the all too human attributes of the transference vehicle, revealed in his speech, manner, and affect, tend quickly to erode these connections, but the detached and silent role of the group leader severely retards such erosion. Insofar as he does nothing and says nothing, the fantasy of his omniscience can be maintained, somewhat after the fashion of George Washington, whose dunderheadedness, according to John Adams, remained undiscovered because of his taciturnity.[32] His nonretaliatory detachment bolsters and colors this fantasy, enabling the members to see him as "invulnerable" and a "superman." But gradually he, too, reveals more and more, and when he speaks he becomes mortal and fallible again and seems quite unsatisfactory by contrast with the idealized paternal image against which he has been silhouetted. Hence the members fluctuate in their attitudes toward him, seeing him now as omniscient, now as incompe-

---

[32] This tendency to magnify the silent is often extended beyond the group leader himself to include the less active members of the group, who are subject to highly dramatic characterizations. The fear is often expressed that if these individuals did speak it would, as one member suggested, ". . . be shattering—a whole new dimension to deal with." Thus while they often complain about their silence, the active members usually make it difficult for the silent members to talk when the opportunity arises.

In addition to serving as a representation of some dreaded expectation of the group leader, the silent members are feared because they represent a latent fantasy structure for the group. There is always in training and therapy groups a lingering semi-conscious conviction that the "real" structure of the group is that of a traditional classroom, in which it is the silent children who are "good," and will be loved and rewarded by the authority, while the active ones are "bad" and will be punished. The explicit nonauthoritarian setting is accepted only partially and with misgivings by most individuals, and the silent members remain a constant reminder that they may be betting on the wrong horse. This is sometimes expressed in the fantasy that the silent ones have a special "in" with the group leader.

Occasionally when the entire group falls silent it seems to be an acting out of this latent fantasy: all sit passively waiting for the group leader to lecture and feed them. But this can only be inferred from the context of the event. Silence is group unconsciousness—as in the sleeping individual cerebration still goes on but we are hard put to get at it. In this darkness many fantasies emerge, and many alternative conceptions of the group's structure are present. All we really know for certain is that the conscious, manifest structure of the group is being rejected when the group falls silent, for this is constructed out of verbal interaction between members. When this interaction ceases, each member can have the fantasy group he wants, a fantasy group which is often shared but need not be.

tent, and circulating bizarre rumors which serve to support both views (cf. Bennis and Shepard, 1956).

In time, the group leader is stripped of his magical image alto- gether—his secrets fathomed, his bag of tricks up-ended—and appears in all his naked mortality, a mere human, although apparently clever and well-intentioned. A revolt occurring this late in the game carries no thrill and yields no sense of triumph. If it is not a god but only a mere human who has been conquered and eaten, then what has the group achieved, and what has it added to itself?

We seem to be dealing here with something akin to the magical force or *mana* of many nonliterate peoples. This force resides in the idealized parental image, and is present in the group leader only so long as he is identified with that image. The "virtue" of the revolt depends upon catching the *mana* while it is still firmly attached to the leader—that is, before the parental image and the percept of the leader have too far diverged, and the *mana* of the leader therefore leaked away. If the group attacks the leader at the point of maximum overlap, they will feel as if they have captured this *mana* and can incorporate it. Revolts occurring later seem to leave the members feeling like the pursuer in a fairy tale who is left with a cloak in his hand, a stone in his sock, or an effigy in place of his presumedly captured quarry.

All of this may seem familiar to the reader, who may recall the following passage from *The Golden Bough* in which Frazer explains the custom of killing the sacred king:

> The divine life, incarnate in a material and mortal body, is liable to be tainted and corrupted by the weakness of the frail medium in which it is for a time enshrined; and if it is to be saved from the increasing enfeeblement which it must necessarily share with its human incarnation as he advances in years, it must be detached from him before, or at least as soon as, he exhibits signs of decay, in order to be transferred to a vigorous successor. This is done by killing the old representative of the god and conveying the divine spirit from him to a new incarnation.
>
> (Frazer-Gaster, 1959, p. 251) [33]

[33] Apropos of Frazer's theory, it is striking how many details in the ritual of executing criminals in our own society correspond to his description of the slay- ing of scapegoats for the sacred king. The final repast, for example, is clearly a vestige of the mock "king for a day" attempt to lend verisimilitude to the substi- tution. The ultimate clue is the electric chair itself, which is built so like a throne. Is it possible to maintain that this is unrelated to ancient customs involving the sacrifice of criminals, who for a brief period held kingly office and gratified their every whim?

The execution of criminals is still an event which arouses enormous public

It is in this sense that we should interpret the objection raised in the seventh-month revolt in Vb that the group leader was "already dead." (See this volume, p. 52.)

The divine life may here be translated as the magical omnipotence inhering in the idealized parental image. As Freud noted in his parable about the ruins of Pompeii, nothing ages or changes in the unconscious, but only when it is dug up and exposed to the corrosive effect of air and light. This is, of course, the essence of psychoanalytic therapy: that this ancient and divine parental image will be "tainted and corrupted" by being "for a time enshrined" in the prosaic corpus of the analyst, and will ultimately dwindle into a contemporary reality to which the patient can respond with somewhat more strength, dignity, and freedom than has been his wont.[34] Transference is at the basis of both approaches and is in each case magnified, but otherwise the views of ancient and modern are diametrically opposed. We now pay to destroy what the ancients murdered to preserve.

The "vigorous successor" to the group leader is usually the group as a whole. The feeling is that they can only become strong if they destroy and incorporate him while they still believe in his mystical power. This same requirement of haste underlies the *omophagia*, as Jane Harrison points out: "The worshippers aim at devouring the victim before the life has left the still warm blood."

" 'The leader . . . before the worshippers [have] finished the

fascination. On the day that Caryl Chessman died all of four groups meeting that day discussed the incident (usually a major war threat is required to stimulate a current events discussion) for the greater part of the meeting. Part of their interest derived from the fact that their own demises were only a day or so away, and there was considerable talk about "reprieves" in the sense of continued meetings, reunions, and so on.

[34] The issue would never arise at all were it not for the capacity of humans to detach this idealized image from the parents themselves. Freud discusses this problem in his paper on the "Family Romance of Neurotics," in which he describes the fantasy that one is an adopted child whose true parents are of higher social rank. "The entire endeavor to replace the real father by a more distinguished one is merely the expression of the child's longing for the vanished happy time, when his father still appeared to be the strongest and greatest man, and the mother seemed the dearest and most beautiful woman. . . . The over-valuation of the earliest years of childhood again claims its own in these fancies" (Rank, 1952, p. 67). It is this early over-valuation, we might add, which attaches itself to the shadowy image of the group leader, until he, also, like the parents themselves, proves to be unworthy of it. The difference between early and late revolts, then, might also be characterized as the difference between attacks on the kingly parents and the lowly peasant foster parents of the hero myth.

song, while the last words [are] still on their lips, draws his sword and smites the neck of the camel and eagerly tastes of the blood. The rest of them in like fashion run up and with their knives some cut off a small bit of the hide with its hairs upon it, others hack at any chance bit of flesh they can get. Others go on to the entrails and inwards and leave no scrap of the victim uneaten that might be seen by the sun at its rising' " (Harrison, 1957, p. 486).

But this feeling is not a mere manifestation of the survival of primitive thought patterns. As in so much magical thinking, it is based to an extent on a psychological reality. What the group wants most when it revolts is to believe in its own strength and dependability. It will be successful as a group insofar as the members are willing to depend on each other rather than on the leader, and this will occur when the group as a whole is perceived as strong and able. Regardless of the objective reality, which presumably is constant, the group that revolts early is attacking not only a real authority figure but also an awesome spectre of the members' own making. Hence far more courage is required to take such a step than would be true later, since not only are they attacking a more formidable opponent but also risk losing more in the way of "parental" protection. In this sense the early revolters are justified in their pride, and the superior yield of their performance is a function of the greater psychological effort which they put forward.

It should be emphasized again, furthermore, that the group members are far from passive in this magnification of the group leader and his *mana*. We have seen that they try to deify him from the beginning, exaggerating his superiority over them by assuming an abject posture. This is an ancient device based on the principle of relativity. A king is weak or powerful only in relation to his people, and he is made great by increasing the social distance between him and his subjects.[35] Thus the way to exalt the king is to crouch down before him, a technique which was exhibited in one group when a member happily remarked, apropos of the leader, "not many fathers have thirteen children!" But in part this process of building up the king and feeding his narcissism is like fattening the lambs for the slaughter—the more mag-

[35] This is the same mechanism we found in Chapter I, in our discussion of deification. A man contemplating the stars with an awareness of the infinite magnitude of the universe feels frightened at his own insignificance. If he posits a deity, however, this feeling of insignificance becomes a way of magnifying the deity by contrast, and the anxiety is converted into the comfortable awe of the dependent and protected infant.

nified his image, the more the "subjects" get to "eat." His symbolic enrichment will ultimately lead to enriching themselves, for the greater the king the more noble the revolutionaries. This is pure magic, and occasionally backfires, the members carrying the posture of helpless self-abasement so far that they are unable ever to rouse themselves from it.

CHAPTER III

Sexual Liberation Through Revolt

Internally, for those who participate in it, the revolt experience is just one of many steps toward independence from parental attachments. At a mundane interpersonal level it simply betokens a transfer of interest from the group leader to the other group members. These simple realities provide the most enduring significance of the revolt, but they can scarcely be understood apart from the sexual overtones they exhibit.

One of the most striking of these—especially mystifying in its resemblance to Freud's primal horde myth—is a change in the sexual economy of the group. This may best be summarized by saying that the group members decathect the group leader and experience a dramatic heightening of sexual interest in one another.

In an odd way, this factor transforms the revolt into a truly Oedipal event. Freud saw the primal revolt of the brother horde as Oedipal in the sense that the goal of the revolt was to get the women away from the sexually monopolistic despot. The women themselves were portrayed as utterly passive in this revolution. Another way to conceptualize this process, however, and one which accords somewhat better with the very active role women actually play in group revolts, is that the "mother" is not simply a collection of female relatives but rather the group as a whole. We may recall the remark made in IIe (see this volume, p. 69) about taking mother out to dinner when father is away.

This latter statement may seem arbitrarily, even obstinately, metaphorical, and it may be felt that we are being tediously and gratuitously symbolic in thus characterizing group events. Yet these equations do appear, as a kind of shorthand if nothing else. Groups with no maternal figure nevertheless make frequent references to such, not only as something of which they are deprived, but also as something from which they are in danger. There is a feeling on the one hand that "the group" is a source of succorance and comfort, even a refuge; yet also there is a fear of being "swallowed up" by "the group" —of losing individuality and separateness. Statements are made about the impossibility of "having a group" with the group leader playing the role he does, and the group is often felt to begin to exist only when he has been expelled.

From this viewpoint, then, the group, as something apart from its constituents, is equivalent to a kind of mother which is being kept away from them by a depriving paternal figure. The purpose of the revolt is to get "her" away from this paternal figure—in other words to make the group what *they* want it to be: comfortable, pleasant, friendly, loving, indulgent, undemanding, etc.[36]

Yet we must not forget that this is metaphor and fantasy only. This "mother" is really something composed of themselves—it is themselves that they wish to take away from the group leader. The relevance of the Oedipal model lies in the fact that the freedom they seek is concerned not simply with dependency but also with sexuality, as the examples below indicate. Furthermore, it is not simply a matter of the men freeing the women from sexual thraldom, but also of the women freeing the men. Let us examine this feeling of thraldom first, and then look at what happens when it disappears.

A. Oedipal Involvement and Sexual Inhibition

In Freud's myth the tyrant possessed all the women in the horde, and a similar fantasy seems to manifest itself in many groups. Sometimes it is expressed merely in male grumbling over the competitive advantage afforded to females by sexual attractiveness and seductive wiles, in the quest for academic achievement and professorial favor. But often it gives rise to fantasies and rumors of teacher-student affairs and even to inhibition of sexual involvement between group mem-

---

[36] Mills suggests in a personal communication that "separating the leader from his love" serves to "clarify . . . the distinction between the leader as a person and the goal that he represents." I have dealt very little with the question of group goals and the leader's relation to them, but my impression is that the primary impulse is a pleasure-seeking one: that the group seeks control and mastery (through knowledge and understanding) for pleasurable purposes, only to discover that in so doing it has cathected the group goal as an end in itself through identification with the group leader. We will encounter this issue again in Chapter IV.

bers—an inhibition which seems to be based on an unconscious conviction that the girls somehow "belong" to the group leader.

IIa. In this group there were rumors that the leader was conducting affairs with several of the girls in the group. During the weeks following the revolt, as the group became more intimate, a number of efforts were made by various boys to date girls in the group. All contact outside the group, however, was surrounded by the most profound taboos. Couples who had dated, or talked of it, never spoke to one another in the group. They sat apart and even confessed in some cases that they avoided looking at one another. (Since most members knew of these relationships individually, it seemed to be from the leader or from the group as a collective, formal, task-oriented entity that they were being hidden.)

Anxiety over this "exogamy taboo" seemed intense in one active male student who dated a popular girl about whom the aforementioned rumors had been particularly lively. Just prior to his first date the student came to the group leader's office and in the course of the conversation casually informed him of his intentions. (This "confession" occurred despite the fact that he did not believe the rumors.) On the first meeting following the date he precipitated an attack on himself by offering himself as a topic for analysis—a gesture which was later referred to as "offering yourself up as a sacrifice." The date, however, was never mentioned.

Ultimately a peer leader emerged in this group—a male student who had, during the course of the year, married a nonmember and was defined by the group members as "noncompetitive." He had conformed to the taboo and was liberated from its effects.

IIb. About nine weeks after the group began there were complaints about how little the members really knew one another, coupled with some typical expressions of resentment at the behavior of the group leader. The latter asked if they felt he was keeping them apart, and this led after a time to some facetious remarks about the possibility of sexual relationships within the group. At this point one boy blurted out, "I wouldn't *dream* of taking out a girl in this group!" When asked why, he seemed at a loss to explain his reaction, suggesting only that people in the group knew too much about one another.

Later in the year other members also expressed a feeling that a taboo existed, but by now it had been violated. Two of the more silent members, it was ultimately revealed, had developed a close relationship which continued until the group terminated. Both were resented by the other group members, although they did nothing while in the group to indicate their relationship—sitting apart and never communicating in any way or showing any interest in each other.

The taboo on public expression of sexual interest between pairs in a group situation is of course more complex in its determinants, as I have noted at length elsewhere (Slater, 1963), and operates firmly even at the societal level. As Stephens observes, "most societies demand a certain amount of public avoidance between husband and wife," and "a good many societies do not even permit husband and wife to call each other by name" (Stephens, 1963, pp. 275–276). More closely related, perhaps, is the following quotation describing love affairs among adolescents in the kibbutz:

> The typical partners give few overt indications of their relationship. They do not appear together in public as a couple nor do they seek each other out informally between classes or at work. All meetings are clandestine. It would be unthinkable to show any physical sign of affection in the presence of other people.
>
> (Talmon, 1964, p. 504)

We cannot, naturally, even attempt to sort out the relative importance of these various contributory factors.

VIII. Several of the girls in this group were married, which seemed to cause a certain amount of discomfort to the males. The feeling was expressed early in the year that the group leader was somehow to blame for allowing this imbalance to have occurred (in fact the group leader had no control over the composition of the group, which should have been obvious from the fact that each individual had chosen his own group, but one widespread form of the experiment myth involves the fantasy that different groups are composed on different principles to test hypotheses regarding composition effects). Marriage was seen as making women "inaccessible" to the group. One boy suggested that the group leader bring his wife to the group but then remarked that it wouldn't be a good idea because they might "take her away from him." When Lillian, one of the married women, later became divorced, however, it seemed to create a great deal of anxiety and confusion among the group members, particularly the males, who felt uncertain about how to respond to her. In the first few weeks of the group there had been a brief "battle of the sexes," and sex roles were discussed at great length during the last two sessions of the group. This was closely tied to the issue of marital and age status, however, for in a session about a month before the end of the group a girl brought up the point that sex role differentiation is minimal in our society in childhood, and that the importance of occupational inequalities was only now becoming clear to her. She argued that sexual equality in the class was assumed but not real, and suggested that the fact that they usually referred to each other as "boys and girls," and rarely as "males and females" or "men and women" was an attempt to preserve the earlier, minimal differentiation. Some of the other females objected that this terminology was almost universal for their age group and that even middle-aged people referred to themselves in these terms—a reflection of the cultural value on youth. A male then expressed the feeling that marriage made people seem and feel older, and that the married women in the group thought of themselves as women and were viewed by others as older by virtue of their presumed greater sexual experience. One of the married girls confirmed this by reminding the group of an incident in which she had been picked up by another girl for referring to herself as a woman. One of the boys then noted that she also referred to males in the group as "boys," and that this differentiation was a challenge to their masculinity. Another boy reported his experience with a friend his own age who had recently been married, and with whom he now felt "six years younger." A few minutes later Lillian remarked that "the time has come for me to be cautious about myself. I feel very, very, very uncomfortable that I'm not married any more."

The last session of this group began with a discussion of the role of the girls in the group and the fact that the "unknown husbands" of the married ones gave them "some kind of mythical power." There was a feeling that all females had some advantage in the group from their ability to ward off masculine hostility with a "sexy look," but that this created a particularly difficult problem in the case of the married girls since the males felt inhibited from responding in kind with some sort of sexual byplay, so that they were at a total disadvantage. Others felt that it was easier, since they could flirt more freely with no expectation of future involvement. One boy said marriage made it possible to put the girl "more in the mother role," and that it was "a different type of flirting that goes on between a mother and child than between a girl and a boy," although he felt unable to describe the difference. They then complained that not only did the girls "play it both ways," being now motherly, now girlish, but that the married ones could "communicate" with the group leader, while "inaccessible" to the other members.

Some of their earlier conflicts were now recalled, particularly the rationalization that girls received higher average grades because they studied all the time. The group leader suggested that behind this lay the feeling that he rewarded the girls more. One of the males replied that they felt "the married girls in the group were more accessible to you because you were married, I mean, you and the married people sort of formed a clique because you had something in common which set you more or less above the unmarried people in the class . . . somehow there is less of a sexual barrier between you and the married women than between you and the rest of the boys and girls. . . ."

The group leader then suggested that Lillian's divorce had upset the group's efforts to make rigid distinctions between married and unmarried girls. Lillian reported that since she was divorced no one in the group ever took her out for coffee, and no one seemed to know what to make of her. Several members then recalled the uncomfortable reaction that occurred when Lillian had invited the group to her house. A boy remarked that all the boys had been trying to put all the girls "in this mother role," and that the reason for this was that in social situations the group leader seemed to be "very attractive to girls" and able to control them, giving rise to the fantasy that they would marry all the girls to the group leader, making them their mothers and thus eliminating their competition as sisters, who had a "tremendous natural advantage" in "trying to please authority." This was discussed for the remainder of the hour, some emphasis being given to the role of women as a buffer preventing the expression of hostility between father and sons.

                                                      (C. P. Whitlock, transcript)

Here we find the fantasy of sexual monopoly quite clearly expressed, along with some of its determinants. The danger of competing with females for the favor of a male, the fear that the females might be not only brighter but also more competent sexually, combine to produce anxiety over masculine adequacy. This anxiety is salved by the device of promoting the girls to the leader's generation. They thus deny that the females are available sexual objects, avoid a competition in which males would be tempted to behave in a passive feminine manner toward the leader, avoid sexual rivalry with the latter, and avoid being rejected as sexually incompetent by the females. If they are seductive with the females it is only as Oedipal little boys flirting with their mothers; nothing is expected of them and they have nothing to lose. Lillian's divorce disturbs the fantasy, however, and she is studiously avoided.

The remark that the girls in a group are "inaccessible" for one reason or another occurs frequently and seems to require only one married girl to touch it off. We will encounter it also in IIb and IIe.

IIg. During a session in which a "displaced" revolt was taking place (see this volume, p. 49), Julie initiated a discussion of the concern of modern corporations with the wives of their young executives. (See Whyte, 1962.) Particular emphasis was placed on an incident in which a corporation "broke up" a marriage. A little later, around a more general discussion of the power of corporations, one of the members suggested that they were talking about the group leader, an interpretation with which they all agreed. There had been some feeling expressed in previous sessions that the competitive pressure of the midyear examination, through which they had just passed, was destroying the solidarity of the group.

IIc. It might be assumed (and was) that in an all-male group such fantasies and taboos would be absent. In this group there were two or three girls present at the first meeting but they did not return. The fantasy subsequently emerged that the group leader had somehow had an active part in preventing the girls from joining the group, just as he withheld help and rewards in general.

Thus the absence of females is no bar to the theme of the sexually monopolistic despot. It is usually visible whenever the group is large and the members have little or no prior acquaintance. But while Freud imagined the primal father as exercising a real sexual monopoly through overt compulsion, he also placed great emphasis (as have most dynamic psychologists since) on the fact that free sexual choice and expression for any individual are achieved only when he is able to detach his libido from parental objects.[37] In a group this parental attachment is transferred onto the group leader, and tends to dilute and distort normal sexual interest among group members.

IIe. About a month after the group began, a discussion arose concerning the general constraint exhibited in talking of sexual matters. Some annoyance was expressed over the tendency to use polite, technical, and circumlocutious terms instead of the four-letter colloquialisms normal among intimates. They wondered if the group leader inhibited them, and this led to a prolonged discussion of his role in the group. Some argued that he was essentially functionless, and the question was even raised briefly as to what might happen if he weren't there. But this was quickly drowned in an attack on the silent members—particularly one or two who did a lot of notetaking. This led to no resolution, however (the nonparticipants rather smugly reaffirming the superiority of their approach), and the discussion moved on to a comparison of the group leader's role with that of a therapist. After some argument about the essential qualities of the latter, they again began to attack the leader, this time in a joking context. Curt, who just prior to the session had encountered him in the local snack bar eating a hasty lunch, made some derogatory comments about his culinary tastes, in which the others soon joined. Mock indignation was expressed at the contrast between this secular weakness and the sacred role in which the group had placed him (see Chapter I of this volume), a discussion which culminated in Paul asking with a rhetorical flourish, "Does God drink chocolate milk?" The group leader, who had acquired a reputation for

[37] It is this interminable struggle for libidinal freedom that seems to provide the psychological foundation for the ubiquitous myth of the dragon combat. As Fontenrose points out, the conflict usually involves both a male and a female dragon, and we may note that it appears most frequently in cultures where the nuclear family is strong and unilineal extensions of the incest taboo weak. Sumer, which produced the earliest known version, had a family system which seems to have been much like ours (cf. Fontenrose, 1959, pp. 9 ff., 146–164, 262 ff., 491 ff.; Campbell, 1949, pp. 352–353 and passim; Linton, 1959, pp. 309 ff.)

physiognomic gravity, was much amused by this image, and participated in the laughter which followed. When Laura, who several times had expressed a fear of looking at the group leader (likening him to her unexpressive father), observed this she burst out: "He laughed! I'm cured! Now we can get back to sex. I'd forgotten what it was like!" A week later Peggy appeared in a new hairdo which everyone admired. Paul suggested that one of the males should now grow a mustache.

This incident illustrates the interaction of individual and group processes. For all members, any attack on the leader, whether a full revolt or simply some consensual sniping, tends to break the transference spell. In part, this seems even to be the goal of such attacks, for inasmuch as mockery and ridicule always constitute a major part of it, the attack serves to remind the members of the fallible humanity of the leader. For the group as a whole, then, in the above example, the derision itself was a transference-breaking phenomenon. For Laura, however, who had devoted so much childhood energy to trying to provoke a reaction from an impassive father, and had been pursuing a similar policy in the group, the crucial incident was the leader's response, the effect of which, although momentary, was so dramatic that she was able to verbalize what was for other members a more vague and limited sensation. But naturally a single incident never resolves such complex problems and this process was repeated many times in this group, as we shall see.

IIe. The group leader's real or imagined capacity to inhibit sexual feelings between members was challenged a month later. Henry voiced the opinion that their recent analysis of a case, which they now saw as entirely sexual in its subject matter, had treated it "as if it were a church picnic." Frank questioned the sexlessness of a church picnic. There was some argument about this and they began citing a long series of examples of the close relationship between sexuality and religion. Mention was made of nuns becoming "brides of Christ," of the sexual nature of religious visions, of *Elmer Gantry*, of the religious injunction to copulate on the Sabbath, and of the use of churches for sexual purposes by young lovers.

The next session was a prolonged discussion of the Twist, some arguing that the dance was unattractive and basically masturbatory, others that it was gracefully sensual. After a time the discussion began to center around Laura, who regarded herself as something of an expert in it, and Paul, who attacked all dancing as a poor substitute for copulation. It was during this debate that Laura made the remark noted above (see this volume, p. 25), about dancing around the leader on a stake. The argument continued, with Laura teasing and coaxing Paul to let her teach him how to Twist, and Paul trying to show the undesirability of casual and unconsummated sexuality. (During this discussion he sat on the arm of his chair, as if by added height to ward off the threat posed by Laura's sexual aggressiveness.) He argued that dancing was analogous to the childhood game of spin-the-bottle—that after a time the participants would "take the bottle away and neck without it," and that dancing similarly became anachronistic with the loss of virginity.

As the argument proceeded the leader commented that the other members seemed to be very absorbed in it, and that perhaps they were hoping Laura and Paul would work out problems common to all. Several of the girls then admitted a strong identification with Laura, being very concerned that Paul not reject her and wanting to tell her how to act in order to prevent this. The males were not so sure of their role and seemed a little jealous of Paul's position. Lorna, who previously had suggested that the group members wanted Laura and Paul to copulate for them, so that they wouldn't have to themselves, now commented that she saw the group as stretched along a linear continuum from Paul to Laura, and felt that if they could only get these two ends united they would have a full and complete circle.

After some further discussion about the Twist the group began to break into subgroups, and when Jim remarked on this, Henry reported that he had been talking aside with Charlotte about how disturbed he had been by her fur-lined glove, which she had turned back as she slid her hand in and out the fingers while listening to the discussion.

At the beginning of the next session Edna reported a dream in which the group leader had been explaining to the group that his wife was upset because she didn't understand what the group was all about and why it absorbed so much of his time and energy. He had then asked the group whether he should "tell her about the group." (Edna associated this dream with an early session in which a graduate student had asked the group leader for permission to sit in and had been referred to the group members for decision. She also mentioned for the first time that she was in analysis.) This led to a discussion of absent members, common deprivations, common differences from friends outside the group, hostility to the group leader, lack of progress, and personality changes they felt had and had not taken place in them.

This sequence expresses the continuing struggle over the distribution of libido in the group. The discussion of sex and religion first stresses the extent to which libido is bound up in the leader: all are "brides of Christ" as in the primal horde. But then it is noted that couples can mate despite the presence of authority: in church, on the Sabbath, and so forth. In the next session this possibility is symbolically enacted, although with consistently greater enthusiasm on the female than on the male side (a phenomenon which will appear again).

Laura associates the dancing with killing the leader, Paul with "taking the bottle away." The third session, with its Oedipal dream, seems to show a libidinal regression, but is actually rather complex in this regard.[38] Edna's dream, for example, seems at first to be a simple transference dream of the type so familiar to the psychotherapist, and we may surmise that the group leader and the group are careless disguises for Edna's analyst and herself respectively. But her having a "therapist all to herself" seems to threaten the group, giving rise to concern over member desertions and preoccupation with the group's allegedly "therapeutic" effect, and since the dream was set in the group and recited to it, it is reasonable to assume that it also echoes some specifically group concerns. Note that in the dream the group is keeping the leader and his wife apart, and is asked to decide whether revealing information is an appropriate solution to this problem. This is a neat inversion of the group feeling that attachment to the leader keeps them apart from one another, but the proposed solution is the same, as is the fact that it is "left up to them." The dream thus expresses both leader-cathecting and group-cathecting tendencies, as does the ensuing discussion with its emphasis on group exclusiveness and superiority combined with frustration and self-disgust.

One accompaniment to the detachment of libido from the group leader is a battle of the sexes, often rather abstract, but occasionally revolving explicitly around the issue of who is most committed to dependence on the leader.

IIe. Most of a session was being spent on the relation between "transference" and "reality." The members reminisced about their relationships with their own fathers, and argued about whether the group leader was really cold or protective, and what *his* fantasies might be like. There then followed a rather teasing attack on the group leader by the girls. Jim accused them of having "incestuous fantasies" to which Edna replied rather complacently that the leader in fact "favored" them. When the leader asked if the boys distrusted the girls' rebelliousness Jim maintained it was nothing but reaction formation. Paul then commented that homosexual feelings toward the leader had also been aroused, and this was followed by some joking between Paul and Jim about homosexual ap-

[38] All "progress" in groups is necessarily temporary, since it produces the confidence to "take it a little deeper," either in the sense of increasing the personal relevance of the issue to individual members or of establishing its connectedness with other group problems. Each "gain" is weighted with new burdens, and the victory seems to peter out like a perfected skill which wavers when an attempt is made to add new elements to it. This is discouraging to group members, who begin to feel that everything is ephemeral.

proaches. Lorna and Andrea then defended Paul's virility and attractiveness, and this led to a confession by Paul that he was attracted to Andrea. They joked a bit about the Oedipal nature of "forbidden" attractions (Andrea was married) and then Jim asked the group leader if he was married. The leader responded with a question and they quickly began again to talk of families and transference, this time with considerable hilarity and solidarity.

Here can be seen again the ambivalent struggle to detach the libido from parental objects. In this incident the girls are ahead of the boys: there is much seductiveness in their attack but it is a *group* seductiveness—which by its very nature betokens a willingness to relinquish individual and private fantasies, to share them, like the confessions of ex-alcoholics. The secret treasure is relegated to the status of a common ailment, and the attitude toward it becomes humorous instead of worshipful. The attack thus represents a beginning of decathexis, as does the allegation of sexual favoritism.

For the males the problem is more difficult. Since libidinal liberation is generally achieved by admission of thraldom, they are put in the more difficult position of having to own up to homosexual feelings. This they can do only in a rather tense joking context and after Jim's attempt to discredit the progress achieved by the girls. Paul's effort is rewarded by the girls, however, and there is a brief blooming of heterosexual engagement within the group. Even this is put in Oedipal terms, however, and Jim quickly turns the topic back onto the leader.

IIe. A month later (the entire Twist episode intervened) a conflict again arose over which sex was most involved with the leader, this time with the girls playing the major accusatory role. For two sessions the members had sat so that the sexes were not intermingled, and the girls were actively "recruiting," i.e., encouraging (even demanding) the participation of the silent members, sneering at attempts to draw out the leader, rejecting the latter's interpretations contemptuously, etc. When Jim discussed his discomfort at his mother skippering his sailboat when he was out with friends, the leader interpreted the satisfaction of the males (who were not only outnumbered but as a group less active and articulate than the females) at having a male leader, and their enjoyment of the impotent rage of the more aggressive females against the leader. After some discussion this was generally accepted, and Andrea suggested that the more rebellious attitude of the girls was due to the fact that they were at an age when they were pulling away from their fathers, while the boys were more involved through their struggles in choosing a career. She suggested, however, that the *latent* hostility of the males was actually more intense, and this call to arms was underlined by Edna, who reported how angry she felt when anyone, but particularly a boy, asked the leader a question.

IIb. An acrimonious if often humorous debate over the role of the modern American woman occurred about a month after this group began, and led to the accusation that girls competed unfairly in academic situations, since their intellectual aggressiveness was coupled with seductiveness and dependency. Incidents in which women had obtained high grades in chemistry and biology by seducing laboratory instructors were solemnly recounted.

Several months later the issue was again discussed following an analysis of Williams' *Cat on a Hot Tin Roof*. Monty had argued that the play would really have been the same even if Maggie were left out, since the play really centered around Big Daddy, and in particular his relationship with Brick. "That quote from Dylan Thomas on the title page indicates something of what Williams was thinking—that's the quote about the dying father—and I wonder why he spent so much time—spent the whole first act on Maggie and then—and then—kind of dropped her." Vic and John disagreed, but Monty argued that Big Daddy was "at the bottom of" all of the relationships in the play, and tried to show that none of the other characters have motives independent of him. "He seems to sit like a big Buddha in the center of everything, which revolves around him." There followed a confused argument over this in which two group members were assuming that Big Daddy was dead at the end of the play. Similarities and differences between Maggie and Mae led to a discussion of the sensitivity of children. Then Monty raised the question as to whether people could change from a conversation. Gordon suggested that it depended upon how hard they were looking for an answer. Len said it was hard to believe that so much could take place in a "one hour discussion" (a phrase that was repeated three times). After some discussion of this the group leader made the obvious interpretation, and John then entered a plea for help, objecting that the group leader would never be a "crutch" for the group (the reference to the play was intentional). Vic said it was the tragedy of the class that they needed a leader so badly but were intolerant of anyone assuming the role. The leader wondered if the discussion of the play hadn't revolved around this issue, and whether the disproportionate emphasis on Maggie over Brick reflected male concern over feminine support.

Shortly after the next session began they started to argue over the relevance of this interpretation. Vic pointed out that in the play Maggie removed not only Brick's bottle and crutch but also his defenses—specifically denial. They recalled the "incest taboo" feeling that had been expressed in the group, and talked of the various "problems" encountered with the females in the group: i.e., one was married, one engaged, one too dogmatic, one too aloof, one too belligerent. Cathy suggested that no one could decide whether the females were females and if so how to treat them. Gordon wondered if the proportion (three boys to every girl) was relevant, and Monty asked what would happen were this male numerical advantage reversed. Much horror was expressed at this possibility and dire visions of henpecking were fashioned. Cathy said perhaps they felt henpecked anyway, while Barry wondered why the girls never felt a need to band together. Cathy said she always looked among males for an ally, and later asked if males felt stronger socially with a female in tow. Except for Barry, who said he felt weaker, they agreed that they did and cited roommate conversations (including, however, some comments which were distinctly derogatory toward females) in support of this. Monty said males were influenced by females to the degree they were trying to be accepted as a "good male." Gordon wondered if the "independence" of the girls made it harder or easier to feel this. The group leader then raised the question of what effect the absence of a formal "mother" role had on this issue. Monty picked this up and asked if there wasn't some way to add a mother figure to sit beside the leader—a life-size drawing or a "visiting stenographer"—so that the girls would not need to fill the vacant role and provide "support" for males, but could be freely competitive. John said this made the problem of sibling rivalry insoluble, but Vic argued that recognition would help. Bob suggested that the girls were competing for the leader's support "as a male" rather than from other males in the group, while the latter were competing for the females. Ralph wondered if this search for feminine affirmation came from doubts generated outside the group, and they began to talk about the prevalence of feelings of inadequacy and fears about homosexuality among Ivy League males, and their own difficulty in identifying with Brick in Williams' drama.

Six weeks later the issue arose anew, with many of the same ideas repeated. There was joking between Roger and Eve over a resolution that males and females be "separate but equal." Cathy again raised the question of "feminine wiles," and argued that it was particularly frequent in college because the age difference between student and teacher was reduced: "They're more equal." Stories of girls seducing instructors and vice versa were again brought up, and led to the question as to whether the seductive and intellectual techniques for gaining approval were combined or used separately. Several girls admitted that covert seductiveness was often added to their competing and striving. Cathy then denied that this was taking place in the group (it had been suggested earlier that neither technique was any use since it wasn't clear what the leader wanted), and Joe asked why the girls weren't looking to the boys for support, claiming that sex antagonism in the group was always based on the intellectual competitiveness of the girls. The leader then asked how girls get approval in the family, and this led to an extended discussion of sex roles and Oedipal competition in the family. Some of the boys discussed their own efforts to assess the likes and dislikes of the leader, and this led to consideration of whether or not girls in fact had the advantage in dealing with fathers, or whether this lay with younger children regardless of sex.

In this case the struggle for libidinal liberation is impeded somewhat by the group leader, who intervenes in the discussion whenever a rapprochement seems imminent. The males' attack on the females, however, does gradually reveal itself as a disguised plea for support. They express (although not directly) the anxiety aroused by the homosexual implications of competing seductively, and ask the girls to abandon their own "wiles" and rescue them from their emasculated condition. Their fear of effeminacy is portrayed in their initial attack on the girls, their attempts to "put them down," and their feeling of being "henpecked." [39]

IIb. The following two sessions were devoted to a discussion of three fairy tales from the Grimm collection: "The Twelve Brothers," "The Seven Ravens," and "The Six Swans." These they analysed in terms of castration and menstruation fantasies, Oedipal competition within the family, and sex antagonism. In the next session they began again to discuss hostility between the sexes, and in particular the subjugation of women. Eve pointed out that in many primitive societies women past the childbearing age were no longer excluded from ceremonies, etc. Angela wondered why this was so, and Roger suggested that sex and childbirth were surrounded with a mystery which made women seem more important. Ralph brought up the fact that women were not allowed in the principal undergraduate library. Roger said he was disturbed by this and wondered if it were based on a feeling that if women knew everything they could dispense with males altogether, even find ways to achieve conception, and men would then become drones. Some of the females in the group then expressed the feeling of wanting men to be dominant but also wanting to be able to be as aggressive as they felt and to achieve as much as they could. After some discussion of sex antagonism in the group they referred to the "Battle of the Sexes" in the fall, and its principal male protagonist, who had since flunked out of college. They talked with some affection about the role he had played in the group and its function for both sexes.

[39] The male reaction in such situations is reminiscent of the anti-feminism in classical Greece and in many primitive societies today. Just as in the group the males feared being outnumbered, so many primitive tribes feel that in the absence of bull-roarers, secret rites, and bogeys, they would be totally unable to control their women, and hence carefully exclude them from religious or (as in the case of the Greeks) political activities. Even in our supposed state of civilized enlightenment we find sex segregation wherever competition from women is deeply feared, as in virtually all athletic contests and in the more fusty corners of academia.

This session marks the beginning of a confrontation of the fears which have divided the sexes in the group.

B. Teaching as an Erotic Irritant

The problem of libidinal enthralment is intensified by the erotic ideas that traditionally surround the transmission of knowledge and the acquisition of understanding. Much has been written about the importance of sexual curiosity as a kind of first-stage rocket for intellectual pursuits, but far less has been said about the extent to which the process of teaching itself is defined in sexual terms. Descriptions of traditional teaching techniques have decidedly phallic-penetrative overtones, using phrases such as "fertile minds," "pregnant with meaning," "planting the seeds" of knowledge, and so on (not to mention such extreme formations as the "Rape of the Mind"). It is small wonder that female college students seem so much less conflicted about learning than do their male counterparts. Being "seduced" by an idea does not de-sex them.[40]

The other side of this sexualization of learning is commented on by Maslow in a recent paper:

At an unconscious level, knowing as an intrusive, penetrating-into, as a kind of masculine sexual equivalent, can help us to understand the archaic complex of conflicting emotions that may cluster around the child's peeping into secrets, into the unknown, some women's feeling of a contradiction between femininity and boldly knowing, of the underdog's feeling that knowing is a prerogative of the master, of the religious man's fear that knowing trespasses on the jurisdiction of the gods. . . .

(Maslow, 1963, p. 121)

He comments on the biblical use of "knowing" as sexual conquest.

(The basis for this sexualization may indeed be biological. All body orifices are highly eroticized, and it is not entirely surprising

[40] The fact that most of the energy in university learning is expended in fighting it is not due entirely to sex role training or sexual definitions of the learning process. The greatest barriers to learning are erected by the teachers themselves, by the priestly monopolism of their methods and attitudes, their fear of youth and approaching obsolescence, and their gatekeeper orientation to their discipline. When experimental programs strip away these barriers some instructors are shocked by the realization that their function as teachers has been merely to inhibit a violent curiosity; and pleading that the new programs take too much time, they return to the more traditional pursuit of opening, with much fanfare and condescension, one little door at a time.

that when the medium of exchange is symbolic rather than material, the orifices of the mind should be symbolically eroticized as well.)

Similarly, there are two ways in which the activities of the group leader tend themselves to generate erotic fantasies. First, his role as one who encourages psychological exploration is often seductively defined. Second, his unexpected interpretive intrusions into the group process are sometimes felt as some sort of rude phallic penetration, and either relished or violently resented as such. Let us examine some examples of both of these processes.

IIa. This meeting took place in the interlude between the beginning and the culmination of the revolt. The group was discussing Freud's case of "Little Hans," and some term papers were to be returned at the end of the meeting. The members were preoccupied, as is usual in such discussions, with the issue of the father acting as therapist, and to so small a boy. Jerry was particularly concerned with the origin of Hans' positive feelings toward his father. "Why should he love his father in the first place? His father's just a doctor." When after some discussion it was suggested by the group leader that according to Freud one loves a source of gratification, Jerry countered that in this instance the father was a source of frustration. He then asked if this love for the father was "completely homosexual." Joe then remarked, "somehow I have the feeling that as a result of this analysis Hans has some mild degree of homosexual tendencies. . . . If he continues to grow up in this type of atmosphere this is what will happen." Duncan agreed, citing Hans' interest in a playmate, but Joe said he meant something more lasting than this. Jay pointed out that Hans was "normal" at 19, to which Joe answered that he had read little of the latter part of Freud's analysis. There was a long pause, and when the group leader suggested verbalizing their thoughts, Betty and Susan expressed a feeling that their discussions were becoming more constrained. Duncan then reflected that "the string holding the sword over our heads is just getting thinner. It'll drop in 11½ minutes."

The concern over positive transference thus derives from the confluence of two forces: first, the difficulty of maintaining their rebellious stance in the face of the imminent receipt of their graded papers; and second, the seductive definition of psychological exploration. "Growing up in this atmosphere" should be taken to refer both to the immediate Damoclean dilemma and the general investigative climate of the group.

IId. Andy reported a dream (see this volume, pp. 174–175) in which he was wandering through a large building filled with movie theatres, looking unsuccessfully for one with an audience which suited his tastes.

Climbing into the attic he came to a man seated at a desk who, without looking up or speaking, motioned him on across the attic to a room which proved to be empty.

XI. A member of an all-female group reported a dream in which she asked the leader for a private conference, a request which he agreed to, but harshly refused when the time came. The leader then went out onto a terrace and stood by a fountain talking happily to some female teachers. The girl pleaded with him that he had promised but he sent her away denying any knowledge of the matter. "Then you came down from the steps, went down the hill and began to run down the path that led to nowhere. I took out after you saying, 'Mr. Jones, you promised me.'"

(Jones, 1960, pp. 47–8)

IIe. Andrea early in the year reported a dream in which the group leader was literally in the "dark at the top of the stairs" (referring to the William Inge play of that name), unseen, saying, "don't be afraid, Andrea, come on upstairs." She was nevertheless frightened. The dream was told in the context of expressing feelings of being trapped by the presence of the group leader and wishing he weren't there.

We shall later examine a second dream reported by Andrea which shows a marked shift from libidinal involvement with the leader to libidinal involvement with other group members.

These dreams define the group leader as one who encourages exploration into the unknown. One is scoptophilic, the others more openly erotic. Here the effect of the group leader is a catalytic one: the Oedipal fantasies are aroused primarily by the nature of the training group situation. In the case of interpretation, the reaction depends more on what the group leader actually does.

Everyone is familiar with the fact that psychological interpretation can be employed for aggressive purposes. The interpreter is at all times, and with the kindest intent, something of an intruder, trying to expose the hidden, presuming to know more about the recipient than he does himself, and essentially invading the structure of his personality and meddling in his "internal affairs." If this occurs in a medical setting it sometimes becomes integrated with the frightened or excited fantasies about the doctor-who-invades-the-body. If it occurs in an academic setting it may be fused with similar notions about the teacher-who-invades-the-fertile-young-mind. It thus at times becomes a sexualized aggression. The recipient feels violated: not only angry and humiliated, but also excited, confused, and disturbed.

Not all styles of interpretation display this quality to an equal extent. The more the group leader confines himself to mild observations about affective behavior and interpersonal relationships the less the interpretation will be experienced in this way. The more the interpretation connects manifest verbal behavior and latent fantasies, the more it involves sexual symbolism or unconscious impulses, the more cryptic and metaphorical it seems, the more the recipients may feel psychically ravished by it. Since most group leaders operate all along this continuum, according to their perception of the issues and needs of the moment, their own behavior is a variable, the consequences of which they must be ready to assess at all times.

The intrusive quality of interpretation is of course what gives rise to the autotomy responses referred to in a previous section. The group leader is felt as a chronic irritant in the orifice of the group: "In and out! In and out!" as one exasperated group member put it. In order to reduce this irritation most groups try both to extrude the leader and to incorporate him entirely as "just another member."

Some groups, however, fall into a pattern in which the leader's interpretations seem simply to be a source of erotic delight. They are neither angrily rejected nor a source of insight and group development. The group interacts, the leader interprets, the group members receive the interpretation passively—smiling when they agree with it, laughing when they do not, looking at all times pleased and rewarded—and then return to the discussion, usually omitting the theme which gave rise to the interpretation. The merest twitch on the part of the group leader suggesting he is about to speak brings a hush, and the members sit with lowered eyes until he has finished. They may even write down what he has said, ignoring persistent comments (also written down) on their so doing. This is a particularly difficult pattern for the group leader to handle, since the best remedy is total silence for a prolonged period—a solution requiring enormous patience and security at a time when the leader is most likely to feel exasperated at the group's lack of progress and insecure about his own competence. If he points out the erotic nature of their response to interpretation this serves merely to provide additional titillation, as will a frank confession of his feelings of helplessness and frustration. This is indeed one of the most interesting aspects of this pattern: by transforming what is normally a minor facet of the interpretation-response interaction into its raison d'être the group members have achieved a kind of covert passive rebellion against the group leader. Through a sexualized response they express hostility, and by treating each interpretation as a gratifying phallus they render it impotent.

Since this syndrome is somewhat rare, and since the fantasies that give rise to it are typically far from awareness, it is difficult to produce examples which lend support to a thesis which almost requires observation for credibility. Fortunately, a member of one group which exhibited this syndrome verbalized a similar view of it, so that one brief discussion is available to us.

IIc. Toward the middle of the year the group members one day expressed considerable resentment over the low grades they had received on an exam. They began questioning the leader about his grading methods and the lack of comments on the returned exams. The leader, who had indeed made fewer comments on the exams than was his wont, and who felt somewhat guilty about the haste with which he had performed this tedious function, became defensive, answering questions, but rather laconically. (A colleague, listening to a recording of the session referred to this incident as "the group undressing the leader.") After a minute or two the leader recovered the initiative by interpreting and deflecting the barrage of questions, and as the group turned to other topics he continued to interpret rather actively throughout the remainder of the hour, as if to compensate for his moment of "weakness." A few minutes before the end Gregory had one of what the other members referred to as his "brainstorms," when he would snap his fingers suddenly and express an idea or interpretation they considered "far out": "Did it strike anybody else that there was something sexual about this exchange, as if we were all sort of trying to work him up to a climax, and then when he spoke everybody sort of sat back and relaxed?" While this produced some laughter and expressions of wonderment, it was not brushed aside, but generated a series of questions.

HAL: In other words, are you saying that we were sexually excited when he talked? (Laughter.)

GREGORY: I say that we're—excited, but not sexually in the—genital sense of the word.

HAL: No, but—I'm just trying to understand what you mean by this sexual—

GREGORY: I'm using sexual in the same way I think Freud uses it, but whether or not I'm right is another matter.

CARL: But whether or not you're right you won't know from this course (laughter), which is another reason why—

STAN: You mean you get gratification of libidinal drives?

GREGORY: Uh—I'm not too sure what libidinal is—I think there's a certain gratification of emotional drives.

STAN: Well—drives.

GREGORY: Same thing?

STAN: Well, yes.

BARRY: Well, *I* sure don't feel any better.

GREGORY: Sorry, Barry (laughter).

STAN: Anyone waiting as eagerly as I am for this period to end? (Many yesses, someone says "looks that way.")

HAL: Why?

STAN: I'm bored. Hey, one question: doesn't the Delphic Oracle usually speak just about the end of the period?

CHRIS: Not until the bell rings—when we're ready to receive it.

PETE: Well, in the minute remaining, I'll say that my roommate read my exam—

ARNOLD: Hey wait, lemme, hold on a second. I want to ask you [Gregory], why did you *say* that, anyway? (Laughter.)

GREGORY: Well, why not? The parallel struck me.

HAL: What gave you the idea?

ARNOLD: Really? Did it really strike you? A lot of times when we say something, we think, well, first we'll see how it will sound.

GREGORY: Oh yeah, I think that's true. But I don't think it was, I don't know.

ARNOLD: We've been talking all the time about things but we didn't really feel we were saying anything. Now all of a sudden you come out with this great new theory—wow!

GREGORY: Well, I don't know. Maybe I just wanted to shake everybody up, sort of.

HAL: Well what made you say this, do you know?

GREGORY: I don't know—during this silence I didn't feel much like being silent, because I was still mad at him. I wondered why everybody else was. I've been reading Freud.

The session ends with Gregory deprecating his idea and the others showing a kind of ambivalent fascination. Note that two efforts to change the subject (both by members usually successful at creating humorous diversions) fail. Note also how boredom with the discussion of the phenomenon is associated with a desire to reexperience it, a desire whose fulfilment, however, is described as bearable only under conditions of immediate flight.

An example of this same definition of the act of interpretation is found in a paper by Rodrigué (1957), concerning the treatment of a three-year-old mute schizophrenic child. After many play sessions in which responses to the therapist's remarks were inferred rather than manifest, the child finally stopped and smiled at him twice in a row following interpretive questions. "The twice-repeated sequence of meaningful responses such as these to a question of mine had never before occurred; never before had he come so near a direct answer. This was followed immediately by his climbing on to the table, lying on his back and opening his legs. It seemed that for him acknowledging my question was the same as the act of receiving the male organ. . . . Thus it might be said that, for Raul, to understand was literally to *conceive*" (Rodrigué, 1957, p. 168).

The fundamental issue in all of this is the gratification of dependency needs, and the sexualization of the member-leader interaction is merely a way of achieving this goal. The phallic definition of the leader's interpretations may be viewed in the same way as the phallic symbolism in the 23rd Psalm of David: "Thy rod and Thy staff they comfort me," which is immediately followed by images of oral plenty. It is, in other words, the cornucopia fantasy familiar from the phallic worship of Mediterranean cultures. It is in the same sense that the following incidents should be understood.

IIb. In the midst of a discussion about a potential revolt (see this volume, pp. 45–46) Madeline was insisting that everything would be easier if the leader would "join the group." Bob maintained that the early member comments in any session were just a process of "groping for approval," and Madeline added, "to see who's going to bite on what." Bob likened this process to turning on a hose: first a spurt of water, then a lot of air, then, after a comment by the leader, a steady stream, and everything was fine—the comment laying a "foundation" for the group.

IIf. It was the last meeting of the group. During the previous three sessions there had been the usual discussions about termination, and these were now continued. There were fantasies of immortality (a group TV program, a group coloring book), fantasies of terminal revelation, jealousy of the leader's having a new group, feelings of failure, concern over whether they had changed or not, etc. In the course of this Aaron suggested jokingly that at the end of the session they would all fall upon the group leader and grab his penis.

We are reminded by this fantasy of the lynching customs described in this volume (page 77) and of the following passage from Zola's *Germinal*, in which the relation between oral deprivation and the attack on the phallus is made rather explicit:

They surrounded the still warm body. They insulted it with laughter . . . vociferating in the face of death the long-stored rancour of their starved lives.

"I owed you sixty francs, now you're paid, thief!" said Maheude, enraged like the others. "You won't refuse me credit any more. Wait! Wait! I must fatten you once more!"

With her fingers she scratched up some earth, took two handfuls and stuffed it violently into his mouth.

"There! eat that! There! eat! eat! you used to eat us!"

The abuse increased, while the dead man, stretched on his back, gazed motionless. . . . This earth heaped in his mouth was the bread he had refused to give. . . .

But the women had another revenge to wreak on him. They moved round, smelling him like she-wolves. They were all seeking for some outrage, some savagery that would relieve them.

Mother Brûlé's shrill voice was heard: "Cut him like a tom-cat! . . ."

Mouquette was already unfastening and drawing off the trousers, while the LeVaque woman raised the legs. And Mother Brûlé with her dry old hands separated the naked thighs and seized this dead virility. She took hold of everything, tearing with an effort which bent her lean spine and made her long arms crack. The soft skin resisted; she had to try again, and at last carried away the fragment, a lump of hairy and bleeding flesh, which she brandished with a laugh of triumph. . . .

Mother Brûlé then planted the whole lump on the end of her stick, and holding it in the air, bore it about like a banner, rushing along the road, followed, helter-skelter, by the yelling troop of women. . . .

(Zola, 1948, pp. 281–2. Excerpted in Coser, 1963)

Yet the fact that the path to gratification of dependency needs is a sexual one must also be explained. It suggests at the very least a regressive orientation to a period in life when sexuality and dependency were not differentiated as they tend to be in adult thinking (although lovers use parent-child kinship terms in every part of the world). Fantasies of reproduction—always active when the issue of the group's death arises—also contributed to the last group example, as we shall see later.

It is at the oral level that interaction in training and therapy groups is most generally focussed, around such concerns as "what am I getting from this group?" and "will it devour me [my individuality]?", and we may note that revolt and the sexualization of the interpretive role of the leader essentially constitute two different solutions to feelings of emptiness. In the revolt the group members in effect form themselves into a mouth, devouring the leader, destroying his authority, incorporating his skills. But in a sense he is now "gone," since an attitude and a view of him as powerful and protective have disappeared. The step appears regressive but is associated with a striving toward maturity and independence. The feeling is that by gaining the leader's powers he can be dispensed with.

Paradoxically, the sexualization of the interpretive role of the leader, although it does not have this primitive cannibalistic quality, is more regressive in its aim. In this case the group members in effect form a vagina for the leader, enticing him to return again and again so that they may be restored and comforted by his "gifts." Here the desired attributes are kept outside, so that they may be absorbed over and over and never "destroyed." The process is basically an oral one, the group waiting for the breast. It obtains its genital veneer only from (a) the accident of having a male leader, (b) the illusorily pro-active and intrusive character of interpretations, which seem to come "out of the blue" to those who have not followed the group leader's thought processes and are unaware of the aspect of the discussion that set them in motion, and (c) the reproductive imagery generally associated with academic and therapeutic endeavors.

Our penultimate example is from the group psychotherapy literature, and illustrates several themes simultaneously.

X. "The ages of the five patients ranged from 29 to 31. They were all timid and self-conscious, and led a very restricted social life. . . . Four of the five were out-patients and came from respectable middle-class homes. . . . Their sexual life had been without obvious blemish. . . . [Miss S.] was an in-patient with a working-class background . . . and the only member with a history of illicit sexual affairs. . . . Some of her early contributions shocked the group. She spoke of homo- and hetero-sexual desires at a time when the other patients shied away from such embarrassing topics. She frequently roused the jealousy of her fellow members by asking for extra interviews with the therapist.

"[After several months] the patients began to show signs of being disturbed by their ambivalent transference feelings for the therapist. They were reluctant to admit and discuss these feelings openly. They turned to a related topic instead. They levelled an attack against a figment of their imagination—the figment of the sexually domineering male. Their discussions livened up as they eagerly aired their aggressive fantasies.

"But the rather nebulous shape of this figment was only a poor substitute for the male therapist, their real target. It was not possible to keep up for long the pretence of completely disregarding the part he played in their dilemma. A timidly daring note of rebellion against his authority was sounded, but its poignancy was disguised by an affecta-tion of playful banter. He was told facetiously that his presence prevented free discussions. Would he please leave the room or, at least, turn his back on them.

"With this change of target . . . the phalanx of feminine solidarity was broken. Individual voices were now heard in defence of the therapist, dreams were reported which clearly indicated erotic transference feelings, signs of jealousy appeared among the members . . . and the appeal for private therapeutic interviews became more frequent." The authors go on to describe how the members used Miss S. as a scapegoat by provoking her to have an adulterous affair outside the group and then criticizing her for it, following which they all began to discuss sexual problems with greater freedom.

(Taylor and Rey, 1953, p. 257)

On the surface, this example seems to go in a direction opposite from that suggested above: a group begins as a solidary one, becoming disunited and Oedipal *following* a mild revolt. Leaving aside for now the unconscious and undifferentiated nature of their bonds (an issue we will take up in Chapter V) we may note simply that this solidarity depended on scapegoating one member and keeping hidden their erotic feelings toward the therapist. Their unity increasingly includes the deviant member as well as their own needs. The fact that it is a one-sex group sets up barriers against erotic involvement with peers, but we may note that following the revolt they express this involvement by their collusion in Miss S.'s affair, and ultimately by their greater verbal freedom with one another. (Note their statement, a revolt cliché, that the therapist's presence "prevented free discussions.")

Of particular importance for the present discussion is the phallic, intrusive image of the therapist which is expressed. Unfortunately we do not have their precise remarks, which would be of great interest, but the fact that they asked the "sexually domineering male" to turn his back (this request was the only atypical part of the entire scene) underlines their phallic perception of the situation, as well as being a provocative exhibitionistic gesture.

We can also see here the operation of Mills' law of identification through aggression: it is only when the middle-class members have attacked the less inhibited Miss S. that they can express their own sexual impulses openly.

The following exchange, from another all-female group with a male leader, also provides a copulatory image of the leader-group relationship. ("G" represents a member, "L" the leader.)

G: You just sit there. You never get excited. You never get angry. We could get up and do the Highland Fling and you'd just sit there.
G: Don't you think if you *did* give more that what you want and what we want would finally come about?
L: You'll bring it about.
G: Do you have *any* opinions of your own?
L: Yes.
G: But they don't belong here?
L: I think there is something in between us here that we don't see.

G: Do you mean that you *and* us don't see, or just us?
L: Just you on this point.
G: *Is it that the group is a she and you're a he?*
L: That's certainly a difference, isn't it?

(Jones, 1960, pp. 58–59; italics his)

C. Oedipal Disengagement and the Group Orgy Theme

We have already seen one example of the transfer of libido from leader to peers in the Twist incident in IIe described above. Let us now examine a few others, beginning with one very early effort and ending with some rather late ones.

IIe. There were in this group three distinct revolt episodes. The first occurred only three weeks after the group began and was generally forgotten by the members even when substantially repeated later on in the year. Whether this amnesia was due to the fact that the early revolt was primarily the work of a woman, or to the fact that it occurred so early as to have little conscious meaning as an aggressive act, cannot be said.

The group leader arrived to find Laura seated in his chair. Most of the other members were crowded with gleeful and expectant smiles around the two ends of the table, as if to force him to take a seat in the middle of one of the long sides. The seat next to Laura, however, had been left vacant, although Frank had his foot in it. The group leader took his usual route toward his own chair and when Laura showed no signs of moving, pulled out the adjacent one, Frank removing his foot as he did so. Almost immediately the members decided to discuss a case study involving an abortive sexual relationship between a rather Pygmalionesque college student and a high school girl. The discussion was rather tense and giggly, with an unusual amount of embarrassment over finding an agreeable level of sexual terminology. After some time and much male resistance they arrived at the conclusion (usual for this case study) that the girl in the case was far more competent sexually than the boy. This seemed to find an echo in the group itself, the girls being rather coquettish, seductive, and "knowing" in the discussion, the boys appearing somewhat stuffy, passive, and negativistic. There was a long discussion of what constituted virginity, with terms such as "technical virginity" and "psychological virginity" being much in use. They wondered whether the sexual norms they now held were a function of their age or of the times. Lorna suggested that whereas now they believed that it was better for a girl to have intercourse with one boy than to tease several, they might embrace the opposite view, now held by their parents, when they themselves became parents. Paul suggested having a reunion in a couple of years to see, and they elaborated a fantasy in which each member would arrive at this reunion dragging a child by the arm.

Attention now focussed on Laura, who had been sitting cross-legged in her chair and was becoming increasingly restless—fidgeting, giggling, shifting her position, crossing and uncrossing her legs, and talking more. She announced that she felt very tense and wanted something to do with her hands. Paul gave her a cigarette, which she smoked (she was a non-smoker). She said she was active because she did not want to look at the group leader, then did so and became somewhat ostentatiously flustered. The other members seemed to enjoy the scene and were clearly egging her on. It was suggested that she had a general tendency to form crushes on instructors and after she had admitted to this weakness they questioned her about these. Charlotte suggested that the altered seating arrangement made the group leader seem more like a student.

In this incident we find the entire revolt cycle played out in miniature, albeit inconclusively. The leader's place is usurped by a girl who demonstrates to him how the group wishes him to be: active, affiliative, sexy. Following this displacement there is a heightening of sexual interest between the members, which is expressed both behaviorally and in choice of subject matter. As the meeting progresses, however, a regression seems to set in, with the major libidinal preoccupation again centering around the leader at the close.

This seems to be an ambivalent effort by the members to free themselves from the leader and at the same time lure him into the group. The discussion of the case study, furthermore, represents not only a desire to express their sexual feelings toward each other, but also their disappointment in the leader for accepting Laura's usurpation so passively. The issue of the male college student's sexual adequacy reflects this disappointment as well as their own shame at having been upstaged by a female revolutionary, and their rather embarrassed response to the seductiveness of the other girls. The unusual tension about sexual terms also expresses their unreadiness to confront each other as free sexual beings. As we shall see, the greater receptiveness of the girls to sexual liberation in the group seems to be a rather general phenomenon.

The virginity discussion seems to have been an effort by the girls to reduce the sexual threat posed to the boys by professing immaturity —an antidote to the anxiety associated with the case discussion. It also seems to be a way of denying or negating any prior libidinal attachment to the leader. But the keynote of the entire session is ambivalence with respect to libidinal distribution. This is most clearly exemplified in the discussion of norms, which in part expresses the feeling that although at the moment the attachment to the leader (the fantasy of an exclusive relationship) is paramount, when they mature they will perhaps be able to cathect each other. The reunion implicitly excludes the leader, but also seems to involve a fantasy of collective impregnation.

Note, however, that the mere mention of the end of the group tips the balance in a regressive direction, with the members turning to Laura and her personal transference problems, in which they all vicariously share. Libidinal freedom is momentarily renounced in favor of Oedipal fantasies.

The reproduction fantasy is interesting in several respects. It is no coincidence that it occurs in the context of a revolt, as we shall see later. Revolt always raises the spectre of group dissolution, and the latter with equal reliability generates fantasies of the group in some way reproducing itself. But fundamentally this is a prospective fantasy about the nature of the training group process in general and the revolt cycle in particular. It says that if the members can incorporate the leader they can do without him—also that thereby the group will never die and they will become parents (teachers, leaders) themselves.

IVc. In one of the later meetings of this group, a meeting which was primarily concerned with sex roles, homosexuality, subgroups, and tolerable degrees of intimacy, the following exchange took place:

MALE: You just said that the leadership group ought to get married and have children.

FEMALE: I said if you have leaders in the group that get married then you will have children (laughter).

FEMALE: You think we're going to be very productive, eh? All fertile people.

Halfway through the next session a remark about "stripping away defenses" led to a discussion of nudist colonies, and the idea that "you can know each other very little even though you are both naked." The conversation soon turned back to the group, and in particular to the silent members:

". . . because if you sit there with half of your clothes off and the other person's sitting there with all their clothes on it's very unfair. So, maybe there are fellows who don't wish to enter into the marriage, who have decided that this is not for me and therefore they are retaining their own modesty—and others wishing to go ahead with the marriage are going right ahead and throwing their clothes to the floor."

(T. M. Mills, transcript)

IIe. It was five months after the episode reported above. The group had been discussing the biblical story of Joseph and his brothers in a desultory way, off and on for several sessions, latterly in response to the fact that the group leader began phrasing his interpretations in metaphorical terms drawn from the story. This was beginning to enrage the members increasingly, in part because it shattered an illusion of attitudinal unity which had been constructed, as often happens in groups, by never discussing the meaning of stimuli common to all. The meeting began with an attempt to decipher one such cryptic interpretation which the group leader had made at the close of the previous meeting. Discovering that they could not even agree on what had been said, they asked the group leader to repeat his statement. The leader demurred, pointing out that his own memory was not necessarily perfect and that their data were as good as his. He suggested that they were attempting again to use him as a final authority, adding rather maliciously that he did recall their having nodded knowingly at the time. Some of the members, especially Paul, were angered by this, but before long became involved in finding fault with each other. Considerable time was devoted to Jim, his role as the youngest member, and his relationship to Paul, the next youngest, who, they felt, expressed Jim's hostility for him. The group leader suggested that they couldn't tell one member from another without a scarlet thread (in reference to the children of Tamar), which produced further anger and utter noncomprehension. Henry, Paul, and Jim then began discussing their feeling that private contacts with the group leader were taboo, and tended to be "punished" by their "siblings." Paul felt that this was "evil" and that the group leader should be available. Jim noted that the girls in the group never dreamed about the group leader any more. Paul then reported a repeated dream that the group leader had lost a leg and that he was helping him to his car and carrying his briefcase. The group became very involved in discussing this dream in relation to Oedipal competition, castration and incest. Edna brought up a dream she had recently had about Antigone, and the group leader's interpretations were compared to the riddle of the Sphinx.[41] The latter was in turn tied to the three-legged ensemble in Paul's dream. Jim asked who Jocasta was in the group situation, and Lorna was repeatedly concerned with the Oedipus myth and what would be won in the group's "Oedipal" struggle.

[41] The sphinx image is of interest in view of the special anxieties attached to the acquisition of knowledge, discussed in the second section of this chapter. Bion has also called attention to this: "Insofar as I am felt to be leader of work group function . . . I . . . am invested with feelings that would be quite appropriate to the enigmatic, brooding, and questioning sphinx from whom disaster emanates. . . . I know of no experience that demonstrates more clearly than the group experience the dread with which a questioning attitude is regarded. . . . My impression is that the group approximates too closely, in the minds of the individuals composing it, to very primitive phantasies about the contents of the mother's body" (Bion, 1957, pp. 455–456).

Here we see a marked sex difference in libidinal distribution, with the group moving into a period of disturbance and change centering in the increasing anger of the males, which grows despite their reluctance to relinquish their dependent orientation toward the leader. The girls seem already to have made the transition, assuming Jim's comment about the dreaming to be correct, but Jim seems almost to be complaining, judging from the context in which the remark arises. He seems to say that if the girls were only more libidinally involved with the leader he would feel unconstrained about seeking him out for private consultation. Only Lorna is dubious among the girls, while Edna seems to be in the process of resolution (thus she dreams of Antigone, who rebels against the father figure for the sake of brother-love). The boys, on the other hand, are still very much authority oriented. Although unable to make much headway in discussing the Joseph myth, they are busily engaged in acting it out. They are deeply concerned, like the authors of Genesis, with whether the elder or younger sibling shall have precedence and what criteria of seniority shall apply. They are fearful of sibling jealousy in their quest for a favored position with the group leader, yet basically seem to prefer Joseph's rather than Reuben's (or Oedipus') approach to family relationships. Note in particular Paul's dream, which constitutes a brilliant acting out of the Joseph fantasy. The dream itself is identical with those of Joseph (he not only becomes the favorite of the father but also reduces the father to a position of dependence and subservience), and telling it to those concerned is a perfect replication of Joseph's near-fatal error (although Paul fortunately escapes with nothing more than a little group analysis).

IIe. A week later the group was discussing sex roles, feminine dominance, the intellectuality of college girls, their drop-out rate, and the sex ratio in their own institution (the girls minimizing their numerical majority). This led by degrees, through a brief discussion about marital infidelity, to the issue of sexuality within the group itself. Several admitted to strong sexual attractions to various members, Paul commenting that he only felt attracted to group members while actually in the group situation. Jim asked how all this related to dependency, while Henry and Paul complained that the girls were all "inaccessible" due to marriage, engagements, or other commitments, but the girls pointed out that this was true of only one or two and in any case irrelevant. They began a half-serious discussion of whether intragroup attractions were felt as incestuous, and how couples paired in the group would feel about lovers outside the group. The discussion of "incest" elicited mention of the film *View from the Bridge* from Andrea and Edna, and Jim asked if the girls "belonged" to the group leader à la *Totem and Taboo*, again recalling the dreams they had reported earlier in the year. Andrea then reported a recent dream in which she was on a slumber party with the group, in which they were also swimming and bathing together, although she could not distinguish individual faces and felt that her brother was also involved in it in some way. When the group leader asked if the members felt he was keeping them apart, Paul said "wait till the vernal equinox." Earlier Paul had confessed a desire to replace the group leader "in every respect," but had been reminded by Jim of his dependency needs and his feelings of inadequacy and helplessness.

In the following meeting a member who had been absent asked what had taken place, and Laura characterized the above session by saying "we all got on the table and screwed." Jim said on the contrary it was very restrained, and he and Paul argued about this, then about who was more prone to defending the group leader. The latter, after this had continued for a bit, remarked once again that accusing one another of being Joseph enabled everyone to play Joseph, and the group members now began to discuss more openly their individual feelings of wanting to be the leader's favorite. Consensus was blocked by Henry, however, who denied any such desire for a private or special relationship, and maintained his position (until weeks later, in fact) in the face of being reminded by other members that in fact he already had such a relationship, since the group leader was his thesis adviser. This seemed to stymie the group to some extent, although the general confession seemed to unite them a great deal in opposition to the leader, and the words "attack" and "without him" occurred frequently during the session, despite the lack of any specific mention or suggestion of revolt.[42]

These two sessions show a further advance in libidinal decathexis of the leader. The first one begins by attacking the central barrier to such decathexis: male fears of being overwhelmed by women. (See Footnote 39.) The girls attempt to minimize this threat and reassure the males that their "marital infidelity" will lead to no terrible consequences for them.

The way is now clear for sexual attractions within the group to be verbalized. The rest of the discussion seems to consist of males raising objections and females trying to dispel them. Note especially Andrea's dream, which, in comparison with the one she reports earlier in the year, shows the process of libidinal transfer quite clearly.

[42] The illusion of unanimity is important in revolt buildups. Groups are far more aggressive toward the leader when all members are present, and two or three consecutive days of full attendance are usually required for a revolt to occur.

Signs of budding mutiny are also apparent in these sessions, Paul being almost converted to the more aggressive female contingent, despite Jim's efforts to hold him back. It is interesting that Paul's "prediction" about when the revolt would occur was rather accurate, suggesting that his own readiness was crucial. Once again it might be emphasized, however, that the actual revolt is simply the ritual expression of a transition taking place in the meetings just described.

IIg. Three weeks after the group had begun a discussion of some case material led to a consideration of the "meaning" of being fat—how it felt, etc. This was a highly atypical preoccupation for this case and the group leader was much puzzled by it. Two sessions later Elizabeth appeared in an empire jumper, which, when Debbie commented upon it, she playfully pulled out in front of her as if it were a maternity dress. Debbie then told a long story about a hysterical pregnancy of which she had heard. Following this they began discussing disturbed children, the work of Bettelheim, pathogenic parents, and a particularly "sick" couple some of them knew, whom they described as "dragging their kid around on marijuana." Neil read a poem by Yeats addressed to the child of a woman who married someone else. The group leader commented upon the concern with disturbed children and referred back to the discussion of fatness, asking whether fatness was equated in their minds with adultness. They thereupon began discussing the case material again, in particular the rather Oedipal father-daughter relationship which it portrayed. Sylvia and Lucy argued with Margo over the correctness of Freud's theories of incestuous attraction, of which they were a little skeptical. Neil became very playful and maintained that the group leader had "joined the group" by virtue of his more frequent interjections. After the meeting was over Debbie came to the group leader's office to ask about the work of John Rosen, who, she had heard, "jumps on top of his patients and says 'I love you!' "

Two weeks later Debbie recounted a dream in which she purchased a fireplace in a store. Deep inside the fireplace she could see a stream in which children were playing. She decided to wear it home, and found that it was upholstered and fit around her middle, becoming "liplike" and with bricks only around the edge. She interpreted this as a vagina dentata, and they went on to discuss dreaming in general. After a pause they turned to Ibsen's *Hedda Gabler*, in which one of the members was playing the title role in a student production. Julie interpreted some of their comments as expressive of a wish to be the "favorite child"—not replaceable like Eilert Lövborg's burned manuscript. Hedda's pregnancy was also raised in this connection. There was some general discussion of group problems, followed by several personal accounts of the difficulties of having fathers who were teachers. The group leader asked if the problem here was not rather one of teachers being viewed as fathers. Roberta and Elizabeth then brought up Toman's book *Family Constellation,* in which the effects of various sibling combinations are assessed. They asked who was an older or younger sibling, who was an only child, etc. Neil asked the group leader if he were an only child, and when this was deflected they began discussing whether or not *they* were expressing a desire to be the only child. Elizabeth then said excitedly that the discussion was "fantastic" in view of the fact that the group leader's wife was "going to have a baby in about two weeks," a fact of which Debbie and Neil were also aware, but Julie was not. Debbie laughed at the latter's surprised expression and said she looked as if it was the dirtiest thing she'd ever heard.

About six weeks later the group held its next to last meeting before Christmas vacation. Penny asked how many were planning to come for the next session, since many students would already have left for their homes. Debbie asked the group leader what he would do if only one person came. When he deflected this question they expressed some annoyance (see this volume, p. 47), asking whether he was in the group or not. Debbie then asked what would happen if the group leader didn't appear, and they argued over the extent to which people remained talking after he left at the end of their regular sessions. While some members now denied that there was an "authority problem," Margo maintained that it was an intense one for her, and to support her argument reported a dream in which the group leader had left the meeting, but before doing so had whispered an interpretation in her ear which she then told to the group. Julie and Paul, who had joined Margo in expressing their difficulties with transference reactions to the group leader, now pointed out to her that the dream also expressed involvement and concern with the group, and a desire to be independent of the group leader.

Three months later, during a similarly penultimate meeting before Spring Vacation, they were discussing a personal experience paper they had turned in the week before. Sylvia and Julie said they felt "prostituted" by giving the group leader the paper, and several either expressed discontent with their performance or complained of the difficulties they had had in writing it. The problem of memory generated a prolonged discussion, which gradually led to the exchanging of childhood misadventures in which they had either been falsely accused or had committed misdeeds which were never discovered. Debbie, for example, told of a childhood incident in which she had put on her father's sneakers at the beach while he was swimming and had broken his glasses which were in one shoe, and another incident in which she had almost caused him to lose his glasses taking her for a roller-coaster ride.

In all of the foregoing there had been a great deal of interpretation by group members of one another's remarks and preoccupations, and of general group themes. This was in marked contrast to the immediately preceding sessions, which were characterized by depression and apathy, with an inability either to share their papers or to talk of anything else, despite occasional efforts to initiate both. The group leader now remarked on the preoccupation with the fallibility of parents, and suggested that interpretation, like glasses, could be worn by anyone. Roberta commented on how inordinately pleased everyone seemed at this, and they began to talk about the ambivalent pressures exerted by parents with regard to grades. Sylvia raised the custom reported in the Bennis and Shepard paper (1956) of having group members grade each other, and the practicality of this was discussed for some time. Sylvia wondered if they wouldn't in any case be grading in terms of what they thought the group leader's opinion was. They then shifted to self-grading, and the difficulties brought on by bad self-concepts, which led to further recitation of childhood incidents.

This series reveals again the halting progress toward libidinal disenthralment. In the earlier sessions we note a variety of typical transference responses centering around the group leader—responses tediously familiar to the psychotherapist. At first the members are entirely unaware of their significance, although gradually they become more so. Yet even in the very beginning we can see elements of independent striving, first in their special fascination with procreation, and second in their continued criticism of pathogenic parents, with its implication that they themselves could do better. While such invidiousness is typically Oedipal, it is also that aspect of the Oedipal constellation which provides the greatest potential for growth. Later the Oedipal fantasies become more conscious and are verbalized—a sign of their waning potency.

The pre-Christmas meeting is a kind of transition point, during which the fantasy of having the group leader all to oneself and the fantasy of doing without him altogether are verbalized in quick succession. More important is the fact that the latter is then discussed in the reality context which really counts: whether group members can define themselves as "still in session" if the group leader is not there. Margo's dream, furthermore, is explicitly and correctly recognized for what it is—a succinct fusion of the two fantasies of favoritism and independence.

The final session is a kind of ritual cleansing, following the disintegrative effect of writing personal papers for the group leader and feeling "prostituted." This is achieved by sharing personal experiences and thus recapturing the group from the leader, by recovering the initiative with regard to interpretation, which they largely do, and by approaching the even more ambitious appropriation of the one currently inaccessible and irrational aspect of the leader's authority: the power to grade. Debbie's story (leaving aside the symbolism which relates to the individual Oedipal relationship) is a fusion of these concerns: standing in Daddy's shoes destroys authority because one sees that authority is based on skills available to everyone, and frighteningly easy to perform. The sense of loss which attends this discovery is counteracted by self-doubt.

In this example disenthralment seems to be taking place without much overt revolt. (See this volume, pp. 46–50.) Consequently we see little expression of sexual feelings between members, whereas post-revolt meetings usually show a marked rise in such feelings. This is particularly true if the revolt is late—post-revolt behavior with early revolts is typically so highly restrained that sexual interest, if present, is invisible. Some examples may serve to illustrate this point.

IId. The revolt in this group occurred in the second month with very little warning, taking the usual form of expulsion of the group leader. When the group met without him they proceeded to go around the table in order, introducing themselves—giving a little background information as well as their motivation for joining the group.

This behavior has several meanings. First, it illustrates the typical group belief that the leader controls hostility in the group. When he is absent some more mechanical device is contrived to perform the same insulating function. It is now unnecessary to "walk on eggs" because no real interaction is taking place. Second, we may observe that the group is behaving as if it were an entirely new group. This fits nicely with the "Oedipal" definition of revolt offered above: the members have taken "the group" away from the leader and are reestablishing its virginity, like Hera bathing in the spring of Canathus. It is not enough that the group be newly theirs, the fact it was not always so must be denied—the group leader's ghost must be obliterated. Third, this new beginning expresses the members' increased libidinal interest in one another. Now that the eliciter of Oedipal responses is gone the feeling is that "we can *really* get to know one another."

Vb. A similar expulsion occurred in this group but almost at the very end of its history. At the beginning of the meeting without the leader there was a good deal of horseplay initiated by the girls, but the boys were very anxious to get to work. Before the male view prevailed, however, there was an interlude in which the lights were turned out, allegedly for the purpose of seeing the observers who they knew regularly watched them from behind a one-way mirror.

When this "work" finally got under way (see this volume, pp. 53–54) it led ultimately to a discussion of Dionysian orgies as "an expression of the id." Initially this discussion was entered into somewhat more enthusiastically by the females, as the following exchange reveals.

FEMALE: . . . I mean drinking and sex orgies and dancing and homo-sexuality—everything: The whole irrational element in the Greeks, when they could really let themselves go and yet have a religious sanction covering the whole thing.

MALE: Actually, there is supposed to be a cultural necessity—some kind of ceremony just to let off steam. There is one in Germany, the October festival.

FEMALE: Well, there is one in Switzerland which is supposed to be the original Mardi Gras and is still going . . . (inaudible) . . . this is the time when really everyone just lets go.

MALE: Well, I suppose the United States would have less of that because there is so much of that Puritan morality.

FEMALE: Well, that's just why they should have more.

MALE: Well, I know, but that's just why they don't.

Another boy then mentioned the Dartmouth Winter Carnival as a safety valve necessitated by being "up in the woods" and a girl brought up the religious ceremonies of the normally celibate Shakers, which she described as "the only place physical contact is allowed and they are great big sex orgies." A boy asked how the sect continued without reproducing and this led to a general discussion of ascetic religious sects and finally back to Frazer's King of the Wood.

(R. F. Bales, transcript)

This incident is again multidetermined. Certainly one reason for turning off the lights was to see if the group leader was in the observation room or if they were truly alone. A second was to turn the tables on the observers, to depose them as the leader had been deposed. The flirtatious, seductive behavior of the girls, however, suggests that an erotic motive was predominant and that the situation was being defined like the petting parties of early adolescents, where the departure of parents is always the signal for the lights to be extinguished and the fun to begin.

The sex difference with regard to erotic motivation is curious, and appears to be universal in groups with male leaders. The female members seem to experience almost no guilt around the revolt, whereas the males evince a great deal. This is not at all surprising at the level of individual psychology, since the females are renouncing an Oedipal fixation while the males are in part acting it out. Yet this is by no means the whole story, since men always seem more sexually inhibited in groups than women. Despite a certain amount of bragging, bravado, and calculated verbal obscenity, when it comes to direct sexual confrontation it is always the females in the group who approach and the males who retreat pleading important engagements. They seem not only depressed in these encounters, but also afraid. It is possible that the passive role of the leader provides a poor sexual model for them. Certainly many males identify in a rather literal fashion with the leader, adopting what they feel is a "strong, silent" pose, which, however, effectively leaves all active initiative to the females. In the long run this puts the males at something of a disadvantage, and the leader may come to represent (as we noted above) a male hero combating the female dragon, rather than the father dragon or ogre who must be overthrown in order to obtain the fair sister-princess. When he is expelled they will feel not liberated but deprived of a prop to their masculinity.

A hint of this masculine need appears in the following report by a male group member of his feelings while observing one of the "battles of the sexes" described earlier. Gary, the male protagonist to whom the writer refers, unfortunately flunked out of college midway in the group's career, casting a mild pall over the entire issue.

IIb. "To me Eve provided a very simple and 'mother type' explanation for the cases. . . . I didn't agree with her explanations but I couldn't attack her or become involved with her on the topic. Gary, since deceased as a member, did attack and I experienced a nervous joy. Biologically it seemed as though everything was tense and excited. I breathed quicker and harder, etc. I was happy for the attack; however, I was greatly relieved when Eve wasn't demolished. . . . I imagine I sort of expected enormous mystical things to occur to her or Gary and they didn't. . . ."

Note the casual lumping of aggression and "involvement," suggesting that the "fight" may have been sexually defined. In general it seems to fit Bion's "pairing group" descriptions rather well (Bion, 1957, pp. 446–7).

Let us now return to IIe and examine the sexual economy of the group following the revolt.

IIe. It will be recalled that the major revolt in this group occurred in the form of two incidents separated by over a week: the second chair-usurping incident and the decision to expel the leader. The meeting without the leader seems to have been more productive than usual, with some useful confrontation and resolution in relationships among particular members. While feelings about the group leader, and about Laura (who came but left early) were also discussed, the bulk of the session was devoted to sexual feelings within the group. The most important exchange, judging by subsequent references to it, occurred between Edna and Henry, who had often shown irritation at each other in the past. The exchange was initiated by one of Henry's frequent denials that feelings experienced by other members were shared by him. This time the feelings in question were sexual, and when some of the members became annoyed at the denial, Edna defended Henry, saying that the girls' aggressiveness made such feelings impossible either to feel or to admit. After some discussion Henry reported that Edna's defense had aroused some erotic feelings toward her, and Edna said this was mutual.

A week later Laura and Lorna opened a session by discussing snakes, and their fear of them. There followed a long discussion of the short time remaining before the end of the group and the academic year (all of the members were graduating except Paul and Jim). They revealed fantasies of trying to find a way to spend another year in college, and wondered what was ahead of them. Sadness and nostalgia were expressed, followed by concern about the present direction and progress of the group. Curt said, with deliberate metaphor, "you'd think after nine months we would have produced something," and they discussed this a little. Jim then complained that they hadn't "really" talked about sex within the group or "done anything about it." Some argument over this point ensued, in the course of which Jim once again complained that the girls no longer talked of their sexual feelings toward the group leader. This produced a general discussion of feelings toward the leader and the extent to which these had been resolved. They wondered if he had changed at all, as Henry suggested, or whether it was merely projection on the part of members, as Edna and Lorna argued. Lorna then suggested that perhaps the more independent orientation of the members had *forced* a change in the leader.

A week later a session began with some talk about other universities and summer plans. Paul expressed an old discomfort about Sandra, and the fact that she had left school just after "coming out" in the group. They then started a long discussion of Laura, who was not present. A number of negative feelings were expressed, along with guilt over doing this in her absence and some discussion about the extent to which the group itself fostered in various ways the behavior that they disliked in her. Andrea and Edna, who were the most critical among the girls (although Paul and Jim, who said she reminded him of his mother, were equally so), placed her at the opposite end of a continuum from Charlotte, whom they viewed as a feminine ideal—to a considerable extent because she was quiet. Since they themselves were among the most active, verbal members of the group they had feared lapsing into the "nonfeminine" pole of the continuum, and hence were made anxious by Laura's boisterousness, an attitude about which they now expressed some guilt. Lorna, who had been acting as the principal defender of Laura, now reported the latter's self-consciousness about her breasts, and chided Paul for calling her "earth-mother" during one of the revolt episodes. Edna argued that dissatisfaction with one's own body was universal, and Paul noted that they had never talked about their bodies. Some of the girls then argued that Laura was threatening because her "aggressive sexuality" challenged the masculinity of the boys, and they recalled Paul asking for help from Andrea in response to one such challenge, and this having increased the tension between them. Paul admitted to these feelings, and he and Andrea then began to discuss their own relationship, which had been strained and hostile throughout much of the group's history. They now expressed the feeling that their conflict had been based entirely on efforts to defend against their sexual attraction to one another, and Andrea said that she wouldn't feel human, or be able to have any feelings at all until she admitted this attraction in the group. During the long interaction between the two which followed, the rest of the group was silent but absorbed. A few sessions later Andrea remarked to Paul that since this mutual confession she could now be "simply friendly" with him.

This series displays the ambivalent quality we have become used to, but ends with a degree of libidinal freedom. Note that thoughts of separation in the middle session yield images of reproduction, which in turn lead to concern about the lack of sexuality in the group. To some extent the "pairing" behavior of these last sessions is a straw-clutching effort to stave off death through a fantasy of procreation. But despite these preoccupations the general trend of the meeting is toward liberation; for although Jim renews his constant effort to displace the group's sexual feelings onto the leader, he expresses contrary attitudes as well this time, and the session ends with a perception of the leader not only as not controlling the group, but also as subject to the group's influence.

The final session in the series recapitulates the long-range process and illustrates in capsule form the issues which must be resolved before libidinal freedom can be achieved.[43] It begins with anxieties

[43] One reason for this recapitulation, of course, is that the initial rapprochement occurred in the absence of the leader. To be certain that the gains were real, it was necessary to repeat them under the least favorable circumstances. This is the exact analogue of the process known in therapeutic settings as "working-through": the initial insight must be de-compartmentalized, that is, applied to more and more aspects of experience, fitted to larger and larger contexts, tied to other insights, and freed of covert qualifications. It is interesting in this connection that in his therapy groups Alexander Wolf has institutionalized the "out-of-school" meetings that arise spontaneously in so many training groups, so that

about separation, the dangers of self-revelation, and sex roles. These are related, the fear being that problems raised now, near the end of the group, would not be resolved in time and would somehow disrupt their future lives. The discussion of Laura has many interesting facets —one way or another she seems to trigger feelings of sexual inadequacy in both males and females, despite her own admissions of difficulty in this area.

The solution to these concerns is the usual one for groups of this kind. When the emphasis shifts from Laura's faults to the fears of the speaker, these fears tend to subside somewhat. Once the girls admit they feel unfeminine, and the boys admit (a little) that they feel unmasculine, they become freer to approach each other.

IIc. In this all-male group no real collective attack on the leader was ever mustered, although occasional individual sniping was not infrequent. One day, about a half hour after the incident with the purse (described in this volume, pp. 65–66), an argument developed regarding the validity and applicability of psychoanalytic theory in particular and psychological interpretations in general. The group leader suggested that the (rather rigid and stereotypical) positions that were being taken reflected their conflict over wishing on the one hand to have an all-embracing theory which would explain everything effortlessly, and on the other wishing to reject the group leader's comments. Some confusion was expressed about this, in the middle of which Gregory offered the following speech, directed alternately to the group and to the group leader:

"Well—you want a wild theory? What do you think about equating this group, and its relation to you [the group leader], to Freud's concept of the primal horde? (Laughter.) The primal chieftain with all his rebel sons— he was the one who ran the whole show, and denied any active sex life to his children, and eventually they all rose and slew him, and that was the origin of the totem pole. It's a very interesting book."

Carl suggested ironically that maybe it "wasn't so crazy" since he had seen a question about the book in a copy of the preceding year's exam. Gregory continued:

"The idea has been expressed in here that he has kept the girls out of this class, and offers us instead Mr. Z. [a graduate student observer. Uproarious laughter followed this sally]. I think we all have the feeling that he is in possession of some superior form of knowledge than we have, and

feelings and thoughts can be expressed in this freer atmosphere, later to be introduced into the plenary "work" meetings. (See Wolf, 1963, pp. 285–6.)

The reader may feel generally that all we are observing here is a shift from what Bion has called the dependency group to what he has called the pairing group. We will deal with this problem in detail in the next chapter.

that he sits on his duff and lords it over us—and refuses to give us what we want, in the intellectual sense, in the social sense—"

Someone at this point interrupted Gregory to say, "Well, you're a married man, what are *you* worried about?"

By this time the atmosphere was one of considerable hilarity. Drew objected to the theory of the group leader's withholding females, on the ground that his sister had reported the girls in the previous year's group as having had "a definite fixation" on the leader, and that clearly he would not wish to miss this important facet of the group. "She says he flashes his eyes at them," he added. "Maybe he *talks* to them," Bud remarked wryly.

Someone now suggested that "along the primal horde idea, how about having a party?" Stan said, "Think what the main course of the meal would be!"

Gregory cut in again: "Another thing, a couple of days ago we had a discussion of Freud and paid no attention to him—we had the power ourselves." Carl objected, however, that they had in fact looked to him early for "definitive answers" and hadn't received any. Stan then observed that *Totem and Taboo* was on the reading list two months hence, and Arnold asked, "What about the idea of following up this theory? Would Dr. Slater have any objections to that?" "What do you mean," Gregory asked, "throwing him out or something?" "No—no—no," Arnold said quickly, "doing some of this reading, discussing this theory." Gregory asked why he was so interested, and Carl said why didn't he read it on his own. Silence fell, and someone suggested leaving early, although in fact the hour had just about ended.

During the period when this meeting occurred (early December) absenteeism was high, and meetings seemed tense and giggly. On several occasions, including the session prior to this, girls from other groups sat in (singly) to observe "what an all-male group was like," a visitation to which the group members reacted rather ambivalently, and expressed their mixed feelings by clowning.

Homosexual anxiety seems pervasive in this example: in the re-mark about the observer, the "married man" retort, the references to female transference reactions. The group is caught in a dilemma, since on the one hand the departure of the women at the beginning of the year, together with their own dependent, submissive approach to the group leader, seems to cast doubt on their masculinity, but on the other hand, a convincing display of aggressiveness in the form of revolt would merely confront them with each other, and the fears associated with their intimacy needs would be intensified. This is ex-pressed in condensed form in the notion that the "prize" of a revolt would be, not the females, but merely the observer.

While this group is of course a special case, it is a general law in groups with which I am familiar that if no attack on the leader of any kind occurs, there is very little overt sexual interest between members (aside, of course, from dyadic affairs conducted outside of the group setting). One could argue either that such interest is a precondition to revolt or that the interest arises from the libidinal release that the revolt generates. My own impression is that both are in part true: that no attack will arise without some degree of intermember attraction, but that both the intensity of and the ability to express such attraction is sharply increased following an attack on the leader, especially among females.[44]

A particularly interesting example of the struggle for Oedipal disenthralment has been reported by Richard Jones. It is peculiarly acute since it takes place in a group composed entirely of adolescent girls, and is thus not merely a recapitulation of an essentially achieved psychological maturation, but a deeply felt current issue.

XI. In the sixth meeting of this group the members began talking, first indirectly and then directly, about their parents. This was apparently touched off by the leader's remark that perhaps the thought of others respecting and depending on one was a little frightening. The members then began discussing the meaning of "maturity." One girl produced a silence by asserting their psychological immaturity relative to the leader. Another silence followed a suggestion that they feared hurting someone in the group. They then became involved in a discussion of parents substituting gifts for love. One girl expressed the feeling that her father punished her when she tried to get close to him, and another expressed similar difficulties with her mother. After considerable sharing of such experiences, including the inability of parents to accept their sexual sophistication, the members expressed gratification over the exchange of confidences and the catharsis.

In the ninth meeting the group began to express hostility toward the leader, although in highly sexualized form. They teased him for being

---

[44] An interesting analogue of this dual influence may be found in Zuckerman's book on baboons (1932). Zuckerman notes (pp. 246–9) that in the absence of females the overlord structure of captive baboons disappears, and that if females are removed from a baboon party the bachelors will also leave. At the same time he also notes that except during times of "sexual fights," when bachelor baboons attack the overlord, the bachelors show very little interest in the females. The relationship between the Oedipal struggle and its sexual rewards is indeed complex. Raphael Patai has observed that in biblical times taking the "fruits" was often utilized as a technique for winning the struggle. Thus Reuben attempted to establish his succession by lying with his father's concubine, as did also Absalom and Adonijah (Patai, 1959, pp. 100–103).

"an introvert," for being "rude" and "obnoxious," for grinning, for blushing. One said that he kept them from "using our fronts," another that he was "afraid to say what he thinks of us because he has to live with us for the rest of the year." One made the following suggestive slip: "I think maybe you're afraid to incriminate yourself because you don't want to have hard feelings toward us. I mean you don't want us to have hard feelings toward you."

In the tenth meeting the group succeeded in getting the leader to agree to answer questions, and proceeded to quiz him about his personal and social life and habits, including his "vices," marital status, income, and whether he had any siblings, etc. They asked if they would be able to help him with his problems, and one member then reported the dream mentioned earlier (p. 101 of this volume). Jones notes that following this meeting the leader was always addressed as "Sir."

In the eleventh meeting one girl reported a long dream in which she married her father. There was some general discussion about sex and why they talked so much about it.

Attacks (often sexually-tinged) on the leader's distant role continued for several sessions, with intermittent interludes of regressed behavior and attempts to seduce him into joining them. The twenty-fourth meeting included a compliment on the leader's haircut, a report that Marlon Brando was dating a nineteen year old girl, followed by anticipations of weekend dates and a rather vituperative discussion of female teachers and a female principal, a discussion which centered around sexual restriction and being "treated like a baby," and was full of remarks suggesting that these maternal figures were themselves immature, unfeminine, and sexually frustrated. This was followed in turn by references to dreams about graduating dresses, college, marriage, and having babies, and a discussion of college life.

(Jones, 1960, pp. 39–47, 49–52, 67–8)

These excerpts provide a sample of the continuous back-and-forth movement between attempts to act out Oedipal transference and attempts to work it through and move beyond it. Each seduce-attack-relinquish sequence is promptly followed by another, and one must either examine the entire history of the group to obtain any sense of ultimate progress, or else do as I have done, and stop arbitrarily at a momentary growth point. It is of course especially difficult to sort out strivings toward maturity from Oedipal competitiveness in this instance, since wanting to be accepted as adult can mean either. Similarly it is difficult to distinguish, in their sexualized attacks, the desire to seduce the leader from the desire to relinquish their dependence on him. The struggle, however, is unmistakable, and receives a poignant statement in the following exchange:

XI. Jones' group, in addition to meeting as such, also met with him under more traditional classroom conditions. These two situations were rigidly differentiated, and the girls' evaluation of their relative merits fluctuated. In the twenty-third meeting, one member argued that the "classes" were better, and "more organized," and another suggested this was because the leader was "more of a teacher."

G: He treats us like little girls in the class.
G: We're even littler in here.
G: But we don't *have* to be.

(Jones, 1960, p. 65)

The experimental group mentioned earlier (p. 22 of this volume) also provides an example of libidinal transfer.

XIII. The group met four times—a morning and an afternoon meeting of three hours' duration each, on each of two successive Saturdays. Much of the second and third sessions was devoted to the issue of how personal they should get with one another. At the beginning of the third meeting there was comment upon Patty's knitting, and Jane, the only other girl in the group, suggested strangling the group leader with it. George then suggested wearing pajamas, so that people would become more "personal." After a few minutes of rather desultory conversation George suggested going outside, and was immediately seconded by several others, including both girls and Alex, who fantasied that "all twelve of us (thus excluding the group leader) will go downstairs, and we'll see twelve people (i.e., observers) following us downstairs, watching." George reminded them that according to the experimenter's instructions, the time was their own. They wondered if the door was locked, then had fantasies of its being wired to electrocute them. They talked of going to Cape Cod and discussed who had a car, parking problems, the extremes of population density on Cape Cod, and the "odd community" in Provincetown. After a short silence Bob mentioned accidents that had happened to him after the last meeting, in particular an auto accident with another car containing two boys and a girl who were "going parking," in response to which Henry remarked that it didn't seem like "a decent combination." Others now related stories of accidents seen and experienced, a discussion which lasted about 15 minutes, becoming increasingly lurid. George then brought up leaving again, but opposition was now expressed, and the topic died after a brief fantasy about taking the observers disguised as rocks. A long silence followed, then Bill suggested playing "Hangman" on the blackboard. Bob immediately asked if anyone had the group leader for an interviewer in the experiment. All agreed that this would be inappropriate, and wondered if the group leader were also getting interviewed following the meetings. Jane expressed pity for the group leader and distress that he was "picked on" so much, but several males objected that this sympathy was unnecessary, and there was another silence. Jane then asked if people had run into each other during the week, and these encounters were then discussed. This led to the long conversation about underground connecting tunnels, alligators in the sewers, Venus' flytraps, etc. (discussed on pp. 211–214 of this volume), then to a discussion of mutual acquaintances, and finally to the question of parietal rules. With much incredulity, laughter, and scorn they exchanged a number of tales of complex rules regarding male visitors in female dorms.

Conversation now became more particularized, focussing on individual members, save for a general discussion of psychology, and of how much personal revelation was useful. Members began expressing feelings aroused by the experiment, particularly Jane, who talked of having been upset all week, and who received a considerable amount of thoughtful sympathy as this was discussed.

Larry then rather abruptly asked the group leader if he were a graduate student, and this generated a lengthy attack on the latter. George wrote his name backward on the blackboard, and when Bob referred to him as a "fixture," suggested "toilet" as an instance. Jane suggested he had lost some of his impartiality, and Patty said he was "not half as God-like as he was at the beginning." Larry talked of seeing him in sports car and sunglasses, and they started to quiz him about the exact nature of the former. Jane said he had "elegant taste," and George suggested he could call up Jane "if he wanted to." This led to embarrassed joking about "etchings," etc., which the group leader cut off with an unrelated interpretation. They then attacked his neutral stance, questioned his humanity, and accused him of "playing God." Gradually they began to wonder whether the problem wasn't that they were viewing him this way. The meeting ended with a discussion of hostility, both toward the group leader and each other, centering largely around incidents of actual or threatened throwing of objects (books, number plates) that had occurred in the last two sessions, but after some joking about this, a brief reporting of more enduring annoyances.

The final afternoon session began with an observation that people had again changed seats, and some comments about who talked the most. There was some joking over a girl that Jane and some of the boys had passed at lunchtime, who the boys said was attractive and Jane said was not. After a silence they began talking about the magazine *Playboy* and the various "Playmates of the Month," and whether magazines of this ilk were "anti-sexual," since they translated sexuality into a consumer commodity—an association which led very quickly to the group leader's sports car and another silence. Silence itself was now discussed, and silent members. One of the latter was drawn into the discussion, although only to confirm his detachment verbally. This was contrasted with the involvement of others, particularly Jane, and some sadness about parting was expressed by several. A remark by the group leader diverted the discussion to the effect of his interpretations, and a return to one of his earlier ones led George to suggest that Jane was an object of generalized sexual competition among the group members, a competition in which the group leader, with his sports car, was seen as having considerable advantage. They wondered whether Jane's emphasis on being personal was sexually motivated, and began asking each other if they had participated in the experiment in order to seek out new sexual objects. They discussed their feelings about this for some time, along with competitive feelings among the males arising out of the presence of females. There followed a long discussion of how personal people felt or should feel in the group, and whether the inevitability of loss should lead to noninvolvement.

(R. D. Mann, transcript)

As is not unusual, the greatest preoccupation with sexuality coincides with the heaviest concentration of hostility toward the leader. Although there is a continual libidinal see-sawing between the group leader and peers, each swing of the pendulum brings the members a little closer to one another and makes them a little more independent of the leader. Attacks on the latter seem to serve as a kind of lever to crank them forward in this progression. While they are at first guilty over this, as exhibited in the "accident" discussion, they become increasingly less so as the conversation shifts from flight fantasies to immediate group concerns.

CHAPTER IV

The New Order

Groups such as those described here must try to accomplish many things at the same time, each one dependent on all of the others having been done first. They often resemble the old shipwrecked sailor in A. A. Milne's poem, who could never decide which of several necessities to procure first, and ended by basking in the sun until he was saved. As long as we deal with broad social psychological concepts such as independence and intimacy we are compelled to recognize that each is a prerequisite of the other, even though the overt emphases of the group may follow an observable sequence. We need not be cowed by this difficulty, however, since there are clear structural changes in groups which have committed themselves to a collective rejection of the group leader, and I should be equivocating if I were to imply that I do not regard a group which makes such a commitment as having developed further than one which has not.

By development I am not referring, however, to any therapeutic or educational gain for the group members. As Stock and Thelen note, "changes may occur in the group without, necessarily, changes occurring in the valency characteristics of individual members" (Stock and Thelen, 1958, p. 190). I would indeed go much further than this and say that I can conceive of a situation in which further group synthesis might be actually detrimental to all individuals concerned.[45]

---

[45] See Appendix I. As an example, we might point out that intellectuals are typically far more fearful of the tyranny of the majority than of autocracy, to which they are often deeply attracted, and many critics of our own society would doubtless feel that the substitution of group authority for that of the leader is a "backward step." I do not share their fear of American "conformity," however, partly because nonconformity in any form other than mere failure has always been the privilege of a very few, almost by definition, and partly because the specific comparisons made with other nations are almost always specious, since by "America" the critic always means Levittown and by "France" he always

But is it not absurd to speak of development at all, if there is no end point in view? The problem here is precisely the same as we encounter in dealing with biological or cultural evolution. We do not know where it is going, or whether we would like it if we did know. But we know a little about where it has been. We cannot, without making a number of value judgments about which cultural products we think are most important, order *cultures* (or species, for that matter) on a continuum of "advancedness" except by carefully selecting extreme cases, since a culture (species, group) which is "advanced" with respect to traits *ABC* may be "primitive" with respect to traits *DEF*, etc. Yet we can make some *quantitative* (more culture is better than less) comparisons, most safely with respect to a single aspect of culture, and most important of all we can say with respect to a vast number of individual characteristics "y could not have existed unless x existed first, and since y is an outgrowth of x it is more 'advanced' than x." [46] It is in this sense that one should attempt to think of "progress" in group development. Naturally, one finds it difficult to do so—even our language constantly betrays us into associating development with "good," complexity with virtue. But it is well to remember that anything here noted as an "advance" could be considered an unfortunate event in terms of some set of human values.

Bion's well-known "basic assumption" theory would seem to contradict the evolutionary view suggested here. Bion stresses the static quality of the basic assumption mentality and refers to "the absence of any process of development" in it (Bion, 1957, p. 453). He makes no temporal distinction between (*a*) the "dependent group," in which the group seems to be assuming that it has met in order to be nourished and protected by a leader, (*b*) the "pairing group," in which the assumption is that the group has met to procreate a Messiah, and (*c*) the "fight-flight" group, which assumes that it has met to fight some-

means Montmartre. (For the average American, of course, there are no French peasants or shopkeepers, neither of whom have ever been famed for bold innovation or unconventional behavior.)

Conformity is of course not the real issue, but rather uniformity, which has increased with rapid transportation, mass communication, and the like. If one loves diversity, however, one must be willing to pay the price for it. I have never heard any of these critics mourn the incipient disappearance of the quaint regional customs hitherto prevailing in the deep South, a change for which mass communication is responsible in very large part. It is a mistake, often made, to assume that because the good society is clearly not here, it is, or ever was, anywhere else.

[46] Cf. Ralph Linton's discussion of cultural evolution in his *The Tree of Culture* (1959, pp. 49 ff.).

thing or run away from it. All are "opposed to development" (Bion, 1957, p. 454). He is vague about the relationship among these types, maintaining that only one assumption can be present at any one time, and is explicitly uncertain about whether they interpenetrate at some more primary level. (See Bion, 1957, pp. 449–450, 454–459. See also 1949a, pp. 20–22.)

While I am in substantial agreement with Bion's formulations about groups—his observations rarely fail to strike a chord of recognition—I also share his feeling that the "basic assumptions" are an incomplete conceptualization. The somewhat truncated description of the fight-flight assumption (i.e., what is the "something" that it is oriented against? The other assumptions are substantive as well as procedural—the group is to do something *in relation to* the leader or a Messiah) might even suggest that it is a different order of construct altogether, a problem that we shall attempt to resolve in the next chapter. (See, e.g., Bion, 1949a, p. 15; 1949b, p. 297.)

Similarly, while it is certainly true that the "pairing group," in the pure form that Bion describes, is entirely lacking in work orientation, this is not in itself incompatible with the notion that it is an outgrowth of the dependent group and at a more advanced stage of development. Neither a primeval fish nor a chimpanzee is a scientist nor can either become one, yet we can still say that, roughly speaking, one is a development from the other and hence more "advanced" in some sense. The future orientation of the pairing group and its desire to produce are themselves evidence of a higher level of development, however unrealistic that orientation may be in the classic case.

Bion himself seems to have some difficulty with this issue. He begins his discussion of the pairing group by describing an instance: the unusual willingness of a group to leave the stage to a pair of members engaged in a conversation tinged with eroticism. He speaks of the "peculiar air of hopefulness and expectation" about such meetings and regards this as the defining characteristic. "It usually finds expression verbally in ideas that marriage would put an end to neurotic disabilities; that group therapy would revolutionize society when it had spread sufficiently; that the coming season . . . will be more agreeable; that some new kind of community—an improved group— should be developed, and so on." He takes pains to discount the possibility that this forward-looking and optimistic view might ultimately lend itself more readily to a transformation into work than would the dependency or fight-flight modalities, but this is made less convincing by the developmental ideas which creep into his exposition, particularly with regard to the group's awakening sexuality. While the hopefulness which Bion is trying to portray may indeed incorporate the most profound passivity, it is one which is less remote from a work orientation than that found in the dependency group. This is implicit in the statement that the feeling of hope is "both a precursor of sexuality and a part of it," since the emergence of sexual interest signifies the release of energy previously bound up in the member-leader relationship (Bion, 1957, pp. 447–448).

There is one further difficulty which arises in this connection, and which we can resolve no more conclusively than those preceding. It may have been observed that virtually all of the examples of pairing we have examined have been clearly associated with thoughts of termination and separation, and Bion also seems to see the pairing group as hope on the verge of despair (Bion, 1957, p. 448). May it not be that the pairing group simply emerges whenever it is necessary to combat the idea of group death with the fantasy of immortality? But when *is* it necessary? Whenever the thought occurs to anyone?

IIe. It was the meeting following spring vacation. The group seemed lethargic and depressed. There was a great deal of talk about how lonely they had felt away from the group, but many seemed to feel that their return had not alleviated the feeling. In part this seemed to be associated with the idea that there was no use bothering to "get going again" since there were only three weeks left. There were fantasies about the final meeting (that there would be a revelation, that there would be an orgy, etc.), and some thoughts about their ultimate separation. There was mention of the previous meeting and the separation fantasies associated with it. (See this volume, p. 72.) Several times they fell silent. Paul said he felt warm in the group, but there was general consensus that in the papers they had written just prior to vacation everything had been said, and that all they could now do was to continue to validate the roles they had evolved—that they did not want to get "involved" again. Peggy, however, attacked this attitude vehemently.

Soon they began talking about getting married, which one or two of the members were contemplating. Andrea said that graduation made her feel "more married," and Laura began questioning her about the difficulty of maintaining a total commitment to a single person. Andrea confirmed Laura's feeling that it was a difficult and uncertain business, and a long discussion of marriage ensued. Edna suggested that the group was looking for a happy ending, wanting to "live happily ever after." Henry said one could not be as involved with a group as with a spouse. They wondered what they would do with the group leader in a "group marriage" and whether he was "more married" than Andrea or Curt.

Charlotte maintained that the marriage discussion was a way of handling
sexual feelings in the group. Paul and Laura then began talking about the
incidence of brother-sister incest, and Paul joked about his attraction to
little girls, particularly some of his female relatives. This led naturally
enough to a discussion of *Lolita*, one which collapsed in confusion, however,
when no one could remember how the novel ended. Henry then switched
the topic from pedophilia to necrophilia, mentioning in particular members
of a Borneo tribe who typically slept with skulls of their mothers and
fathers. The group leader remarked that they seemed to be bewailing
the fact that it was impossible to marry everyone, which reminded Paul
that he had had a dream about Curt. Amid much hilarity Paul then made
a spirited advocation of polygamy, saying that he wanted first to marry
Andrea, and then Curt.

While there are, as usual, many complexities to this meeting, the
relevant issue for the moment is the constant occurrence of pairing
fantasies as an antidote to separation. What is particularly interesting,
however, is the "return of the repressed" in these fantasies, as marriage
becomes equated with graduation and is defined primarily in terms of
losses: loss of childhood, loss of sexual variety, loss of nonresponsi-
bility, loss of incestuous attachments. In this context the inability to
remember the ending of *Lolita* is rather transparent, since the recol-
lection of Humbert's loss of Lolita, as well as Lolita's own maturation,
marriage, and pregnancy, would have destroyed this fantasy as well.

Looking back over our examples another relationship is striking:
thoughts of termination only seem to occur at three different times,
(1) when it is imminent, (2) during or soon after an attack on the
leader, (3) when such an attack is being contemplated. In other words,
the eventual death of the group is a fact which tends to be ignored
as long as possible, except that when the group is in the process of
liberating itself from the leader, awareness of its ultimate demise suddenly and dramatically forces itself upon the group's attention. But
why is this so? Could it be that prior to this time [47] the group is not
aware of itself as an entity and therefore cannot imagine the termination of that entity? Let us recall again the passage from Bennis and
Shepard quoted in the Introduction, dealing with member reactions
to the revolt: "The event is always marked in group history as 'a
turning point,' *'the time we became a group,' 'when I first got involved,'* etc." (Bennis and Shepard, 1956, italics mine).

[47] It may of course happen repeatedly. All three of the revolts in IIe were
accompanied by thoughts of separation (*and* "pairing" manifestations), with intervals of "forgetting" in between.

The dependent group does not fear termination because the group members have vested all their group feeling in the leader, and group death has no meaning. When this feeling is withdrawn, and vested in fellow members, the pangs of group mortality begin acutely to be felt.[48] One might indeed wonder if the dependent stance is not a way of warding off group self-awareness and its attendant anxieties. This would, of course, be the position taken by Erich Fromm.

It will undoubtedly have struck the reader that sharp parallels may be drawn between these changes in the orientation of group members to the group as an entity and those which characterize self-perception in the development of the individual psyche. Bion argues that groups operating on any of the basic assumptions are totally devoid of any conception of time and operate largely in nonverbal modes of interaction (Bion, 1957, pp. 464, 473–4). We would modify this view somewhat relative to the pairing group and argue that there is a continuum of increasing consciousness involved in the three basic assumptions. It may also be observed that the basic assumptions correspond closely to the different categories of religious orientation, but we must postpone consideration of this parallel until the next chapter. Suffice it to say that self-awareness is associated with extensive transformations in all three domains and that the achievement of such self-awareness occurs primarily in relation to conflict of one kind or another. As Jung points out, "identity does not make consciousness possible; it is only separation, detachment, and agonizing confrontation through opposition that produces consciousness and insight" (Jung, 1958, p. 136). The attack on the leader is produced by an anguished awareness of his separateness and in turn reinforces that separateness. Concomitantly, the group's *own* separateness is fostered by this event and gives rise to feelings of aloneness and a sense of group mortality and finiteness. The desire for immortality arises only at this point and with these feelings.

[48] Bion also notes the essential parallelism of the dependent group's deity and the pairing group's Messiah (1957, pp. 458–9). It might be pointed out that many therapeutic groups are open and continuous—the group is there when the patient comes and goes on after he leaves. For members of such groups, the group never dies, and although their personal separation is an important issue, the finiteness of the group is not. The analogue with the individual organism is hence lost, and pairing may have an entirely different significance. Furthermore, although it may be more cohesive, the members more involved, and the group more under the control of the members than in a mortal group, there is this one important sense in which it is never theirs.

IIb. The principal attack on the leader in this group (p. 143 of this volume) was associated with reading the Bennis and Shepard paper, which had focussed their concern about progress, and made them a little rebellious about being predictable. Some argued that regularities occurred in all relationships, without making people anxious about it. Tom pointed specifically to the regular pattern of increasing intimacy in dating situations, which was universally noted but not upsetting. Roger countered with the fantasy of returning from each date and opening a little envelope which told what had happened.

In the next meeting an ambiguous question by the group leader touched off a discussion, first of the irrelevance of his comments and their inability to ignore them, then of the relationship between their homes and the group. Some wondered if they were trying to use the group to acquire techniques to master home situations, or at least obtain better awareness of them—reenacting in the group things that didn't work out at home. Eve suggested that the same applied to the group itself. Roger said he'd hate to feel as unhappy and unsuccessful about his family as he did about the group at times. Eve suggested a general fear of mentioning family problems that would lead to being viewed as sick. Someone then suggested that perhaps the converse might also hold, and Roger agreed, citing his own mother's insensitivity regarding a friend of his who had been hospitalized, and his consequent inability to talk to her about it. The feeling was expressed that the course and the local community in general provided a healthy view that no one was really "normal."

Eve, however, felt that home was a haven while the group was not, and wanted to avoid contaminating this view with comparisons. Angela and Cathy objected to the notion of home as a haven and Eve qualified her remark by saying she had only viewed it this way since she had been away from it, returning only for short visits. Len predicted that they would one day feel this about the group, whereupon Roger said "we'll never get away from it." They continued talking somewhat nostalgically about their homes, and their ability to preserve their unrealistic views of them during short vacations despite underlying awareness that things had really changed.

Here amidst nostalgic thoughts we find a mixture of group chauvinism and distress over the loss of naiveté, together with a feeling of the separation from others that their collective knowledge has caused. A similar effect can be produced by the loss of a member:

IId. It was the next to last day before Christmas vacation. At the beginning of the session the group leader reported having received official notice of Ed's having withdrawn from the university. (It was Ed who had initiated the revolt six weeks earlier. His absence during the past two weeks had been the object of much comment and rumor.) The group began discussing Baruch's *One Little Boy* which they had been reading, and particularly their anxieties about the effects of such psychotherapy, whether it could possibly have any destructive consequences. As one member put it: "How far do you disassociate him (the patient) from the things which have worked for him, and leave him without? You see, my whole approach to this thing is bad, because I have a feeling that you are tearing away from him—not replacing it—whereas probably at the same time you are replacing it." This set the tone of the discussion, which was serious, thoughtful, and ambivalently positive about the therapeutic process. Most of it centered around the fear of regression, which the majority felt was a necessary prelude to cure, although they argued about whether it occurred concurrently with or prior to the latter, and how much of the structure remained intact while the rest was being rearranged. This took them deeper and deeper into the intricacies of psychoanalytic theory, until Shirley asked, "Doesn't this discussion show the various degrees of fear of the consequences of the experience of this course?" Most agreed that it did, and the departure of Ed was mentioned. They then returned to the Baruch study and raised the issue of therapeutic results having an upsetting effect on other persons in the patient's life. Ted brought it back to the group, suggesting that all the anxiety was generated by their motivation to change, since "there's no fear of losing something unless you really want to lose it." The group leader interpreted guilt over Ed's leaving and a desire to absolve the group of responsibility for this, and this led to references to "a bunch of amateur people playing around with fairly powerful emotions, and fear of doing the wrong thing— not being able to handle it, or going too far, or not knowing when to stop." They then began comparing self-revelation inside the group with the "prescribed," "superficial," "ritualized" kind of interaction occurring between friends and acquaintances on the outside. "This is something which doesn't go in gatherings of a social nature. People don't like to be disturbed emotionally, and they don't like for you to show great emotion." Maria recalled that, "Before I took [this course] I talked to one person who had taken it, who was highly in favor of it and about ten who hadn't, who thought it was a terrible thing—that it was morbid." Others recounted similar tales of people who had referred to it as "dangerous," and after some laughter over a former member who "went around analyzing everyone," Jack raised the question as to the extent to which one could "take the things you learn here into society. . . . How much can we assume that [the assumptions and discoveries of psychology] have become a part of our life. I think . . . very little has." He mentioned that through Feiffer and other humorists much had penetrated the larger world, but that in general one had to keep these ideas "completely apart from life when you walk out of this door." The group leader then pointed out their concern about going home and feeling different during vacation, and they continued for a short time to talk of the hostility toward and fascination with psychology evinced by friends and associates. During this discussion David began to talk of his special problems of dealing with what he had learned in the group, and for the remaining fifteen minutes they discussed this, along with David's relationship with Carol. David and Carol had entered the group together, always sat together (unlike the usual pattern of couples in a group), and seemed to arouse tension on the part of other members, who alternated between ridiculing David's psychological naiveté and wistfully encouraging him. Today the latter seemed to predominate, to the point where Maria referred to "this business of trying to set up David as strong and masculine."

While there are many themes running through this meeting, the major one seems to be a kind of Frommian loss of innocence—a feeling that what the members have learned has set them apart from other people and made communication difficult. A similar experience was reported earlier in IIe, when members returning from a spring vacation shortly after their revolt reported having felt very lonely while at home.[49] The departure of Ed in the present case generates a high degree of group self-consciousness, some of which may come from Ed's identification with the revolt. Through Ed they left the "Garden of Eden," and his departure reminds them of their mortality. Although almost smugly "ingroup" at times and confident of their ability to change themselves for the better, they are also fearful of losing defenses and becoming too detached from the "outside (unsophisticated) world." Thus they begin to court David, who symbolizes what they have left behind.

Let us now turn to some of the specific manifestations found in post-revolt groups, dividing them arbitrarily into those involving attitudes toward the leader and those involving relationships among fellow members.

A. The Totem Feast

The most general statement one could make about member attitudes toward the leader after a revolt or its equivalent is that sometimes they behave just as they did before it, sometimes they seem to view him in a far more realistic and secular fashion, and sometimes they act as if he were dead.

The first impression one receives after a revolt is that little has changed in the leader-member relationship. Things seem to return

[49] Similarly, subjects taking drugs like LSD often feel alienated from friends who have not undergone the experience, and seek out fellow subjects.

quickly to normal, and there is nothing very remarkable going on in the group except a slight increase in independence among the members, a kind of breathholding caution about intermember hostility, and occasional manifestations of what appears like overdetermined remorse.

The leader then begins to become aware that he no longer plays so necessary a role in the group. He more often finds that he has nothing to add to what is being said, that the interpretations that coalesce in his mind are all verbalized before he gets ready to express them, and that those few interpretations he does make seem a little tangential and not very helpful.[50] He appears to be most useful when he is repeating, i.e., pointing out the continued relevance in a slightly new context of some old saw that the group has long since accepted (in other words, in "working through"). Far from producing groans, as repetitions so often do, these are now accepted in a matter-of-fact way as helpful reminders from a friendly source. Indeed, the entire interpretation sequence is profoundly altered, in a way which is startling when it first happens. For by this time the group leader is accustomed to getting some sort of response when he speaks or to being totally and deliberately ignored. His speech either has a jolting effect on the interaction, producing silence, laughter, anger, scorn, guilty smiles, depressed sighs—at the very least a change of topic—or this effect is warded off by not listening and continuing on as if he had not spoken at all. (All of which is in keeping with the phallic definition of interpretation described in the last chapter.) But now his speaking seems to have no special impact on the group, whether his ideas are considered and used, or rejected, or ignored. It is as if they contained for the group only their intended intellectual significance —as if they had been divested of all sacred or libidinal overtones. In other words, it no longer matters who said it.

This, then, is the second impression the group leader receives: that he is no longer being deified. For as long as the group members can maintain their lethargic dream of the leader's magic, they will not think of adopting his techniques and functions. A primitive tribe will see the colonial invader as a god only until it understands and

[50] This is not to be confused with the usual bad days experienced by every group leader, when things seem to be at a prolonged standstill and he is unable to illuminate the problem. One feels no *need* of contributing anything so far as the objective situation is concerned, and the only tension present springs from the narcissism of the leader. For although the group leader feels rewarded at the group's achievements and successes, he also undergoes a sharp loss here. Being deified, despite the attendant annoyance, frustration, and despair, always provides some narcissistic gratification; being useful and needed provide even more.

can replicate the tools of civilization, and it will be able to do the latter only when it has stopped viewing the invader as a god. The situation in the group is very similar.

The third impression the leader receives, however, is that the worshipful attitude is still present, despite being detached from his own person. It is perhaps less frequently in evidence than before, but it is nevertheless quite visible at times. The attitude may attach itself to many things, even something outside the group, but usually to an object which both represents the group as a whole and also has some temporal-spatial association with the leader.

Bion notes, for example, that "in the dependent group the place of leader may be filled by the history of the group. A group, complaining of an inability to remember what took place on a previous occasion, sets about making a record of its meetings. This record then becomes a 'bible' . . ." (Bion, 1957, p. 450). Bion sees this as emotionally indistinguishable from dependence on the leader himself, even a search for a more ideal leader. Historically, however, the distinction between the rule of law and the rule of men has been important, and we may regard the use of a written record as an important step in substituting appeal to data for appeal to authority, even if the data in this case appear in the intermediate form of a record of a venerated past.[51] Bion is correct in insisting on the essential emotional identity between the two attitudes, but it is of equal significance that the person of the leader no longer stands for the group as a whole.

A second possibility is that a group member may be invested with some of the leader's attributes. It is rare for this to occur for more than a few moments without the more usual responses of sibling jealousy and democratic leveling reasserting themselves, but it is visible on occasion.

IIa. It will be recalled that Joe had played a kind of "doctor's assistant" role in the group prior to the revolt, and that when it came, although he did not oppose it, he also was attacked. When the group met alone, furthermore, he was absent.

---

[51] During the revolt in IIa there was, as noted, a great deal of talk about who would be the leader in the assigned leader's absence, whether the interpretive function could be performed and how discussion could be controlled. One member suggested a kind of rotary speaking system which he defended vigorously but unsuccessfully against attack. When asked if he was trying to say it would improve discussion he replied, "I didn't say it would *improve* it. I was just trying to think of some *mechanism* that might possibly take the place of Mr. Slater." In a similar way, a group will often sanctify a book or paper on group processes.

Months later, Joe was rather explicitly accepted as a peer leader, and no sooner was this position certified than echoes of the group's earlier relation to the formal leader began to be noticeable. On two or three occasions when the discussion was active and it was difficult for the less aggressive to break into it, members raised their hands, looking to Joe to be called upon—an unconscious gesture which caused considerable embarrassment when a member became aware of having done it.[52] Even the fantasy of tyrannical monopolization of the women was transferred to Joe, in the form of male complaints that the girls always sat near him and talked aside to him. These incidents occurred during the three or four sessions following verbal recognition of Joe's special position.

What seems to be involved here is another kind of halfway point between that state in which the group leader is worshipped and seen as indistinguishable from the group as a whole, and that in which clear distinctions are made between leader and group and between secular and sacred. In the final phase there is very little in the everyday internal workings of the group which is contaminated by sacred ideas. Indeed, this is perhaps the essence of the revolt process, and the reason why learning, therapy, and group development all depend on it: as long as the idea of the sacred pervades the leader-member relationship, rationality and adaptation are impossible. Through the revolt process this relationship is secularized. The sacred sphere is detached from workaday affairs and confined to an area where it cannot impinge on these affairs. This is essentially what the primal horde is supposed to have achieved. Instead of involuntary subordination to a powerful leader they substituted voluntary subordination to the totem—a purely symbolic representation of the group as a whole.[53]

[52] I have never known an academic group in which unconscious handraising did not occur. A habit of so many years' duration is difficult to break; the hand seems to rise almost of its own accord as the individual listens intently, waiting for an opportunity to express his idea. He is often astounded when someone points out his hand in the air and looks at it as if it did not belong to him. In early meetings handraising tends to be directed toward the group leader, but later it seems directed toward those who are doing most of the talking. IIa was something of a special case, since it took place during a period of transition in the course, which had previously been run with a different format, and prior to the revolt the leader had in fact channeled the discussion to a considerable extent. The handraising thus had a historical significance specific to the group, and the incidents with Joe were correspondingly more dramatic.

[53] It goes without saying that today successful adaptation requires further diminution of the sphere of the sacred. Even though the flag is the most limited of emblems, interfering hardly at all in the instrumental activities of the society, still the veneration in which such emblems are held threatens to destroy the world.

But fragments of the original orientation still cling to the first totemic representations. The mere fact that a person is chosen rather than a pure symbol reflects this, and it is not surprising that he reveals so many associations to the leader. Indeed, there is even an element of expiation in choosing such an individual, but perhaps more important than this is the notion that by virtue of these resemblances the peer leader contains more *mana* or, in Durkheim's terms, more of the "totemic principle" (Durkheim, pp. 190 ff.). In time such a solution becomes nearly as cumbersome as the original state of affairs, however, and instrumental effectiveness will depend on channeling the "totemic principle" into some kind of symbol which will leave all interpersonal relationships in the group free of sacred ideas.

IIg. An example of an ambivalent attempt to circumscribe the sphere of the sacred occurred in this group following the midyear examination. Sylvia, attacked for having in the previous session made some remarks about gaining insight from the exam, vigorously defended herself by pointing out that in so doing she was not making a bid for the group leader's approval, but on the contrary was discarding the "private" examination relationship by making it public. Art suggested that the group regarded the examination relationship as sacred, group interaction as profane.

Actually, Sylvia's remarks about the examination and the group's response are both ambivalent with regard to the dependency issue. The aggression against her is based both on her "eager student" performance and on her attempt to secularize the sacred extragroup relationship to the group leader. Needless to say, as long as the examination relationship *is* regarded as sacred, the group's independence of the leader remains largely spurious.

This is the same ambiguity we encountered in the Messiah fantasy of the pairing group, but we may here recall Bion's notion that the Messiah must never be embodied in a living representation or the characteristic hopefulness of the pairing group will be destroyed.[54] My own feeling is that the fantasy of the unborn Messiah is a more viable orientation for the group when it is nothing more than that. Fantasy is after all harmful only when it distorts reality. We can even say that the revolt is nothing more than a process of separating fantasy from reality. The "totemic principle," the *mana*, the fantasy of an om-

---

[54] Robert Gordon in a personal communication offers the interesting suggestion that perhaps Jesus was "more readily accepted by Gentiles than Jews because in their case this did not mean surrendering such a pre-existing hope."

nipotent force—whatever one wishes to call it—is detached from the group leader and isolated as a totem or a Messiah fantasy. If the peer leader becomes invested with all this he is of little use to his fellow members as a leader, since they will become "hung up" on the dependency issue all over again. Fortunately, this never seems to happen to any marked extent. Once the work of secularizing the leader is carried through to the point where a real substitution can be tolerated, there is likely to be correspondingly little *mana* left in the group leader to be transferred to the substitute, and any secondary deification is likely to be short-lived. We must also remember that there is little mystery attached to any of the group members by the time substitution is likely to take place, and mystery is almost a prerequisite to deification. Silent members sometimes become associated with Messiah fantasies, but only so long as they remain silent. If a silent member attempts to act on these fantasies he is doomed to immediate ridicule and scorn, since up to this point he has not "carried his share of the burden." Realistically, the group needs talkers, with or without, before or after the revolt, and no member who is inactive is ever in serious contention for a leadership position. This tends to mean that attitudes toward peer leaders are most likely to be secular and realistic from the start, since perceptions of these individuals are based on a great deal of behavioral data, and any feelings of respect and admiration are founded on tangible benefits collectively received.

For this reason the connection between the old group deity of the dependent group, incarnated in the person of the group leader, and the hero of the post-revolt group, is likely to be far more marked in prospect than in reality. Groups considering expulsion of the group leader invariably express the feeling that some sort of peer leader will of necessity emerge when they meet alone, and usually discuss the possibilities at some length, though often with little reference to names. Sometimes this is even given as an argument against expulsion, as if equality were intrinsically valued. All of this involves the interesting assumptions that (*a*) heretofore the group leader has been directing the discussion, and (*b*) as yet there are no peer leaders, both of which are usually false.

IIb. This group had two partial revolts, neither of them really consummated. (See this volume, pp. 45–46.) The second incident occurred at about the halfway mark, and expulsion was considered in some detail. By this time, however, a few of the members had read the Bennis and Shepard paper quoted in the Introduction, and there was a feeling that expulsion would be not only a futile ritual, but also an expression of dependency, inasmuch as it would constitute a carrying out of an apparently pre-ordained pattern of behavior. This frustration seemed to add to the general fury.

In the course of the discussion of expulsion, the usual issue arose as to what sort of peer leader might emerge in the absence of the formal leader. Roger was much excited by this and exclaimed, "It's so—so *religious* almost!" (Laughter.) "Somebody coming up from the ashes to lead us across the Red Sea or something."

This mythological eclecticism shows clearly the close connection between the leader and his replacement on the one hand, and Frazer's discussion of "dying and reviving gods" on the other (Frazer, 1959, pp. 283–369).

A third possible vehicle for the residual worshipful attitude is the group leader himself—that is, he can be split in some way so that both sacred and secular attitudes toward him can be expressed. This is the same kind of compromise effort to separate reality and fantasy we saw in the case of the peer leader, but is perhaps more primitive. The most usual approach to the splitting is a temporal one—the group leader's past remarks are oft-quoted and treated with great veneration, as if they were sacred texts, while his current interpretations are treated in a highly secular and realistic fashion.

All of these tendencies are simply various expressions of two changes: (1) the actual skills of the group leader have been diffused among the group members; (2) the group leader and the group deity, once identical, have been separated. In a sense these changes are simply two sides of the same coin—a secular process and a magical definition of it.

But as we have noted, this definition has many variants, not necessarily associated with the same outcome. If some notion akin to *mana* is attached to the leader's skills, then it would seem most appropriate to conceive of this force as now residing in everyone, or (since this is not a particularly compelling metaphor) as endowing the group as a whole, and by extension, some emblem of the group as a whole. As such, the totem of the group is simply an expression of group pride, of a sense of collective power and achievement.

The separation of reality from fantasy is a one-way process. What we really mean by it is that a portion of reality has been captured from the realm of fantasy, for initially, in the history of individual, of species, of group, or of any relationship, all is fantasy. Development is simply a matter of rescuing more and more pieces of reality, like bits of dry land emerging from the sea. When we say that the image of the leader has been detached from the fantasy of an all-powerful deity we mean that he can be perceived realistically, and that interaction with him will be correspondingly more rational, less predictable, more tension-free.

Yet this should not be interpreted to mean that the realm of fantasy is at the same time diminished—that the more light the less darkness. On the contrary, the brighter the light the deeper the darkness by contrast, or, to return to an earlier metaphor, the greater the area of dry land, the deeper the pools into which the sea must be distributed. By detaching reality from it, the fantasy is purified and intensified, just as the living sacred king is slain so that the god (fantasy) in him may be preserved and purified of his contaminating influence. We may recall the remark in IIe (see this volume, p. 68) that the group leader might "be more really here" if he were expelled.

This is why it is so difficult to characterize the post-revolt period in groups. While on the one hand the group seems to be secularized and enlightened, on the other hand its sacred sphere sometimes seems deeper and darker, if narrower, than ever.

What if, in other words, the "goal" of the attack were not to capture *mana* from the group leader but simply to create a better oracle by killing him before his *mana* departs from him? It is after all an axiom of oracular religion that the most effective prophets are dead ones, by virtue of their connection with the nether world and their having been purged of the slag of reality. The popularity of severed heads and heroes' tombs as oracles in ancient times exemplifies this rule (cf. Jung, 1958, pp. 188–193; Harrison, 1957). Is not the notion that the prophet will know more when dead a reflection of the desire to loose fantasy from its mortal mooring? Hence is not the attack on the leader perhaps the expression of a fantasy that this will rid the group deity of its mortal prison? Instead of absorbing the *mana* of the image of the leader are they not perhaps keeping it outside? Fantasy is separated from reality in this case not for instrumental benefit but to safeguard a dream and preserve an infantile state.

It is not at all unlikely that some such motivation contributes to the revolt. But it should be noted that even primitive responses such as this have their developmental side. The primitive men who severed the prophet's head gained a measure of independence thereby, since they now had to rely on their own imagination rather than someone else's, at least until they relapsed (as they usually did) and delegated this task to an interpreter-priest, thus reestablishing the initial dependence. Insofar as this relapse was avoided the process is a little like the evolutionary theories of Ferenczi and Freud, in which the maladroit efforts of living matter to return to the inorganic state continually drive it farther from its goal (Ferenczi, 1938; Freud, 1950). All we can say is that the motivational and fantasy components of the revolt are multi-faceted and strange; the most sophisticated, civilized, and rational desires for growth being combined with the most primitive and irrational drives toward permanent darkness and passivity.

There is still another way to interpret this separation of the worshipful attitude and its original object. When an ancient hero like Heracles is deified, he must be immolated, and his mortal aspect burned away. The destruction and apotheosis of the original group leader image constitute a separation of what is valued and desired in the leader from what is rejected and resented. This is what "killing and eating" symbolize in this situation—the separation of good and bad, love and hate, so that one may be taken into oneself and the other destroyed. What is valued is distilled out as an abstract principle, while the impure vehicle is eliminated. It is for this reason that aggression leads to identification—in fantasy the attack is a freeing of the desirable attributes from the hateful shell that prevents their acquisition.

Let us now try to summarize all of these complexities. Prior to the revolt three entities are bound together: the person of the group leader, the group deity (i.e., the object of the worshipful attitude, dependency needs, or whatever of the group members), and a set of abstract skills, qualities, or powers which are desired by the members. After the revolt process has run its course these three entities are separated. The qualities of wisdom, understanding, and interpretive skill are now emotionally recognized as abstract principles, no longer inherent in any particular person, and hence capable of being shared by all. Prior to this time there is a deep conviction, for example, that only the leader knows what is going on in the group. He may assure them that, after all, the same data are available to everyone and that it is simply a question of keeping one's eyes and ears open. They will reply with earnest intensity that he has more knowledge and experience in these matters, a view that in no way mitigates their steadfast rejection of his interpretations or their feeling that his is an absurd way to conduct a group or teach a course. The·revolt reverses to a considerable extent all three of these attitudes. Although the instructor may be a more skillful interpreter than they, this is now seen in a more balanced fashion, as a function of his having "been at it longer."

They are able to admit that they also have the power to interpret, even to interpret the behavior of the leader himself.

The symbolic ideas of communal killing and communal devouring express the fact that before a group can become united around a set of principles it must (a) rid itself of the fantasy of a *living* omnipotent protector, (b) separate the valued principles from their living vehicle, and (c) make them available to all on an equal basis. The cannibalistic fantasy thus leads to the idea that the "totemic principle" resides in every group member, and this in turn necessitates collective acceptance of the unprotected situation in which the group functions, and of responsibility for what has happened and will happen in the group.

All of this leaves one separation still unaccounted for. The group deity and the desired attributes have both been detached from the person of the leader but not from each other. When sought, the attributes are magically defined. It is only after they have actually been attained that the attributes are secularized. It requires great imagination and energy to maintain a magical view of one's own skills, and it becomes impossible when everyone else possesses them, too. So gradually, detached and disembodied, the group deity drifts off on its own, making sporadic appearances as a kind of group totem, a symbol of group unity and group pride.

One of these manifestations might best be described as a totemic feast—a ritual recapitulation of the revolt with attendant expressions of group solidarity. It is interesting because it tends to occur whenever there is strong pressure to regress to the earlier state of dependence and rivalry.

IIa. Several meetings after the group met alone, a session was devoted to reviewing material in preparation for a midyear examination. The group leader, in releasing the case material which would provide the basis for a segment of the examination, had sanctioned discussion of it, but had pointed out that he could in no way participate in such a discussion. When the day of the anticipated discussion arrived, the group leader made a few remarks about the structure of the examination and then fell silent. The members talked in a desultory fashion about several other matters, and the group leader remarked that they seemed to be avoiding the discussion they had planned, and wondered if the threat of intermember competition was inhibiting them. In reply, the members complained that "nonparticipation" on the part of the group leader could not be achieved so long as he was seated in his usual chair, and that it would be necessary for him to move to the side of the room. He promptly did so, and with audible sighs of relief they commenced a lively discussion.

The threat of regression here is quite clear. The group was about to separate temporarily, and during this separation would be examined as individuals rather than as a group. The desire to cooperate in discussion clashed sharply with the competitive wish to withhold ideas that might be snatched up by others and used on the exam. Furthermore, they had seemed unable to face up to this conflict, and had been obliged to have the group leader point it out to them. In every way they seemed to be slipping back into their old dependent and rivalrous pattern. The solution was to recapitulate the event which had established their solidarity, by once again expelling the leader, whereupon, reassured, they were able to work cooperatively despite the spectre of grades. The *need* to take this step is indicative of the group's fragility, but the *ability* to take it is a measure of its resiliency.

IIa. It was the last session prior to spring vacation. The preceding weeks had been rather typical of this period in groups of this sort—full of conflict, of the expression of negative feelings, of mutual analysis and confrontation that was often bitter, of high anxiety and feelings of failure, of high absenteeism. The session began with comments about the many absentees. Then one member suggested that the real question should not be, why were the absentees absent, but, why were the participants present? Someone then wondered what would happen if they all got up and left. Everyone laughed, and it was suggested that it would be even better if they all stayed and the group leader left. Everyone again laughed, the atmosphere livened, and amidst joking and laughter the group began to reminisce over the original revolt. After two or three minutes thus spent, they began to analyse the difficulties they had been having, and continued in what the leader felt was a highly productive discussion for the rest of the hour.

Once again solidarity is achieved by a ritual reenactment of the revolt. Confidence is restored, tensions evaporate, productive effort is engendered, simply by reliving this early experience. How do we explain this phenomenon? Is it simply a matter of completing, through repetition, an emotional process begun by the revolt? As we have said, the revolt is in most cases more a beginning than a culmination of group self-sufficiency.

Durkheim's analysis of totemism throws the greatest light on this question: "There can be no society which does not feel the need of upholding and reaffirming at regular intervals the collective sentiments and the collective ideas which make its unity and its personality"

(Durkheim, p. 427). But "individual minds cannot come into contact and communicate with each other except by coming out of themselves; but they cannot do this except by movements. So it is the homogeneity of these movements that gives the group consciousness of itself and consequently makes it exist" (Durkheim, pp. 230–231). Furthermore, "collective sentiments can become conscious of themselves only by fixing themselves upon external objects" (Durkheim, p. 419). In other words, consciousness of the group as such originated in common action toward an external object, the old, overinvested image of the leader, and whenever its collective self-awareness seemed to flag, it was necessary to relive this experience in order to strengthen itself. Durkheim adds: "On feast days . . . their thoughts are centered upon their common . . . traditions . . . the collective ideal of which they are the incarnation. . . . Men do not deceive themselves when they feel at this time that there is something outside of them which is born again, that there are forces which are reanimated and a life which reawakens" (Durkheim, pp. 348–349).[55] And again, "The rite serves . . . to sustain the vitality of these beliefs, to keep them from being effaced from memory and, in sum, to revivify the most essential elements of the collective consciousness. Through it, the group periodically renews the sentiment which it has of itself and of its unity; at the same time, individuals are strengthened in their social natures. The glorious souvenirs which are made to live again before their eyes, and with which they feel that they have a kinship, give them a feeling of strength and confidence" (Durkhem, p. 375). Even the hilarity and excitement of the group during these occasions finds its primitive prototype, for Durkheim says the effect of every feast is to "excite a state of effervescence."

As noted above, all of these "feasts" occurred when the solidarity of the group seemed to need renewal or, in Durkheim's terms, "revivification." In both of the examples given, the group was about to separate temporarily. In both cases external forces tended to reactivate individual dependence on the group leader. In both cases there was internal friction in the group. By the ritual act of collective recapitulation of its great traditions, the group set these threats at naught.

[55] It is worth noting that several of the major nations in the world today have as their principal holiday the celebration of a revolution, including the United States, France, and the Soviet Union. In no case, moreover, does this revolution coincide with the nation's origin. Our own totemic feast—July 4—does not even commemorate the achievement of independence but only the declaration of same. Similarly, in IIa it was the moment when the leader was asked to leave, rather than the moment of his departure, which was commemorated.

B. Equality, Fraternity, and Autonomy

In the last analysis independence cannot be conferred; it can only be seized. For independence is first of all a state of mind, and we can only say that it has become manifest in an individual or group when it no longer occurs to that group or individual to seek the solution of its problems by an agent outside itself. To "demand one's independence," a phrase often heard from college students struggling ambivalently to loosen familial bonds, is of course a contradiction in terms.

Similarly, we cannot characterize a group as "independent" whose unity is based entirely on a common attitude toward an external object. If a group *consistently* needed to attack the leader in order to stay together, we would feel that they had not progressed very far beyond their initial dependent state.

This produces the interesting paradox that intermember hostility can be symptomatic either of dependence on or independence of the leader. This is because there are really three different stages in the structural development of the member-member-leader triangle. In the first stage, as a result of normal social training, there is a generalized inhibition of hostile sentiments, but since throughout their lives expression of hostility toward peers has been sanctioned less rigidly than manifest hostility toward authority, there is a certain amount of displacement from the latter to the former. As the revolt builds up this process is increasingly reversed, and, as we have seen, a successful revolt depends on near unanimity of animosity toward the leader. Following the revolt this demand for unanimity of feeling continues, and there is an intense taboo on intermember conflict. Gradually, however, this restriction is relaxed, and there is again a great deal of hostility expressed between individual members. This coincides with more or less universal acceptance of the usual training group value on free and candid expression of feelings in interpersonal relationships.

As usual, this description hardly does justice to the chronological complexity of the matter. Some work on member-member relationships must take place in order to achieve the necessary consensus for expelling the leader, and obviously only a part of the intermember hostility in the first stage is displaced from the leader. It would be pleasant to announce that there is a marked difference between intermember fighting in the pre-revolt and post-revolt stages, but in reality there is little to distinguish them. The most we can say, and this very impressionistically, is that while the level of emotional intensity is the same in both, there seems to be more *interest* in the later conflicts—more cognitive involvement, libidinal cathexis, or whatever. For this reason it is much more difficult for the leader to attract hostility to himself in the later stage than in the earlier one.

Nothing is more startling and impressive about leading groups of this kind than the fluidity of aggression, the ease with which it changes from object to object, and the utter irrelevancy of the object's appropriateness as a target. This even presents something of a problem for the group leader, who often finds it altogether too easy to deflect an attack on himself merely by appearing a shade too benign or too punitive, with the consequence that the members begin snarling and snapping at each other like trapped foxes. Or, conversely, the slightest comment on his part during some quarrel between members will recreate the comic scene so popular in American farce, in which two physical combatants turn on and pummel the peacemaker who tries to separate them.[56] Usually, of course, it is the former problem which is the more serious, since warding off hostility is an almost automatic response. Ogilvie, in the study cited above, reports great difficulty in training his experimental stooge to absorb hostility (Ogilvie, 1961). The problem is acute in training and therapy groups, where the explicit encouragement of forthright and unvarnished interchange of personal sentiments provides a particularly favorable milieu for displacing hostility from authority to peers.

As an example of the difference in the hostility economy between the pre- and post-revolt stages let us consider the simple and not uncommon situation in which most of the group members are vigorously attacking one of their peers whom the leader feels rightly or wrongly to be a scapegoat for himself. If he voices this feeling in the earlier stage he will be more likely to be attacked himself with equal vigor for making such a stupid, irrelevant, narcissistic, and paranoid remark. The "scapegoat" will be forgotten in the mutual commiseration over having to put up with so troublesome and unhelpful a group leader.

If the leader voices this feeling in the post-revolt period, it is more likely to have the exact opposite effect. The members will listen

[56] Cf. Blake Higgs' calypso song, "Never Interfere with Man and Wife." It is strange that a phenomenon so well known as to be a popular comic subject should only recently become the subject of serious study. Cf. Mills' research on the effect of hostility toward authority on intermember cooperation (Mills, 1964a).

very calmly, agree that there is much in what he says, suggest that they probably are annoyed with him for this, that, and the other reason, and begin to reconsider their feelings about the "scapegoat" in this light. By imperceptible degrees, however, this reconsideration becomes indistinguishable from the original attack and continues thus until some understanding is gained by the "scapegoat" about how he provokes people or by the attackers about why they are so threatened by him. Thus in the first stage the members tend more often to disagree with the leader and then "prove" him right, while in the third stage they tend more often to agree with him and then "prove" him wrong.[57]

Consider for a moment to what these changes correspond in the primal horde myth. Freud's theory seems absurd in part because the transition between the Darwinian horde state and the moment of overthrow is so abrupt and apparently unpredictable. His acceptance of Atkinson's formulation, in which normally each son eventually establishes his own horde, leaves insufficient motivation for change, and Freud is thrown back upon vague suggestions of new weapons and cultural advance (Freud, 1950, pp. 126, 141).

For the primal horde is fundamentally nothing more than a slightly extended pecking order. Everyone is for himself, the strongest takes all, and when the strongest weakens, the next strongest takes all. If we think in terms of sons, it will usually be the eldest who replaces the father. It is difficult to see how under these conditions the idea of cooperative effort could arise. The disadvantageous position of the eldest son is made palatable by his power over his brothers, so there would be little motive for him to relinquish this power. It would take exceptionally stupid brothers, moreover, to agree to cooperate in effecting a change of despots, from which they would gain nothing. Cooperation arises among people who are in the same boat, to which nothing could be more foreign than a pecking order.

Mills, in his paper on the primal horde,[58] has attempted to trans-

[57] This question of correctness is of course meaningless as well as unanswerable. As in psychotherapy, an interpretation can never be incorrect, unless it is stated comparatively or quantitatively, since human beings are so complex and ambivalent that any statement will be accurate at some level. (This follows from the psychological law that every motive has an equal and opposite contramotive.) From a theoretical viewpoint, the issue is whether it is *salient* or not; from the practical one it is whether or not it is well timed.

[58] The discussion which follows is derived almost entirely from Mills' paper on the primal horde (Mills, 1959) and personal communications. Not only is the idea of attempting to abstract structural phases from Freud's metaphorical

late Freud's mythical narration into a sociological process, replacing events with structural stages, which is ultimately the only way in which these ideas can become scientifically useful. But his analysis encounters precisely the same difficulty just noted—that there seems to be no logical developmental bridge between a structure based on sheer power (pecking order) and one involving cooperation and a normative structure of some kind.

In the groups we have described the revolt is not preceded by a pecking order but by a patriarchy, i.e., a group centered around a single leader and competing for a favored position with him. It might be more useful to think in terms of a four-stage process, the first of which (pecking order) would rarely be found in a group of adult humans, for whom legitimization of leadership is normally a prerequisite to membership.

The transition from this first structure to a true patriarchy will not be brought about by the disadvantaged but by the dominant tyrant. Among the brothers, the eldest and strongest dogs hope to have their day, while the rest are too intimidated and browbeaten to hope anything. Only the "father" has the power and desire to bring about social change, in order to preserve and consolidate a position which is ultimately doomed. He will attempt to delay his overthrow by conferring benefits upon his followers, making their position less intolerable and making it seem as if the few benefits they *do* have will be taken away if they do anything to threaten or displease the despot. That this is a highly successful technique is obvious from innumerable historical examples. While it carries within itself the seeds of its own destruction, as we shall see, it is also true that generally a patriarchal despotism only comes to an end (as a system, not in the individual case, where incompetence takes its usual toll) when some new source of power, external to the system, upsets the balance of things. (This is doubtless where Freud's idea of a new weapon or technique comes in, but anything creating new wealth would have the same effect.)

Now the principal tactic used by the despot to maintain his position is "divide and rule" in the specific form of "the last shall be first and the first shall be last." In other words, he upsets the pecking order below him, bolstering the weaker and weakening the stronger. He favors the weak, gives him benefits and uses him as a spy. When it is

ideas his, as well as most of the specific translations made, but even the few departures from his formulation spring from consideration of material to the fathomless relevance of which he first called my attention: the myth of Joseph and his brethren.

seen by everyone except the strongest contender (eldest son) that more immediate and tangible benefits are to be gained through despotic favor than through the usual channel of succession, the pecking order structure is defunct and the courtier or patriarchal structure established. What seems on the surface to be the most highly developed form of the latter is familiar to us from the *Arabian Nights,* in which anyone can become wealthy or penniless through the whims and preferences of the Caliph. Its prototypical expression is also found in the Middle East, in the biblical story of Joseph and his brethren.

Before discussing the latter, however, let us note two recurrent ideas in Freud's primal horde theory. The first is that all the sons were *equally* persecuted by the father (Freud, 1951, p. 95). Mills, in his translation of the primal horde myth, sees the demand for equal treatment as a crucial factor in moving from the "pre-murder" to the "post-murder" structure of the horde (Mills, 1959, pp. 14, 17), and compulsive equality is characteristic of groups during and immediately after revolts, so that the variable is perhaps important but simply misplaced in Freud's theory. Second (and not unrelated to the first), Freud speaks of the *youngest* son as the one who replaces the father in the primordial condition, as a result of his mother's favoritism (Freud, 1951, p. 93; 1958, p. 103). This seems absurd in a true pecking order setting, since it would be the eldest and strongest who would be the first to "profit by his father's advancing years," while the youngest would have to wait for all the others to decline as well. It would seem as if Freud in his theory collapsed the pecking order horde and the patriarchal horde into one, with a great deal of confusion resulting.

When we turn to the story of Joseph, we find the missing link in the entire sequence. In the pecking order structure a rough de facto primogeniture exists. True primogeniture is a legitimization of this situation, an attempt to stabilize the pecking order structure under cultural conditions favorable to it. But as we have seen, it is ultimogeniture which appeals most to the would-be patriarchal despot himself, both because it lengthens his term, and because by favoring the youngest or weakest he can bind him to himself and perhaps avoid his overthrow altogether. This view is epitomized by the Baganda, who typically strangle the firstborn of a chief if it is male, believing that otherwise the chief will die (Queen et al., p. 75).

What we see in the book of *Genesis* is an endless struggle between the old pecking order structure and the newer courtier structure, with endless rivalry and strife as a result. Cain and Abel, Esau and Jacob, Reuben and Joseph, Manasseh and Ephraim, Zerah and Perez all partake of the struggle. Usually the youngest is favored by the father (Jacob is an exception), and usually the youngest wins out (Abel is an exception here). Often there is ambiguity about the order. Thus Jacob and Esau are twins, while the case of Perez and Zerah is one to whet the appetite of legal philosophers everywhere. Joseph himself is an ambiguous case, being the next youngest of the father's children but the oldest of the mother's. (Although on the surface he seems to be identified with the favored younger sibling, his overcompensated but nonetheless ill-concealed hatred for Benjamin —exhibited in the cup episode and his anger over Ephraim's blessing —show that he is fighting on both sides of the conflict.)

The pecking order and courtier structures are clearly exemplified in Reuben and Joseph, respectively. Reuben, the firstborn, copulates with his father's concubine and is cursed by Jacob for his challenge. Joseph, the fawning and backbiting flatterer, is favored by Jacob for his unfailing submissiveness to authority. Reuben's sexual aggressiveness is contrasted with Joseph's pious rejection of Potiphar's wife. The message of the story (although it is extraordinarily complex and full of unresolved ambivalences) is clearly that the wild and free nature of the Bedouin must be curbed—that success in life is only possible within the framework of patriarchal despotism.

Raphael Patai notes that "the patriarchal family, with the practically unlimited powers vested in the family head, is a social environment eminently suited for the emergence of sibling rivalry, often in violent form. The sons' position, indeed their entire future, depends in such a setup on the wish and will of the father" (Patai, 1959, p. 215). This is of course the situation which the patriarchal despot is trying to bring about, and he does it largely by manipulating favors and creating divisions among the sons. Patai notes that even today in the Middle East intense sibling rivalry is not only expected but even fostered deliberately as a culturally valuable trait. He stresses the essential role of the absolute authority of the father in generating this rivalry and shows how hostility toward him and jealousy of his power is displaced onto siblings in the hope of gaining rewards for good behavior. He suggests that in biblical times also sibling rivalry was consciously fostered, in part through the preferential treatment of the younger sons (Patai, 1959, pp. 219–220).

As we suggested before, however, this technique contains within itself the seeds of its own destruction. The raising up of the weak and the casting down of the strong tends to equalize the positions of all the sons, and the whimsical giving and taking away of favors will if too extreme make everyone feel that his position is too insecure to make the effort to flatter the despot worthwhile. Under ideal conditions, then, a sense of equality will be achieved or seen as a desirable goal, and when that goal has been reached, the despot will be overthrown. This is by no means inevitable, of course—a courtier structure can be kept going indefinitely in a stable setting. It is merely possible.

The story of Joseph illustrates this point as well. For we see most of Jacob's sons already united, not against Jacob, but against Joseph. Furthermore, there are many resemblances to the myth of the primal horde: the despot with many women, the restless and deprived sons, the collective attack, the group slaying, the animal substituted for a human, the exaltation of the "slain." But the attack is against a scapegoat, the slaying is feigned, and the exalted is not dead but simply a successful expatriate. The story of Joseph thus takes us from the pecking order stage to the courtier stage, plays with the next stage, and then draws back, reinforcing the patriarchal order through the displacement of hostility. Note in particular the generality of Joseph's revenge: in return for being sold into slavery, he in effect sells the entire nation into slavery, from which only another great patriarch can rescue them. But one can conceive of the possibility that if all could combine against one brother, they might combine against the father also—that the success of the united effort of equals might be so impressive that they would carry it a step further and end the system altogether. Cooperative effort was not all that strange to them. Does not the Middle Eastern proverb say "I and my cousins against the world; I and my brothers against my cousins; I against my brothers" (Patai, 1959, p. 218)? By the same token, of course, there would be a strong tendency to dissolve once the deed was done, and only a continuation of the compulsive equality expressed in the collective attack on the despot would lead to a real change in the system.

Thus the third stage, following upon the courtier or patriarchal stage, might be called the stage of equality. It is inaugurated by equal treatment, for equal treatment always leads to a coalition against whoever dispenses it. In the training group the attack on the leader occurs as frequently as it does precisely because he is neutral and impartial. Favoritism will always undermine it. Furthermore, the attack occurs at the moment when the active majority feels that there are no special groups still operating in terms of the courtier structure. (Thus silent members and females must always be checked.) It is then maintained by equal guilt, responsibility, and renunciation, as in Freud's myth, although this renunciation refers primarily to the despot's power, while other spoils, material or imagined, are shared.[59]

One meaning of the primal horde myth seems to be that the stage of equality is so unstable as to produce the danger of relapse into the penultimately primitive structure of the pecking order and the regicidal transmission of power.

Vb. During the discussion which took place on the first day of the leader's expulsion (see this volume, pp. 53–54) there was a great deal of wonderment expressed at the voluntary acceptance of the role of "King of the Wood" in Frazer's famous example of the Sacred Grove of Diana. Likened to the endless revolutions of the children's game "King of the Mountain" or "King of the Castle," they saw the role as entirely uninviting. One girl wondered if "the fact that none of *us* want to be 'King of the Wood,' whether this is affecting our judgment of this, because my reaction was that the King of the Wood was binding himself in a terrible kind of slavery—this horrible business of running around the tree every night looking for someone who is going to attack you. . . ."

(R. F. Bales, transcript)

The stage of equality cannot in any case be forever maintained. Sooner or later some differentiation creeps back in. It is interesting that in Freud's myth there are many different outcomes: fratricidal strife, matriarchy, totemism, and essentially all of the social and religious phenomena that we find in the world today and in historical records. Perhaps the most useful way of thinking about the primal horde myth is not as an historical description or a theory of the foundation of civilization, but rather as simply a general paradigm of social change, similar to the more particularized ones so popular with the Greek philosophers. Stage four, the stage of redifferentiation, is simply the new order and is identical with the first stage of the old order. Thus:

	Stage 1:	stratification on homogeneous criteria (old)
Old Era	Stage 2:	stratification on heterogeneous criteria
	Stage 3:	leveling
New Era	Stage 4:	stratification on homogeneous criteria (new), etc.

Our discussion began with the criteria of physical strength and dominance, which yielded the pecking order structure. In stage two,

[59] Theodore Mills points out that it is interesting to think of Freud and his early disciples in this connection. The difficulties in his theory may reflect his peculiar difficulty in handling these relationships. Note that *Totem and Taboo* was his first major work after acquiring a following.

the courtier patriarchy, a divergent set of criteria was added: unctuousness, obsequiousness, and cajolery. (In some instances, for example the caliphates of the Middle East, this may be the only criterion, and produce a stable system.) The confusion generated by divergent criteria tends to fuse together all but the most advantaged individuals, and the former then attack and destroy the latter. Equality now reigns until differentiation begins again, perhaps on old criteria, perhaps on new. After a time a second set of criteria undermines this differentiation, and a new revolution occurs. It is no accident, furthermore, that the second set of criteria in our example is almost the exact opposite of the first.[60] Any hierarchy has an inherent tendency to generate its opposite. Conscious human thought is perversely one-sided, and the "return of the repressed" has social as well as psychological manifestations. Side by side with every hierarchy is an inverted ghost, only awaiting some cultural invention to become fully manifest. We can see such a ghost amid the overwhelming sycophancy of the *Arabian Nights,* in the frequency with which rude and irreverent wild Arabs, impertinent sharpers, and brazen usurpers are rewarded or succeed in their endeavors.

Let us now return to our discussion of the changes in peer relationships associated with the revolt in our training groups. If we apply the system of stages outlined above, the nature of these changes may be clarified somewhat. In our groups we essentially have no stage one, since there are two sets of criteria to begin with. Since the group leader plays such an ambiguous role, the members can assume either that (1) the situation is really just like any classroom where the rewards go to the good little boy or girl who keeps his or her mouth shut, flatters the teacher, laughs at his jokes, listens carefully to what he says, and feeds it all back to him at the proper time (the strange silent role is just a paternal eccentricity—the teacher is trying to show by example how to behave, or perhaps is playing a game with us), or (2) the group leader is really leaving everything up to the members, and since he is not going to assume a leadership role in the group, one should act as if he were not there, in which case the most active and dominant member will gain the rewards, just as in any peer group.

Neither of these, however, is definitively rewarded. The leader seems to give no rewards, and as long as he is present, no one will

[60] It might be mentioned here that the Hegelian quality of this scheme was only perceived in retrospect.

fully accept a peer leader. Everyone hedges his bets to some degree, and confusion reigns. "Sibling" rivalry is intense.

At the time of the revolt (the equality or leveling stage) hostility is all funneled onto the leader, with intermember hostility prohibited. This continues for some time after the revolt, gradually giving way to the final stage, in which new criteria of differentiation emerge and hostility between members is open and tolerated. Since these criteria differ considerably from group to group, however, it is difficult to make many generalizations about this last stage.[61] It is probably fair to say, however, that in many groups understanding and perceptiveness (now freed by the revolt from the stigma of either competition with or seeking favor from the leader) become important elements in the status structure of the group.

One cannot regard the stage of equality without realizing how ephemeral it must be. There is a quality of brittleness and tenseness about it which is best expressed in its negative emphasis. In the section on the totem feast we referred to the "valued principles" being made "available to all on an equal basis" but the initial concern seems to be merely that no one should get too much of anything. In part this emphasis may arise from a desire to avoid guilt, but the biggest issue seems to be a fear of defection and dependency.

IIa. During the meeting without the leader, four members got up and left. Two went to the group leader's office but failed to find him. The first departure produced an explosion of laughter but no comment; the others were ignored, although remembered. Several members reported later a strong feeling that silence could not have been tolerated in this session, since this would have demonstrated that the group had no purpose without the leader, and the group would immediately have disintegrated. Many felt they were talking just to fill a space. Several members raised their hands at some point or other in the meeting. One member accounted for the concern with orderliness during this session by explaining that, "if the group was disorganized a leader would *have* to emerge." This was not only seen as ipso facto deleterious, but also as a prelude to a struggle over leadership, which would be disintegrating. Indeed, there was no open conflict of any kind in the group for several weeks after this session. Members who attempted to become prominent in any way were

[61] Since the reader no doubt feels overrun with stages at this point, it would perhaps be useful to note that stages one, two, and three of the hostility-distribution paradigm described at the beginning of this section correspond to stages two, three, and four in the more general scheme just advanced. The reader should be warned, however, of still another trinity, only partially related to these, which is discussed in Chapter V.

quickly squelched and ridiculed. This taboo even seemed to apply retro-actively, for no one seemed able to recollect who had been most active in precipitating the revolt, and the guesses made regarding who said what during the episode were inaccurate.

One is most impressed in these concerns with the feeling that it would take little to restore the pre-revolt status quo. Leadership is distrusted because dependent strivings are still so intense as to trans-form the most democratic peer leader into a potential tyrant. The lingering desire for autocracy is counteracted by a compulsive avoid-ance of any kind of leadership. In the example just given the early defections and the handraising lend validity to these fears.

Yet there is also guilt in this fear of leadership, this avoidance of silence, this inability to recall the "ringleaders" of the revolt. Too much prominence means too much of the spoils and hence a dis-proportionate share of guilt over the revolt. Scapegoating potential leaders reduces the burden of guilt on the group as a whole.

But without conflict, without leaders, a large group of this kind (i.e., 36 members) can accomplish little, and these taboos were not destined to last forever. Little by little long-postponed battles among various individuals began to break out, and finally the leadership taboo also dissolved.

IIa. That Joe should have been selected as leader was not surprising. He would talk when no one else did and was relied upon for this. He was intelligent, frank, and outspoken. But these qualities were recognized long before his leadership was accepted. It will be recalled that a "totem feast" took place just prior to spring vacation. The day after this vacation the group was trying to choose a case, from among those they had already discussed, to re-analyze as a group. One of the first proposed was the story of Joseph and his brothers, with which the group had had no little trouble, in part because of the very close parallels it presented with the group's own history. The proposal was made by Joe himself. After some discussion it was put to a vote and rejected by all but a small minority, consisting, however, of Joe and the most active members of the group. Several other cases were then proposed, and the group prepared to vote among them. At this point it became apparent that Joe had assumed leadership in the proceedings—recording votes, putting the questions, defining the issues, and all of the other activities pertinent to a chairman's role—and this was later commented upon without animosity. During the discussion, however, Joe found a pretext for asking for a revote on the *Joseph* case. It was again rejected by a large margin, and the group went on to make its selection among the remaining cases.

The group thus granted leadership to Joe at the same time that it rejected his substantive suggestion and the case that bore his name (and with which he naturally was strongly associated). This selective acceptance had several facets:

(1) Rejection of the suggestion was a rejection of those attributes of Joe which had been a source of antagonism in the past. Saying "let us discuss *Joseph*" was equivalent to saying "let us discuss me," a notion reminiscent of the remark which had led to his suggested expulsion on the day of the revolt. Furthermore, it was probably apparent from his frequent comments on their failure to discuss it that *Joseph* would have been the group leader's preference. Joe's nomination of the case thus raised again the question of his independence of the leader. This issue became explicit during the following session when he was challenged more directly about having been something of a company man in the past. His frank admission of this seemed from the group's viewpoint satisfactorily to differentiate him from his sycophantic biblical namesake. (When the case was first discussed Joe several times referred to him as "Joshua" by mistake.)

(2) Rejection of the suggestion was a rejection of the group leader. In order to tolerate this change in the group it was necessary once again to reaffirm the group's solidarity by an expression of hostility toward the common enemy. The group in a sense was flexing its muscles in resisting this outside force and having demonstrated its ability to do so could now undergo internal readjustments.

(3) Rejection of *Joseph* was a way of defining the limits of Joe's leadership. It indicated that while on procedural matters his suggestions would generally be followed, on substantive questions he was just another group member.

IIa. After a few sessions there began a series of challenges to Joe's leadership. All of these were defeated, but all of them tended to raise the status of the challengers and seemed to restore a sense of reality to the group's perception of Joe's position. They also brought into an active role one or two students, highly valued by the group, who had been relatively silent and passive in recent meetings.

Thus the final structural solution in this group was a fairly typical democratic leadership structure. We have no way of knowing, of course, what would have happened had the group continued meeting indefinitely, but the group was large enough so that solution of purely mechanical and procedural issues of communication management was crucial.

In smaller groups (that is, a dozen or less) the demand for
equality is likely to be less rigid and intense, and there is correspondingly less tendency toward hierarchy and formality when the stage
of equality passes. The preoccupation in such cases tends to be less
with the issue of hierarchy versus equality than with that of rigidity
versus flexibility of roles.

IIe. The second meeting after the leader's return began with a
discussion of the idea of sexual envy in Bettelheim's *Symbolic Wounds*
and the influence of sex differences in the group. This broadened out into
a discussion of similarities and differences of all kinds, of barriers between
people, etc., and then narrowed again to the question of sex roles, via a comment that the group leader was both male and female in the group.
Edna and Andrea expressed the feeling that the girls in the group used
psychological insight in an aggressive and controlling way, while the boys
used withdrawal as a defense. Jim complained that the girls were being
masculine now. The discussion became more particularized as they turned
to the roles of individuals, and whether these were determined more by
the group or the individual. There was some consensus that the group as
a whole was more conservative than individuals, who often showed signs
of change only to be pushed back into older patterns by the other members.
A few days later the feeling was expressed that it shouldn't make such a
difference if specific people were absent—that the group should be competent enough to carry on as usual regardless of its particular composition.

We see here an increasing concern with role flexibility in the
group—a restiveness with "assigned" patterns of behavior and a desire
to see the group as an organic unit with interchangeable parts. But
the emphasis is not so much on holding everyone to the same level
as it is on broadening everyone's behavioral repertory.

In part this is an expression of the desire for closeness. Since
differences create barriers between people, the differences must be
eliminated. If everyone can play everyone else's role then everyone
will understand everyone else, and all can fuse together into a solidary
mass.

At the same time this desire for interchangeability is clearly linked
to separation. Everyone wishes to incorporate everyone else in order
to ward off the losses they will soon undergo. Note that the first expression of this desire, the wish to escape the constraints of sex roles,
is associated with the perception of the group leader as playing both
mother and father in the group, so that their wish involves, as a corollary, an identification with him, and through him with all members of
the group. In addition, the wish to increase their role repertories is

simply a desire to get as much as possible from the group in the way of self-development before it terminates.

But we can also observe in this process a sense of expansiveness, of increased potentiality, as if the definition of the group situation had changed in some way. Warren Bennis suggests, in a personal communication, that a revolt results in a total increase in power in the group. Defining power as the ability to influence, everyone, including the group leader, has more influence on everyone else. There is a change, limited and halting to be sure, from a view of the group as operating under conditions of scarcity, with only so much love, understanding, wisdom, and power to go around, to one of the group as an expanding economy, with potentially limitless resources [cf. Maslow's discussion of "synergy" (1964), and Likert (1961), pp. 179 ff.]. This view is severely tempered by the approaching demise of the group but is nonetheless striking. We are reminded of Spencer's description of the transition from the militant to the industrial society: "But with the cessation of those needs that initiate and preserve the militant type of structure . . . social organization loses its rigidity . . . changes of structure follow when men, not bound to prescribed functions, acquire the functions for which they have proved themselves most fit. Easily modified in its arrangements, the industrial type of society is therefore one which adapts itself with facility to new requirements." Spencer also notes that in addition to this augmented plasticity there is an increase in decentralization, mobility, activity, learning, individuality, tolerance, humanitarianism, and equalitarianism—all of which we also tend to find in the post-revolt group (Spencer, 1896, II, pp. 602 ff.) [62]

If Bennis' argument seems too utopian for the reader it can be buttressed by looking at its obverse. For it can hardly be questioned that large discrepancies in status or power create a *loss* of power for everyone. Perhaps the most famous examples of this are Frazer's descriptions of kings unable to move about or eat or drink freely or inter-

---

[62] Indeed, the interchangeability of roles seems to be strongly associated with both democratization and modern technological development (cf. Slater, 1961b; Bennis, 1962; Slater and Bennis, 1964). It would seem as if the need to be able to make rapid adjustments to unpredictably changing conditions is the primary element, with democracy and role flexibility as two social techniques for ensuring such capacity. This is the social form of the individual problem noted by Bion, i.e., that "the dependent group, with its characteristic elevation of one person, makes difficulties for the ambitious, or indeed for anyone who wishes to get a hearing" (Bion, 1949b, p. 296).

act with whom they pleased for fear of affecting the weather adversely or destroying commoners with their overwhelming *mana* (Frazer-Gaster, 1959, pp. 56–59, 145 ff.), and we are all familiar with the tyranny to which public figures are subject in respect to their private lives. But as Stephens has pointed out, this is equally true at the more mundane level of family relationships: "*Extreme* power inequality seems to beget inhibited 'formal' behavior. Curiously, it is not merely the submissive person who is restrained. The *dominant* person is also 'formal,' withdrawn, and rather inhibited in his dealings with the submissive person." He quotes Yang's description of the relaxed family gathering in the traditional Chinese peasant household, a gathering from which the father had to remain aloof in order to maintain his patriarchal status (Stephens, 1963, pp. 316–318). Psychiatrists who assume the traditional physician's role (refined by psychoanalytic doctrine) when dealing with certain types of expressive or hyperactive psychotics and psychopaths often find themselves crippled and made to look ridiculous by the narrow range of rather stuffy behavior which their superior status leaves open to them in these interactions. The technical theories of John Rosen seem to have been in part a reaction to this difficulty (Rosen, 1953).

The striving for augmented plasticity is also expressed in the recruitment of silent members (see this volume, pp. 42–45, and footnote 32) and in the reshuffling of seating patterns whenever these have become fixed. We have encountered the latter in several instances (e.g., see this volume, p. 26), at least once in direct connection with the revolt (see this volume, p. 41). In many cases (most of the academic ones) this desire is a complex interaction between the wish to wrest the group from the leader and the wish to make it more organic. Both may derive in part from the fact that some group leaders duplicate a seating chart, based on the early choice of seats, and ask the members to keep these positions for two or three weeks until the names become familiar. Usually most seats become relatively permanent until some conscious effort at change is made, a change which symbolizes the transition from a formal and authority-oriented structure to an informal, group-oriented, and flexible structure.

In therapy groups the dedifferentiation of roles tends to go unnoticed as a sociological phenomenon, since the discarding of rigid behavior patterns is an explicit goal of the therapy.

XIII. In the third meeting of this experimental, four-session group, there was a good deal of aggression toward the group leader and a marked increase in intimacy among the members. (See this volume, pp. 127–129.) During a discussion of the goals and possible limits of psychological investigation, the following exchange took place.

BOB: But no, seriously, the group is just like another kind—another species of entity, because it is made up of the variables which you can't measure by brain waves and the fact of the glass, J. B. [the group leader], and the fact that we're all here for various reasons. . . .

PATTY: But you could set that up with another group.

BOB: Yes, that's right.

PATTY: Set it up with any group of randomly selected people.

GEORGE: Let's do it.

PATTY: Let's all be someone else (laughter).

(R. D. Mann, transcript)

IIf. It was three weeks before the end of the group, and the discussion was sporadic and desultory, with lapses into depressed silences and multiple conversations among pairs. Feelings of failure were expressed, and Miriam wondered if they could achieve anything in the 9 or 10 more sessions (she said weeks at first, which caused some comment) remaining. Gil said that if they were beginning all over again they could progress as far in 9 sessions as they already had, and this led to some joking about starting again with their names changed. Miriam then suggested that they all exchange roles, and there were several remarks about who wanted to be who, and who would be the group leader. They explored this quite seriously for a while, trying to decide what it meant, whether it was a substitute for getting close, whether there was a difference between imitating and impersonating (i.e., replacing), and whether it all simply expressed a desire for someone to replace the group leader. Miriam said that her suggestion had not been serious, but the expression of an idea that she felt was hostile and grotesque, and they wondered if it was simply a desire to spread and confirm their self-disgust.

On the next-to-last day they talked of the approaching end and their inability to drop defenses. Fantasies of continuation led to a discussion of what would have happened if they had had different names (they seemed not to remember the earlier discussion). They then wondered who would be the group leader.

Later in response to expressions of feelings of incompleteness the group leader asked what it was they felt they must do before they could end the group. Aaron said all that came to his mind was copulating, and there was some desultory talk of seeking unity, letting go, etc. Miriam joked aside to Tom about a group orgasm, and whether it would produce a child. Tom promptly suggested that she was indulging in fantasies about the group leader and she giggled, attracting the attention of other members, to whom she reported this exchange.

These discussions seem on the surface to be the same as those in IIe, and we may note that, like the latter, they are intimately associated with the issue of separation. On closer inspection, however, differences begin to emerge. Whereas in IIe they discuss how role changes have been resisted by group pressure, in XIII and IIf they ask, "What would happen if we started again and were different?" Furthermore, in IIe there is little and decreasing concern with the group leader, while in IIf every discussion turns back to this preoccupation. Finally, in IIf it is not a question of enlarging the scope of one's behavioral repertoire, but of a wish not to be oneself at all. One might suspect that the revolt plays some part in producing these differences —in generating a desire for specific and partial rather than global and diffuse change. To understand why this should be so, however, we must turn to a whole new set of considerations.

PART TWO

The Evolution of
Boundary-Awareness

CHAPTER V

The Evolution of Conscious Bonds and
Its Reflection in Fantasy

Stock and Thelen, and indeed Bion himself (1957, p. 456), point out
that there are times when Bion's "basic assumption" paradigm fails
to illuminate group events, and suggest that "some more fundamental
assumption that integrates the modalities within a simple theme is
needed." They observe that one modality is often "used to express concern over another" (Stock and Thelen, 1958, p. 238). This raises a
question as to whether the three "assumptions" do not really represent
two different levels of conceptualization: that on the one hand they
are simply points on some sort of continuum, but at the same time
they also express different techniques for responding to or coping with
the phenomena to which this continuum pertains. As we noted in the
previous chapter, "fight-flight" seems less an "assumption" than a mechanism for dealing with a state of affairs which has not been specified.
Unlike the dependency and pairing groups, even the object of this
mechanism (e.g., leader, couple, Messiah) is unknown.

Could it be, in fact, that the lack of an object in the fight-flight
definition is not accidental but reflects some important facet of its
nature? It will be recalled that in the last chapter a developmental
view of the basic assumptions was suggested—one based on the notion
of increasing self-awareness and separation. Does the fight-flight group
perhaps represent the most "primitive" stage in this evolution, one in
which the distinction between self and object is altogether blurred?
Our idea of the basic assumptions might then be as follows: (1) there
is a continuum of group evolution, involving the increasing awareness
of individual and group identity and separateness; (2) there are several defensive mechanisms—fight, flight, pairing, dependency—which
periodically become a shared property of the group—a group culture.
Specific mechanisms are especially appropriate to particular points
on the continuum, presumably points of actual or incipient transition.

(It is these mechanisms which provide the static quality noted by Bion, rather than the underlying continuum which gives rise to them.) This paradigm would fit Bion's suggestion that the basic assumptions "may not be fundamental phenomena, but rather expressions of, or reactions against, some state more worthy of being regarded as primary" (Bion, 1957, p. 456).

We hypothesized in the last chapter (pp. 134–135) that "pairing" as a group phenomenon was a response to a growing awareness of the group as a mortal entity separate from and independent of the leader, and that the dependency group was not subject to this degree of awareness inasmuch as all group feeling was vested in the leader. Let us now see if it is possible to generalize this process in a way that will anchor the occurrence of the fight-flight group.

Piaget's work on cognitive development in children provides considerable assistance, particularly his studies of the way in which the child's orientation toward rules changes with age. Piaget distinguishes four stages in the application of rules and three stages of consciousness of rules, but he describes their progression as "elusive" and warns that "the facts present themselves as a continuum which cannot be cut up into sections"—a warning which we may well keep in mind for our own continuum, remembering that the points we have chosen to outline this continuum are entirely extrinsic to it (Piaget, 1932, p. 17).[63]

In Piaget's first stage of consciousness of rules (the most relevant continuum for our purposes) the child plays "in its own way, seeking merely to satisfy its motor interests or its symbolic fantasy. Only, it very soon contracts habits which constitute individual rules of a sort" (Piaget, p. 42). In the second stage the child begins to want to play as others do and imitates their rules, although the result is often idiosyncratic. But "no matter how egocentric in practice his play may be, he regards the rules of the game as sacred and untouchable" (Piaget, pp. 45–6). In the third stage, "the rule of a game appears to the child no longer as an external law, sacred in so far as it has been laid down by adults; but as the outcome of a free decision and worthy of respect in the measure that it has enlisted mutual consent" (Piaget, p. 57). Piaget notes that the decay of the attitude of sacred immutability is paradoxically (from a common sense viewpoint, at least)

---

[63] A subsequent warning is also worth quoting: "And if language and discursive thought which, according to a famous metaphor, are necessarily cinematographic in character, tend to lay too much emphasis on discontinuity, let it be understood once and for all, that any over-sharp discontinuities are analytical devices and not objective results" (p. 80).

accompanied by a sharp increase in adherence to the rules (Piaget, p. 62).[64]

This transition from the second to the third stage, from a "morality of constraint" to a "morality of cooperation," is sufficiently reminiscent of the revolt process—of the change from the "dependent group" to the "pairing group"—that we may perhaps be forgiven for looking for other points of correspondence. We recall, for example, that viewing the group leader as a divinity was combined with an utter inability to learn anything from him or follow his leads, a condition that was reversed when he was cast out. But can we find anything in Piaget's analysis which will carry us beyond such superficial analogical resemblances? Consider the following quotation, which relates to Piaget's second stage:

. . . Each child plays for himself, he pays no attention to his neighbor, does not seek to control him and is not controlled by him, does not even try to beat him—"to win" simply means to succeed in hitting the marbles one has aimed at. And yet these same children harbour an almost mystical respect for rules: rules are eternal, due to the authority of parents, of the Gentlemen of the Commune, and even of an almighty God. It is forbidden to change them, and even if the whole of general opinion supported such a change, general opinion would be in the wrong: the unanimous consent of all the children would be powerless against the truth of Tradition.

(Piaget, pp. 52–3)

[64] He quotes one boy who sees such adherence as necessary to avoid constant quarreling—an entirely secular attitude. The feeling that one should conform to rules even though they can be altered at any time by mutual consent is worth stressing, considering the sentimental confusion that often arises in connection with Riesman's distinction between "inner-directed" and "other-directed" modes of conformity (1955). It is frequently assumed that in contrast to the inner-directed man, the other-directed individual has no internalized norms but simply responds to any kind of group pressure. This is a serious distortion of Riesman's position. The inner-directed man had a single set of internalized rules which he took with him everywhere. He either wore his dinner jacket in the jungle or disintegrated and "went native." The other-directed man has internalized not one set of norms but a meta-norm which says: "although groups differ in their customs, one should adhere to whatever customs are present." This is obviously a far more complex and sophisticated piece of internalization, appropriate to a complex and mobile civilization. It permits an ethical relativism while ensuring some kind of social conformity. Although it creates a number of its own problems, other-direction should never be confused with the lack of internalization found in tradition-direction, which depends altogether on external sanctions and is still prevalent in much of the working class.

A training group, of course, does not consist of children, but of well socialized adults, who know perfectly well how to play a game with one another, and that rules can be cooperatively invented and altered. Yet with respect to those characteristics most unique to the training group situation the Piaget model does not fit so badly. We have observed, for example, that member expectations of the leader are utterly irrational. The difficulty in applying the model is that given levels of awareness with respect to given sets of variables are achieved at different times, so that a group of adults may be at Piaget's third stage with respect to the rules of an intellectual group task but at the first stage in their awareness of the emotional boundaries and connections between people.

It is commonly observed, for example, that people who come together in a training or therapy group interact initially almost entirely in terms of transference. (This is of course true of all groups of strangers, but in most groups a variety of cultural conventions serve to mask these responses.) Regardless of the sophistication of their task behavior, emotionally they are operating in terms of Piaget's motor stage ("seeking merely to satisfy . . . motor interests or symbolic fantasy"), or in his second stage, in which rules are imitated but the child "pays no attention to his neighbor." Ezriel remarks (1950, p. 68) that "when several people meet in a group, each member projects his unconscious phantasy-objects upon various other group members and then tries to manipulate them accordingly. Each member will stay in a role assigned to him by another only if it happens to coincide with his own unconscious phantasy. . . ." In other words, the group member tends to approach a new group setting by merely repeating old patterns of behavior with new materials. This also is true of neophyte marble players, as Piaget points out: "The child begins by incorporating the marbles into one or other of the schemas of assimilation already known to him, such as making a nest, hiding under earth, etc. [But] then he adapts these schemas to the nature of the object," that is, he is forced to take into account the fact that the objects are round and small, will roll away, etc. (Piaget, 80–81).

A similar process occurs in the group setting, for while on the one hand, through trial and error, a culture evolves which maximizes the opportunity of most members to play their cherished private performances, on the other hand, as time goes by, more and more reality begins to intrude itself gratingly into their perceptions of one another.

The most dramatic change, however, is brought about through the leverage provided by having a common object for fantasy projection. The presence of an ambiguous authority figure allows the members to share a fantasy, and as they become increasingly engrossed in this sharing, they are gradually seduced into sharing a reality instead and are thereby freed realistically to confront one another. That is, in order to realize the enjoyment of a shared fantasy they are led to invest it increasingly with group-relevant elements and decreasingly with personal-familial elements, until it becomes dangerously susceptible to disconfirmation.

We might, therefore, tentatively consider the earliest period of atomistic fantasy as roughly similar to Piaget's motor stage, the period of fantasy convergence as similar to Piaget's second stage, and the period of emergent realism as similar to Piaget's third stage. Note that it is in the stage corresponding to the period of fantasy convergence that egocentrism is combined with a sacred attitude toward the rules.

Piaget makes an interesting point about this combination. He points out that "up til the age of 6–7 the child has great difficulty in knowing what comes from himself and what from others in his own fund of knowledge" and that at this age "society is not so much a successful cooperation between equals as a feeling of continuous communion between the ego and the Word of the Elder or Adult. . . . Just as the mystic can no longer dissociate his own wishes from the will of his God, so the little child cannot differentiate between the impulses of his personal fancy and the rules imposed on him from above" (Piaget, pp. 48–9). In other words, the fusion of egocentrism with the sacred attitude is not at all accidental, but the expression of a fundamental law. Piaget continues:

> Egocentrism in so far as it means confusion of the ego and the external world, and egocentrism in so far as it means lack of cooperation, constitute one and the same phenomenon. So long as the child does not dissociate his ego from the suggestions coming from the physical and from the social world he cannot cooperate, for in order to cooperate one must be conscious of one's ego and situate it in relation to thought in general. And in order to become conscious of one's ego, it is necessary to liberate oneself from the thought and will of others.
>
> (Piaget, p. 87)

This is a crucial passage for our purposes, for Piaget is saying that cooperation is based on consciousness and separateness—that one must have an awareness of boundaries in order to communicate with others. If ego and the social environment are not differentiated, "the mind is unwittingly dominated by its own tendencies," i.e., by unconscious fantasies and reflexive interpersonal responses, and rational group effort is impossible. Normally, however, as the child grows older, "he will not only discover the boundaries that separate his self from the other person, but will learn to understand the other person and be understood by him" (Piaget, p. 90).

IId. It was early in April, and the group was discussing Shaw's *Man and Superman*, with particular attention being devoted to Don Juan's search for meaning, for an ideal mate, etc. Andy reported the following dream:

ANDY: In relation to this I'd like to tell you about a dream *I* had. Reason I can't explain this, I guess, is because I feel very much involved in this case. It seems to *me* to have many similarities. I had a dream about a month ago—or two weeks ago, that—I was in a big building— and it was a huge building: it wasn't just one movie theatre it was 10 or 12 movie theatres. And there were maybe 3 or 4—maybe 2 or 3 movie houses on each floor, and there were about, oh, five or six floors. And I remember there wasn't any elevator and I had to keep climbing. And I'd walk into elevators—I mean I'd walk into movie places, and people would turn and look at me, very funny, and I'd feel very out of place, and I wouldn't have—this wasn't the movie I was looking for. So I'd go to another one, and I kept going up and up and up and up, and finally, I came to the last one, way up on the— really top floor, and I went in, and there were very strange-looking people in there—you know—it was really way out—beards and every- thing—and I walked in, and you know I really tried, I mean, after all this was the last one. I mean I really tried to fit in, and really tried to enjoy this movie, and I didn't even sit down. It wasn't what I was looking for, you know. So I went out, and I was really feeling kind of bad, you know, 'cause I'd already paid my money to get into this house. See you could take your choice of a movie but you had to pay when you came in the front door. And so I went out, and you know how often in an old building all the staircases will be nice staircases until the top floor, and there'll be sort of an attic floor up there, in which you go up sort of a stair ladder? It's not as nice as the other stair- cases. Well, I saw this thing and so I went up there, and it was really weird, 'cause there was this low-ceilinged place, dark, you know, and there was this guy sitting at this desk, and he was writing, or something, and when I came in, he went like that. He just pointed. He didn't say a word, and he didn't seem concerned with me. He noticed me and went like that and then he sort of dissolved—he went back to his work. He had no effect on me whatsoever. And I went up this very rickety ladder and there was a board across the rafters, and I had to follow this board across these rafters, and I was getting scared, you know, after all this was a strange place, and I didn't know what was happening. I kept getting cobwebs on me—it was really bad, really getting miserable up there. But I went on and I got over to this little place where he pointed at, and it was a little bitty room. And there wasn't anything there. There wasn't anything at all in this room. It was empty. So there I was.

JACK: Did you wake up or what?

ANDY: No. That was the end of the dream. I remember I sort of walked around confused for a while and looked back at him. And he was either gone, or he was paying no attention to me at all.

He added that it seemed related to the individual search for an ideal, that he felt better even at the end of the dream than after leaving the last movie where he couldn't fit in.

Ted suggested that it was related to the problem of trying to fit into a coherent group, and the group leader asked if they were saying that the ideal group was an empty room. They laughed, and Ted said, "Well, there's certainly the minimum of difficulty in interpersonal relations in it."

A long, still silence followed.

MARIA: So, let's be an empty room.

SHIRLEY AND CAROL (overlapping):   We *are* being one.

An individual who enters a group for the first time tends to perceive it as an undifferentiated mass. He may pick one or two individuals for special attention, but this will perforce be on the basis of unconscious fantasies—of transference. Thus insofar as he is discriminating he distorts, and insofar as he is empirical he is vague. At the same time, all other group members are perceiving the group in a similar way, so that the first shared perception of the group members is that the group, with one exception (different in each case), is an undifferentiated mass. Furthermore, not only is this perception not in the forefront of consciousness, but also there is no awareness that it is shared. Finally, as we shall see later on, the *definition* of this undifferentiated mass may also be unconsciously shared.

This creates a rather tenuous state of affairs. If a member acts on his perception of specific individuals in the group, his distorted view of them will be likely to produce an abortive and confused interaction. If he acts on his perception of the group as an undifferentiated mass, however, he may suddenly hear a rather overwhelming echo from the other members. This will be unnerving, since it blurs the boundary between himself and the group as a whole. He will thus find himself in a position similar to Piaget's very small child, and this will be reinforced by unconscious transference reactions of various kinds, which, since he cannot accept them as coming from himself, will seem to be produced by powerful but ambiguous pressures from the group.

The sharing of fantasies about the leader tends to rescue the members from this horror, but initially it is a desperate remedy. The leader is differentiated out from the mass partly because it is perceptually easy to do so, but partly in order to counterbalance this mass—to create a hero to ward off the devouring dragon.[65] But the differentiation of the leader does not immediately produce clear differentiations among members, and many groups do not progress far beyond this point. It is worth noting that a successful revolt usually involves a period in which the *differences* in members' attitudes toward the leader are brought forward. A group, in other words, cannot effectively revolt so long as it perceives itself as a mob or mass, but only when it can differentiate clearly among its members. This conflicts, of course, with the need for equality in and following the revolt, when a whole new set of anxieties emerges, touched off by the new awareness of the members' separateness from the leader.

Another way of viewing this process is to think of the group as attempting to substitute conscious bonds for unconscious ones. A conscious attachment is based, by definition, on an awareness of differences, whereas unconscious ones always entail mystical fusion. Group development is thus the gradual encroachment of light on shadow, with the various "basic assumptions" being techniques applied at different points to defend against whichever shadows seem most fearsome at a given moment.

Before going any further with this thought, however, we must cope with a problem which arises whenever we study any developmental sequence, whether phylogenetic or ontogenetic, biological or cultural. In biological evolution, organs and capabilities appear all up and down the evolutionary "tree," like independent inventions. If we observed a higher species in stage one of the evolution of some capacity or other, and a lower species in stage two of the same process, we might draw erroneous conclusions about the relative complexity of the two species, supposing this were all the data available to us. Yet the lower species *is* more complex than the higher with

[65] We can observe the working out of the same ambivalence in the widespread popularity of children's games in which one person stands in the center of a ring or is in some other way set off from the group for a time, only to be replaced by another.

respect to this specific capacity. Similarly, a child might appear aggressive and rebellious at ages 2, 4, 6, 13, and 15 and docile and accommodating at 1, 3, 7, 12, and 17. If we observe the child from 1 to 2 we would conclude that aggressiveness was more "advanced" than docility, while if we observed him from 2 to 3 we would infer the opposite, and so on. In one sense we would be making foolish and all too familiar errors (such as occur when people compare the "primitiveness" of cultures without making explicit which traits they are using as criteria), but if we made our conclusions more specific each would be correct.

Piaget struggles with this difficulty throughout the section from which we quoted so heavily above. He notes that the ritualization which occurs in the "motor stage" is also found in the infant, while "at the same time, and this is where the analysis becomes so difficult, it is obvious that by the time a child can speak, even if it has never seen marbles before, it is already permeated with rules and regulations due to the environment, and this in the most varied spheres" (Piaget, pp. 42, 44). Our group members, of course, are even more advanced, and talking of them as if they were groping infants in the early meetings of the group does great violence to the observable data.

Piaget then notes that children in the motor stage take the same casual attitude toward rules as do the older children in the third stage, although this casualness has an entirely different meaning (Piaget, p. 46). This problem plagues him repeatedly, and he finally warns that "things are motor, individual and social all at once," that constraint and cooperation are both present at birth. "Here again, it is not so much a question of these successive features themselves as of the proportions in which they are present. Moreover, the way in which conscious realization and the time-lag from one level to another come into play is a further bar to our arranging these phenomena in a strict sequence, as though they made a single appearance and then disappeared from the scene once and for all" (Piaget, p. 79).

Our problem is precisely the same. We cannot look at a bit of pairing behavior and say that the group is "at stage three on the boundary-awareness continuum." We can only say that around some issue, and at some level, it has reached a high degree of consciousness of the separateness of people and things. As Freud pointed out long ago, the same patient in therapy may have the same insight more than once and experience it as new. Moreover, he will be correct insofar as each time more ideas are attached to it. Indeed, we may well question whether it is not true for *all* individuals (not just obsessive neurotics)

that ". . . 'forgetting' consists mostly of a falling away of the links between various ideas, a failure to draw conclusions . . ." (Freud, 1956,
p. 368). Perhaps the best model of the mind is not the vertical-depth
model of traditional psychoanalytic theory, but rather a simple three-
dimensional spatial model, with an insight being a link between any
two ideas, irrespective of time, consciousness, or abstractness. If we
think of the mind as a map of the relations among objects, then any
absent connection in the mind will produce a blurring of the boundaries between objects in the environment (including oneself). This
is why the extension of consciousness is accompanied by a sense of
loss, separation and isolation, and why its contraction brings about the
pleasures of mystical fusion and the terrors of identity-dissolution.

Another problem is created by our suggestion that fight-flight pertains to the most primitive level of boundary-awareness, so that, subject to the profound qualifications just noted, we might expect to see
rather more of it in the earlier sessions of a group. Actually, however,
although we see a good deal of it during the early meetings, it seldom
takes particularly dramatic forms. To infer its presence seems more far-
fetched at such times, because of the polite and civilized veneer which
groups display when their acquaintance is still casual. While it may be
true that at the commencement of a group the members are least
aware of their specific connections with and differences from other
people, objects, and ideas in the situation, they are also least involved
and have easiest access to cultural definitions of the situation which
render it familiar and harmless. True, there are sometimes long and
tense silences, in which unconscious fears of group envelopment may
be pressing on them, and there are manic flights in which no one
listens to anyone else but only talks loudly to himself. But can we
really hypothesize such fears at these times?

This is a most difficult problem. For on the one hand, as the group
continues, involvement increases, and more layers of the personality
are engaged in the group situation. Customary cultural techniques of
interpersonal asepsis fall away, and deeper feelings nudge consciousness. But at the same time self-awareness, awareness of group identity,
and intragroup differentiation are all increasing, so that at the point
where these most primitive fears about the group might become most
visible, they are already in a state of decay. The phenomenon is
similar to the problem of the unrecoverability of "experiences which
took place in very early childhood, before they could be compre-
hended" (Freud, 1956, p. 368), a problem which has been most fully
treated by Schachtel (1949). Indeed, it is very common for groups to

report considerable amnesia for events occurring at the beginning of the group, before the conceptual tools for understanding them were available.

We suggested above, however, that the blurring of boundaries between oneself and the group tends to occur when the group member experiences sudden reinforcement by the group of feelings, impulses, and fantasies of which he is not fully conscious. At such a time he will feel swept away by forces that seem to come both from within and from without. He will experience a sense of envelopment, which, unless he can somehow translate the unconscious material into something pleasant or at least familiar, will induce a feeling of incipient terror. Presumably this could occur at any time in a group, although realistic and individuated knowledge of other group members and an image of the leader as differentiated from the group would both serve as points of orientation in such antigravitational states.

Fight and flight are both mechanisms for warding off this state when it arises. Both serve to protect the boundaries that distinguish one individual from another. Fighting is a way of saying "this is me, I am different (in fact opposite) from you." It is like pinching oneself to be sure one is not dreaming, except that the members pinch one another, saying, as it were, "I hurt, therefore I am." We might here recall Lorenz' argument that only species characterized by intraspecific aggression are capable of forming personal bonds (Lorenz, 1959, pp. 182 ff.). Flight, of course, simply removes the individual from the morass altogether. Instead of demonstrating separateness through contradiction, he does it through distance. This may be achieved through individual withdrawal from other members or by all members fleeing from the impulse which produced the sense of boundary loss.[66]

It should be emphasized that the feeling that one is dissolving is not merely frightening but also pleasurable. The maintenance of

[66] The fight-flight mechanism is also familiar to mental hospital personnel involved in admitting new patients, since it is so frequent a response to the combination of inner turmoil and a disorienting environment. Organic deterioration alone may produce it, but since some sort of change of locale generally eventuates from such behavior, the internal disorientation is quickly compounded. I have always been impressed with the rapidity with which death frequently follows such transfers in the case of elderly patients.

A separation may perhaps be made here between the fight and flight defenses, since the latter leaves the situation unchanged, while the former has consequences which serve to diminish the threat which gave rise to it. Fighting does in fact serve to discriminate among members—the notions of friend and enemy create a more benign and differentiated group image.

boundaries by living organisms is enormously energy-consuming and tension-inducing. Indeed, it might not be altogether incorrect to say that boundaries *are* tension, that all tension is a function of the preservation of boundaries, and that all tension-release involves the reduction of boundary-maintenance, like water seeking its own level. In the most primitive layers of the unconscious this may even be the motive for joining a group. The individual member, like the mystic and the psychotomimetic drug cultist, hopes to achieve ecstasy through the effusion of emotional energy and the release of tension which follows in the wake of a relinquishment of boundary armor and machinery.

There is always, in other words, a rather intense ambivalence about boundary maintenance, so that loss of individuality is at once a tempting yearning and an overwhelming terror. In most individuals, emotional boundary loss seldom proceeds any great distance before anxiety sounds a warning bell, and the fight-flight mechanism goes into effect. The fight-flight *group* arises when mutual reinforcement of some unconscious fantasy seduces all or most members into moving farther in the direction of loss of individuality than they desired or anticipated. As students of mobs well know, groups elicit feelings of which people ordinarily manage to remain unaware. Confronted with his participation in some riot or other, a usually controlled individual will say, shamefacedly, "I don't know what got into me," thus revealing in a simple phrase the two most fundamental threats which group life poses to the individual: the loss of boundaries (". . . what got *into* me") and the submersion of conscious motives by unconscious ones ("I don't *know* what . . ."). Since consciousness is here equated with the boundary of the self, and unconscious impulses are seen as coming from without, it may even be redundant to speak of these threats additively. The idiom itself, of course, is a survival from the medieval idea of demonic possession, and its persistence in popular speech is a grim reminder of the strength of unconscious motivation. Our culture has many patterns which normally protect us from such extreme manifestations of possession as the dancing manias of the middle ages, but mob reinforcement can hardly be said to have disappeared from modern life.

The most rational person, upon hearing the shouting of a large crowd nearby, will experience an emotional response to it, whatever his intellectual attitudes. Excitement, fascination, and fear will all make themselves known, at least at the autonomic level. Now although this emotional responsiveness is far more dramatic in large crowds, it operates in identical fashion in small groups. Even the techniques, fight and flight, are the same. A rioting mob, for example, is having its cake and eating it, too—losing the tense, inhibiting effects of individual boundary-maintenance but at the same time preserving some primitive sense of separateness through direct and aggressive physical contact with the environment. Similarly, a panic is fundamentally a concatenation of individual efforts to achieve separation from the collectivity.

Let us now summarize our tentative formulations thus far. We have suggested that Bion's fight-flight group is attempting to deal with the relation between the individual and the group at times when individuals find it difficult to differentiate between the two. The dependency group seems to be concerned with a somewhat more advanced stage, in which individuality is at once acknowledged and denied, through an attempt at symbiotic union with authority after the fashion made classic by Frommian theory.[67] The pairing group is an attempt to make palatable full individuation and separateness by maintaining a disembodied fantasy of mystical unity and immortality in the form of a distant future Messiah.

We then struggled with the difficulty produced by the fact that no group of adult individuals really begins as Piaget's child does—unable to distinguish between himself and his social environment. Although we frequently observe a clear transition between dependency and pairing as a correlate of some area of increasing boundary-awareness, we cannot really imagine an adult group emerging from some primeval haze in which fight-flight was a chronic necessity. As a solution to this we suggested that moments in which the individual-group boundary is temporarily lost often do occur, although the increasing involvement of the individual in the group through time obscures the frequency of this phenomenon in the early life of the group. What changes most profoundly over time, we suggested, is the balance between conscious and unconscious bonds between members, the latter decreasing and the former increasing, if we hold constant the degree of personal involvement.

We might then think of Bion's mechanisms as attempts to maintain individual and group boundaries under conditions of constant flux: a flux produced on the one hand by increasing emotional involvement,[68] and on the other by increasing secularity, consciousness, dif-

[67] See Fromm (1942). Indeed, Fromm's concepts of destructiveness, authoritarianism, and automaton conformity bear some resemblance to Bion's triad.

[68] "Involvement" is of course difficult to assess, and in terms of fantastic

ferentiation, and separateness. The uneasy feeling, which I share with Bion, that the mechanisms sometimes seem to merge with one another or to be expressions of the same thing is explained by the fact that they *are* expressions of the same problem, that they represent different combinations of the same variables, all oriented toward maintaining a constant environment. I am suggesting, in other words, that the pairing group is an attempt to maintain the same balance between individual and group identity (under conditions of maximum consciousness and maximum involvement) that the fight-flight group is attempting to maintain under conditions of minimum consciousness and minimum involvement.

Note, for example, that although all of the mechanisms deal with the same ambivalence, they seem to be differentially oriented to the poles of this ambivalence. Fight-flight seems primarily directed toward protecting against loss of individuality, while pairing seems primarily directed against too great a degree of individuation. This reflects the varying conditions in these two kinds of groups. The fight-flight group is faced with the alternative of group dissolution or individual engulfment—there is no clearly visible middle ground. Either of these possibilities will produce panic, but if the former has been buttressed against to any extent by some institutional structuring, it is the latter which becomes most threatening. In the pairing group both possibilities seem less likely, in the sense that some sort of considered commitment to the group exists, but one based on conscious and familiar ties. The danger of engulfment is less important because it is no longer the sole basis for unity. But the secularization of the group, the leader, and other members, while generating greater rationality, autonomy, and understanding, also raises the threat that perhaps there is no emotionally intense reason for being together at all. Thus the pairing group—although the most secular of the three types in most respects—attempts to reintroduce the sphere of the sacred in a noninterfering way, by placing it in the future and divesting it of all practical consequences save for an oversanguine mood and a certain passivity.

The dependency group is intermediate with respect to both the involvement and the consciousness dimensions, and its ambivalence

unconscious expectations of the group as something that will change one's life or personality (a not too uncommon notion), one might argue that "involvement" is greatest before the group even starts. At the same time there is typically a reasonably stable and consistent increase for most members in most groups in the extent to which the group and its participants become "significant others," in the sense in which that term is usually employed.

over boundary maintenance is firmly anchored in its relation to the leader. Indeed, ambivalence is the keynote of the dependency group, in which intermediacy seems to express itself through antipodal exaggerations, like the storms of adolescence. On the one hand we see a passionate involvement in the group, but on the other hand we observe that the "group" means primarily the leader, as shown in the constant readiness to betray one's peers in order to obtain special favor with him. Yet in addition, this involvement with the leader is itself split between deification and derogation, as we have seen.

Most important of all these antitheses is one which finds its echo in Piaget's children at a comparable developmental period. Piaget observes that children in his second stage have in part established the boundary between inside and outside. They are, for example, realistically interested and involved in learning what others do and imitating this. The brittleness of this expansion of awareness, however, is expressed on the one hand in the exaggerated force and prestige attributed to what comes from without—the sanctity, antiquity, and immutability assigned to rules—and on the other hand by the egocentricity of actual play and by the persistent difficulty in distinguishing between what is indeed a learned rule and what is in fact a spontaneous invention. The dependency group exhibits an identical contradiction in its perception of the leader, whose utter apartness is stressed at the same time that his identity is totally submerged in individual fantasies.

One might indeed raise the question whether this tendency for group development to take the form of decreasing extremeness in oscillation—of closer and closer approximation to its own average state—is not an important factor obscuring our vision of group process.

The following example illustrates how the same conflict may express itself at different levels of boundary awareness.

IIh. It was the last meeting before spring vacation. There were several absentees, including all of the males in the group except the group leader. Some opening comments among the girls on hairdos led Barbara to remark that her hairpiece was actually her own hair—that she had been unable to part with it when it was cut years ago, and had kept it shut away in a drawer until recently. Angela recounted a similar story of a friend who had saved a pair of ten-inch braids (initially for purely sentimental reasons) in a plastic bag, and Beverly said she used a similar container for her own braid. Angela remarked that it was like keeping a dead body around, while others compared it with saving tonsils and fingernail clippings. Emily likened it to keeping rose petals, and

Angela told of a friend who still had his appendix in a jar. Beverly said she had kept the eyes from a frog she had dissected in high school, and they discussed the difficulty in getting at the brain of a frog and the extra grade points it yielded in biology labs. Angela told of helping camp children dissect large bullfrogs so they wouldn't "slit their wrists," and Ruth asked if they reacted with an "ugh!" when they got a female. Angela said most of the frogs *were* female, and that one child had thought there was something wrong with her frog because it was male. She then told of a "parents' day" lecture when a number of frogs got loose and were hopping all over the room. Barbara described how her father had once brought home six goose eggs and a hen to hatch them, which led Angela to tell of pigeon eggs about to hatch outside her window. Barbara then remarked that the hen had refused to let the goslings go in water. There was a long silence, broken briefly once by Ruth saying the group leader was "awfully left out" of this discussion of hatching eggs, etc., and once by Beverly asking Angela about a diagram she seemed to be drawing. Finally, after several minutes, Ruth wondered why they couldn't talk as easily as they had before the meeting "started," and suggested that they felt the need to discuss something "deeper." The group leader suggested that what they had been discussing seemed "pretty deep," and mentioned their preoccupation with the losing and retaining of body parts. Ruth said that this content "fits nicely into the group," in connection with their missing members, but expressed skepticism about the group situation determining these associations. After some discussion of this another silence fell. This time Emily broke it by announcing her anxiety about coming to the meeting. She talked of her difficulty in resolving her feelings about the group leader and, ultimately, her father, from whom she was in the process of establishing greater independence, preparatory to her marriage. This was discussed for some time, interspersed with other stories of parents who "hung onto their children," even when they were middle-aged, and prevented maturity and independence. Evelyn suggested that establishing a life independent of one's parents was necessary since otherwise one would be left with nothing when the parents died.

In content this is a typical pre-separation meeting. The discussion reflects the loss felt at the absence of key male figures and the imminent if temporary dissolution of the group. This is heightened and deepened by the fact that several members were in the process of making important marital and career decisions, and all were concerned with relinquishing close dependent ties with their parents (and, in the immediate situation, with the group leader). The symbolism in the early part of the meeting is too complex to unravel here, condensing feelings of loss and abandonment, of anger, of self-hatred, of feminism, of nostalgia, of oral sadism. The loss of male peers produces castration fantasies and a strong ambivalence over being feminine that is finally resolved positively. Some of the "body-parts" material seems to have a cannibalistic aim: the parting members wish to take pieces of one another and of the group leader home with them as souvenirs. Furthermore, as the group nears its end the question, "What have I gotten out of it?" is often given rather literal expression.

But while the symbols can be endlessly interpreted, the issue of separation and loss is at the root of every one. This is treated metaphorically and unconsciously in the first part of the meeting, directly and consciously in the second. The first part deals with segmented entities, the latter with the complex feelings of whole persons. The first confuses individual and group boundaries, the latter differentiates them. The first attempts to ward off the threat of separation through fantasies of reproduction, the second by bolstering individuality and autonomy and projecting dependent feelings onto others. Thus while the problem, the conflict, and the preoccupations are the same, a higher level of boundary-awareness is displayed in the second part of the discussion.[69]

A. Some Mythological Parallels

While the reader may feel justifiably annoyed at the thought of trying to stuff any more parallel content into so ramshackle a conceptual scheme, we must now take another leap afield, this time into the murky realm of schizophrenic fantasy and mythology, in an effort to make somewhat more corporeal the shadowy notion of "loss of individuality."

It might be appropriate to begin with the unelaborated remark by

[69] We should not leave this topic without noting the debt which the scheme we have outlined owes to an unpublished paper by Warren Bennis entitled "Working Paper on Group Development" (1957). Frankly treating the group as an organism, Bennis develops a series of postulates and presents a genetic theory based in part on psychoanalytic theory. He calls his three phases oral, anal, and genital, although describing them in terms similar to those used here. In the "oral" phase: "the organism is veritably undifferentiated. . . . There seems to be high permeability to the environment and no differentiation among Ego . . . , Object . . . , and Leader . . ." (1957, p. 4). The major fear is one of abandonment. In the second or "anal" phase the leader is differentiated out and the members bound together in opposition to him and the environment. The third or "genital" phase involves pairing behavior, greater differentiation, and greater (conscious) integration. In general, however, Bennis' scheme is oriented more toward the emotional needs of group members than is mine.

Bion that "the group approximates too closely, in the minds of the individuals composing it, to very primitive phantasies about the contents of the mother's body." What is perhaps most frightening, however, is not what these contents include, but the analogy itself—the equation of the group-as-a-whole with the body of the mother, and hence on the one hand with warmth, security, closeness, and belonging, but on the other hand with envelopment, boundary destruction, loss of identity, loss of consciousness, and death.

These latter associations have been most thoroughly examined by Neumann (1955), to whose ideas we will now briefly turn, without at the moment troubling ourselves with the assumptions on which they are based:

> . . . the consciousness of man arises in the course of the first years of life, and is in part molded by the social bond of the infant with the group, but particularly with its most prominent representative, the mother.
>
> (Neumann, 1955, p. 43)

> [The equation of "woman" with "world"] is the basic formula of the matriarchal stage . . . in which . . . the unconscious [is preponderant] over the ego and consciousness.
>
> (Ibid.)

> . . . the Terrible Devouring Mother, whose psychic attraction is so great . . . that the . . . ego complex, unable to withstand it, "sinks" and is "swallowed up."
>
> A contrary movement may be represented symbolically as follows: the hero devoured by the monster *cuts off a piece of its heart and so slays it.* This symbolic process corresponds, on the image plane, *to a conscious realization.*
>
> (Neumann, 1955, p. 27. Italics mine)

Here we see the notion that the social context of the individual is experienced as a maternal envelope to the extent that conscious awareness is not highly developed, and that this enveloping "mother" is felt to be irresistible in such a state. The moment a piece of the undifferentiated mass is differentiated out, however, the "monster" is overcome. It is in this manner that we may interpret many of the creation myths, especially the earth-diver myths in which a god or animal dives into the endless water of chaos and after much time and difficulty (and often death) returns to the surface with a tiny fragment of earth from the bottom of the water, held in the mouth or under the fingernails. From this fragment grows the entire universe (Long, 1963, pp. 188–216).

Neumann continues:

The phases in the development of consciousness appear then as embryonic containment in the mother, as childlike dependence on the mother, as the relation of the beloved son to the Great Mother, and finally as the heroic struggle of the male hero against the Great Mother. In other words, the dialectical relation of consciousness to the unconscious takes the symbolic, mythological form of a struggle between the Maternal-Feminine and the male child. . . .

(1955, p. 148)

Thus the womb of the earth becomes the deadly devouring maw of the underworld, and beside the fecundated womb and the protecting cave of earth and mountain gapes the abyss of hell, the dark hole of the depths, the devouring womb of the grave and of death, of darkness without light, of nothingness. For this woman who generates life and all living things on earth is the same who takes them back into herself. . . . This Terrible Mother is the hungry earth, which devours its own children and fattens on their corpses; it is . . . the flesh-eating sarcophagus voraciously licking up the blood seed of men and beasts and, once fecundated and sated, casting it out again in new birth, hurling it to death, and over and over again to death.

(1955, pp. 149–150)

Neumann regales the reader with some deliciously gruesome representations of this aspect of the "Great Mother," but we shall content ourselves here with merely noting the ubiquity of the "Terrible Mother" image in folklore, and its emphasis on boundary destruction.

Whether or not consciousness should be considered "masculine" is a matter best relegated to metaphysicians and belligerents in the war of the sexes. It is incidental to our argument, which simply says that the psychological experience of emotional submersion in a group tends to ignite in the individual the fantasy of merging with, or being devoured by, the mother, which in turn is associated with loss of consciousness and death. There is nothing mystical about this: the emergence of consciousness is for most human beings inextricably intertwined with separation from the mother, and the individual need have no memory of this process in order to associate them. Indeed, emotional separation from the mother is a very gradual process, and children of fairly advanced ages still have difficulties at times in distinguishing their own wishes from those of their mothers. The strong fight-flight tendencies of adolescents are symptomatic of this difficulty. Combat in particular helps establish their separateness from the mother. As

Jung argues in the passage quoted above (this volume, p. 135) it is opposition that produces consciousness.

For some individuals the separation is not complete even in adulthood:

> Joseph stated that if he were to remain with his mother for the rest of his life, his life would be effortless as far as feelings were concerned. He felt that he and she were living for each other, that she treated him like a part of her body, an object to be used for her own purposes, and that she did not want him to grow up. . . . "My mother . . . feels for me. . . . I don't even have to open my mouth to understand her feelings toward me. . . ."
>
> [In the words "Siamese twins"] he was expressing the feeling of being with his mother two persons in one. . . .
>
> Mary stated that she could not distinguish herself from her mother since she was so much like her. In a dream her mother was crawling all over her and getting inside her. . . .
>
> (Limentani, 1956, p. 232)

The confusion of self and object is most impressive in the final remark of the first of these three schizophrenic patients.[70] Such difficulties in establishing clear boundaries between mother and child are usually experienced by both parties to the relationship, as innumerable clinicians have pointed out (see, e.g., Searles, 1961; Caplan, 1955a), and the fact that their unity was once physical and actual

[70] One often feels a deep chord of satire in utterances of this kind, which resemble the pregnant and magnificently ironic metaphors that schizophrenics so often produce. Sometimes it seems as if the patient is quite aware of an interpersonal dilemma and is making a bitter joke about it, rather than being actually uncertain about, say, the boundary between himself and his mother. The savage brilliance with which he may occasionally expose the pervasive professional and institutional hypocrisy around him lends weight to this view. At other times, however, his confusion is utterly convincing, although he is then unable to verbalize anything about it.

It will be recalled that groups tend similarly to express their most profound feelings in humorous guise (indeed, someone, I do not recall who, once suggested that a group can best be thought of as a schizophrenic patient) or not to be aware of them at all. The principal difference is that joking remarks in the group setting are immediately defined as such, while we tend to assume that a schizophrenic is serious until proven otherwise. The effect of this mental set can be demonstrated dramatically by imagining Joseph's last quoted remark being delivered with the inflections of a Jewish comedian. This pathetic confusion becomes humorous the moment we assume conscious control. Although neither a group nor a schizophrenic is fully in the cognitive position of the groping infant, each recapitulates this position in certain restricted areas—hence the ambiguity as to the depth of insight into the difficulty.

is perhaps important (although obviously not a sufficient condition) in this regard (cf., e.g., Caplan, 1955b, pp. 103–112).

The group, then, is both sought and feared in terms of unconscious associations with a very primitive image of the mother, one which involves fantasies of being swallowed and enveloped. Not only is the group as a whole viewed this way, but also the leader, who either is not individuated at all or else is defined purely in maternal terms. Characteristic of this state of mind is an unusual fear of group silence, which is too closely analogous to unconsciousness, and during which susceptibility to fantasies of the sort just described is heightened. In a group, after all, "consciousness" presupposes talk; silence can provide only unconscious union. Silence permits no differentiation among members, for all are behaving identically. It is thus possible for an individual to fear that everyone else is thinking the thought that he is trying not to think, and hence to become frightened of being overwhelmed by forces which seem both to be breaking into him and bursting out of him.

Without necessarily implying a standard temporal sequence, let us examine how this kind of unconscious definition of the situation might evolve into one appropriate to the pairing group.[71] First, as we have several times suggested, the leader is differentiated out. In Chapter III (see this volume, pp. 102 ff.) we argued that in the dependency group, this differentiation takes the form of defining the leader as a male hero, either fighting with or copulating with (at the level we are discussing the distinction is no longer germane) the dragon-mother image of the group as a whole, with the members assuming the role of the child before the primal scene.

What is peculiar to the dependency group is that it is oriented toward an indefinitely postponed outcome to this scene (thus the static quality to which Bion refers). It cannot tolerate the prospect either of the leader being reduced to impotence and helplessness by the unconscious unity of the group, nor of group unity being altogether destroyed or overwhelmed by the power of the leader. Normally, however, the "Great Mother" image of the group is subject to more rapid erosion than the image of the leader, since his shadowy role and real

[71] In Chapter IV we noted that hostility between peers tended to occur at some distance before and after the revolt, and intimacy among peers is also a significant issue at these times. But as we noted then, and as Piaget shows for his stages, these resemblances between earlier and later developments mask profound differences. Intimacy in the pairing group is more a question of conscious sharing than of fusion. De Rougemont's discussion of *eros* and *agape* is one way of viewing this difference (1957, passim).

authority act as a kind of refrigeration, retarding decay. The give-and-take of member-member interaction, however, establishes differentiations and conscious linkages which gradually encroach on the vacuum filled by the "Great Mother" fantasy. As we have already suggested (see this volume, p. 176), such awareness of personal differences seems almost to be a prerequisite to revolt, and we might hypothesize that in the absence of this awareness the "Mother" image would be the more frightening of the two and hence the leader's "power" highly comforting and reassuring.[72] When the "Mother" image decays, however, revolt becomes imminent, in order for the members to stave off their fear of being overwhelmed by their helpless dependence on a leader who now appears liberated from the bonds which held him. It is as if the preening bird described by Lorenz (see Footnote 31) suddenly found that the impulse toward flight had artificially been decreased and thereupon ceased his preening and flew to the attack.

Up to this point the evolution of fantasy images of the group situation seems to follow the sequence quoted from Neumann above regarding the evolution of consciousness: ". . . embryonic containment in the mother . . . childlike dependence on the mother . . . relation of the beloved son to the Great Mother . . . heroic struggle of the male hero against the Great Mother." Neumann does not take us beyond this point, however, and we must still determine what kind of fantasy product underlies the pairing group.

What immediately strikes our attention is the fact that as we have defined it, the dependency group is behaving in a manner identical to the pairing group, i.e., passively watching the interaction between a couple. Three factors discriminate between the two situations, however. First, in the pairing group there is no power issue, and the participants are defined as noncombative equals. The "pair" in the dependency group recreate the true primal scene—the child's definition of parental copulation as a cosmic struggle. The couple in the pairing group seem devoid of these most archaic overtones, even though other aspects of the primal scene are present.

[72] It is my impression that homogeneous groups are more inclined to get "stuck" in the dependency group modality. If so, we might explain it on the grounds that homogeneity reinforces the archaic, undifferentiated, "Mother" image of the group, and hence the leader must be made powerful (through member submissiveness) in order to combat this image. The most important kinds of homogeneity would seem to be those which involve common unconscious fantasy-structures, as in therapy groups of patients with identical pathology (cf. Wolf, 1953, 274–5). At the same time, however, revolt is often defined as a prerequisite to individuation (cf. Vb, pp. 51–53 above).

The second and closely related difference is that in the pairing group the fantasy preoccupation is not with who will win but with the product—with reproduction. Whereas in the dependency group any decisive outcome will produce anxiety, in the pairing group the only conceivable outcome (if so outrageous a pun may be forgiven) is one which would induce rejoicing, as proof of the immortality of the group and the fertility of all good things. In other words, in the dependency group the fantasy couple is sadomasochistically defined, and the preoccupation is with hostility and danger, while in the pairing group, purged of hostility through the revolt against the leader (see this volume, p. 78), sexuality emerges in pure form and attaches itself to the wish for eternal life and constant renewal.

The third difference is not at the fantasy level at all, but bears reemphasizing here. In the pairing group the members are differentiated from one another in actuality to the extent that the idea of submersion has lost some of its sting. Indeed, as we saw in Chapter IV, equality and interchangeability of roles are actually sought. What is significant about the pairing group is that any couple can play the sacred roles. (For example, see IIe, this volume, pp. 92–3, 122.) The sacredness, in other words, does not inhere in the participants but is external to them and can be invested in anyone. The dependency group is dominated by the sacred attitude, which is rooted in its feelings about the leader and about its own unity. The pairing group, on the contrary, is free to be sacred and secular by turns. The dependency group resembles a priesthood in a state of perpetual ceremonial, while the pairing group more closely approximates a peasant village, which on the occasion of certain festivals selects some couple to simulate a *hieros gamos*.[73] The couple is not intrinsically sacred, but only as a function of their selection for this single ritual. Once the ritual is over, they are immediately secularized again.

Now it may already have struck the reader that these fantasy images of the group show a fairly close correspondence with common mythological themes, particularly those familiar to us from the great Mediterranean civilizations. Consider, for example, *Enuma Elish*, the Babylonian creation epic, in which the god Marduk battles and destroys the goddess Tiamat and fashions the world from her corpse:

As Tiamat opened her mouth to its full extent,
He drove in the evil wind, while as yet she had not shut her lips.

[73] For the applicability to training groups of the sacred marriage theme I am indebted to Francis de Sales Powell.

The terrible winds filled her belly,
And her courage was taken from her, and her mouth she opened wide.
He seized the spear and burst her belly,
He severed her inward parts, he pierced (her) heart.
He overcame her and cut off her life;
He cast down her body and stood upon it.

(King, 1902, pp. 71–73)

The lord trod upon her hinder part,
With his toothed sickle he split (her) scalp.
He severed the arteries of her blood.
The north-wind carried it away unto hidden places. . . .
He split her into two parts, like an oyster.
Half of her he set up and made the heavens as a covering.

(Langdon, 1923, p. 147)

Here we have a clear analogue of the process of differentiation and separation. Tiamat is a fearful being because she represents that stage of development in which there are no boundaries between objects. It is when Marduk, "peering into the inward parts" of Tiamat, sees her husband Kingu inside that he falters and becomes frightened (Tablet IV, 65–68), and it is believed by some that in early forms of the myth Tiamat actually swallows Marduk, as she attempts to do in *Enuma Elish* (cf. Fontenrose, 1959, p. 162).

As is typical of such conflicts, the hero essentially fights from within. Usually he is swallowed by the monster and cuts his way out (cf. Campbell, 1949, pp. 90 ff.). But what is essential is his escape and the division of the undifferentiated whole into several differentiated components. "The combat-myth is a myth of beginnings, a tale of conflict between order and disorder, chaos and cosmos. Chaos was dark and watery, the habitation of monsters and demons, the land of the dead; it preceded the cosmos and still surrounds it" (Fontenrose, pp. 465–6). For group members this struggle is the attempt to substitute conscious for unconscious bonds—to conquer the spectre of absorption into the mass and obtain a clear vision of its separate particles. Forming the universe from pieces of Tiamat is the analogue of forming a group of individuals from a mob.

The emergence of the leader-father from the undifferentiated maternal totality is expressed in several related myths, which also show the subsequent differentiation of the many from the one:

At the beginning of all things Mother Earth emerged from Chaos and bore her son Uranus as she slept. Gazing down fondly at her from the mountains, he showered fertile rain upon her secret clefts, and she bore grass, flowers, and trees, with the beasts and birds proper to each. This same rain made the rivers flow and filled the hollow places with water, so that lakes and seas came into being.

(Graves, 1955, I, p. 31)

In the beginning, Eurynome, the Goddess of All Things, rose naked from Chaos, but found nothing substantial for her feet to rest upon, and therefore divided the sea from the sky, dancing lonely upon the waves. She danced toward the south, and the wind set in motion behind her seemed something new and apart with which to begin a work of creation. Wheeling about, she caught hold of this north wind, rubbed it between her hands, and behold! the great serpent Ophion. Eurynome danced to warm herself, wildly and more wildly, until Ophion, grown lustful, coiled about those divine limbs and was moved to couple with her. . . .

Next, she assumed the form of a dove, brooding on the waves and, in due process of time, laid the Universal Egg. At her bidding, Ophion coiled seven times about this egg, until it hatched and split in two. Out tumbled all things that exist, her children: sun, moon, planets, stars, the earth with its mountains and rivers, its trees, herbs, and living creatures.

(Graves, 1955, I, p. 27)

In both of these myths the goddess ultimately encompasses the destruction of the god, and indeed it is typical of these tales of beginnings that the male figure is initially overcome. Note also that it seems immaterial whether the process of differentiation is achieved by impregnating or by destroying the goddess. It is this primitive and combative quality in the relations between the primeval couple that distinguishes them from the deities which figure in the *hieros gamos*.

But no sooner is the leader-father differentiated out from the mass than he becomes almost as threatening as the mass itself (although, as Fontenrose points out, in the battle between the hero and the dragon pair, it is the female dragon that is always a little more terrible. See Fontenrose, *op. cit.*, p. 465). Since he inherits the gravitational pull of the group on the dependency needs of individuals, he also inherits the devouring tendencies of the female dragon and becomes himself a dragon or an ogre-ish giant. The ego can identify with this leader-figure only when it is in opposition to a more powerful mass, that is, when it is in the process of becoming differentiated. Once the mass loses some of its fearful aspect, the leader-figure is the more overwhelming, and now the individual must differentiate himself from *it*, in the form of the son-hero who fights against the father-ogre— as Cronus castrating Uranus or Zeus overthrowing Cronus.

But Rhea was subject in love to Cronos and bare splendid children.
. . . These great Cronos swallowed as each came forth from the womb
to his mother's knees. . . .

(Hesiod, *Theogony*, 453 ff.)

But when Zeus was full-grown, he took Metis, daughter of Ocean,
to help him, and she gave Cronus a drug to swallow, which forced him
to disgorge first the stone and then the children whom he had swallowed.
. . .

(Apollodorus, I.2.1)

Here we see recreated the original disgorgement of individuals
from the mass. No sooner is this first individuation achieved than it
is lost again in their common immersion in the fantasy of an all-encompassing father, and must soon be rewon. The fate of Tiamat may then
be re-enacted on the paternal figure:

The sons of Borr slew Ymir the giant. . . . They took Ymir and bore
him into the middle of the Yawning Void, and made of him the earth: of
his blood the sea and the waters; the land was made of his flesh, and the
crags of his bones; gravel and stones they fashioned from his teeth and his
grinders and from those bones that were broken . . . of the blood . . .
they made the sea. . . .

(Sturluson, 1916, pp. 19–20)

Thus while female corpses seem more frequently to provide the
raw material for creation of the world, male ones are not altogether
lacking, and the processes metaphorically described seem identical.
In discussing some of these myths Long comments: "The killing or
sacrifice of these powerful beings effects a redistribution of power.
Instead of the power residing in one being, it now flows into every
part of the universe. It is made accessible to all beings" (1963, p. 224).

This calls to mind our interpretation of the meaning of the group
revolt and suggests that all of these symbolic events share a common
evolutionary dimension: what is won is always greater consciousness.

Characteristically, it is a female who helps bring about the leader-father's demise (in Hesiod it is Gaia), and indeed the hero seldom
stands alone in these matters. If he does not have a troop at his back,
it is likely that he will be aided by a helpful male in fighting the female dragon and vice versa.

One cannot, in fact, help observing the seesaw quality of these
struggles—the constant alternation between "group" and "leader" orientations. This is hardly surprising, since human beings have never found
a way to achieve a sense of unity without either a leader figure (or

figures) of some kind or a symbolic image of the group as a whole. Furthermore, the formation of conscious bonds in place of unconscious ones, by making possible a more stable and viable group structure, may effectively *reduce* the physical autonomy of the individual. In other words, his awareness of his emotional separateness may correspond to its incipient disappearance in actuality. The two figures with which he contends never disappear, but only alter their shape and disposition.[74] The terrible goddess of one drama becomes the helpful one of the next, and the prize of still another (cf. this volume, p. 86).

But although the alternation of group and leader conjures up the image of a highly static dualistic equilibrium, this is not the only dimension determining the emotional and mythic structure of groups. For while the two figures are in a state of perpetual exchange of positive and negative attributes, *both* experience a continual decline in awesomeness and uncanny potency. Thus although Hera, for example, is fully as malevolent as Rhea or Gaia, she is not nearly as terrible a figure, simply because her malevolence is understandable in human terms. The many boudoir myths concerning the Olympians have removed from them their supernatural aura.

This is essentially the dimension which discriminates most decisively between the *hieros gamos* myths and the cosmic matings of the great procreators, just as the dimension of boundary-awareness distinguishes the pairing group from the dependency group. In the *hieros gamos* the couple have shrunk to a mere echo of their former combat. No longer is the entire world embraced in their relationship; the couple is now merely a symbol of the existence of this dualism, and their peaceful nuptials represent the achievement of some kind of balance in their impact on the individual. Since they have both been secularized to so great a degree, it is no longer essential that either one be defeated.

In the group situation the transition from dependency to pairing group is marked by the revolt against the leader, and we of course find this theme in Greek mythology also, in the Titan revolt against Uranus and in the Olympian conquest of Cronus. Both are incomplete, however, as revolts tend to be, and in both instances there is a con-

[74] By the same token the disappearance of the fearful ogre in the fantasy-life of any group may justify referring to it in organic terms. An organism, after all, does not have a "leader." It is united without it—there is no "master cell." Similarly, when one cannot easily locate the center and source of power in his society it is not merely metaphorical to admit that he has become part of an organism.

siderable return to the prior state of affairs after the deed is consummated.

The *hieros gamos* itself appears not infrequently in mythology and ritual, the mating of Zeus and Hera being particularly noteworthy:

All the gods brought gifts to the wedding; notably Mother Earth gave Hera a tree with golden apples. . . . She and Zeus spent their wedding night on Samos, and it lasted three hundred years.

(Graves, 1955, I, p. 50)

. . . the son of Kronos clasped his consort in his arms. And beneath them the divine earth sent forth fresh new grass, and dewy lotus, and crocus, and hyacinth, thick and soft, that raised them aloft from the ground. Therein they lay, and were clad on with a fair golden cloud, whence fell drops of glittering dew.

(Homer, *Iliad*, XIV, 346 ff.)

That vegetation should be generally associated with these divine nuptials could be anticipated both from our knowledge of the pro-creative-messianic orientation of the pairing group and from Frazer's explicit interpretation of all such ceremonies as fertility magic: "The marriage of Zeus and Hera was acted at annual festivals in various parts of Greece, and it is at least a fair conjecture that Zeus and Hera at these festivals were the Greek equivalents of the Lord and Lady of the May" (Frazer, 1959, p. 93).

"Again the spirit of vegetation is sometimes represented by a king and queen, a lord and lady, or a bridegroom and bride" (Frazer, 1959, p. 87). Numerous examples are presented in which couples are chosen according to some criterion, such as beauty, to play the parts assigned. In some cases, one partner is a deity or representation thereof, the other a privileged mortal. (See Frazer, 1959, pp. 92 ff., 299, 302–3, 409.)

While, as we have seen, the pairing phenomenon takes place frequently in groups it might be illuminating to present one example in which we find not only the ritual but an incipient mythology as well.

IId. It was the second week in December. The group had revolted a month before, but had tended to reject Ed, the principal instigator of this revolt. Ed dropped out of school three weeks later—a fact which was just now coming to the attention of the group members. A series of three meetings ended in a prolonged discussion of Ed, his role in the group, and the members' feelings toward him. In the first of these sessions the group was discussing the same case mentioned above in connection with the revolt in IIa. (See this volume, p. 27.) But whereas IIa had been especially concerned with the topic of death wishes, this group was most preoccupied with the question of whether conflicts between family members in childhood can ever be entirely resolved in adulthood. Starting from the mother-daughter conflict in the case, the conversation eventually drifted into sibling relationships, with a number of personal examples.

The next session began with the discussion of another case, this one concerning a male college student who was involved in a relationship with a girl they characterized as "bitchy"—a relationship in which they felt he was entirely inadequate. This led to a discussion of difficulties in learning the male role in our society, with the father absent from the house and performing work not understood by the male child. There was some argument over whether initiation rites or some functional equivalent thereof did or did not exist in our society. David argued that a male model was unnecessary, since he himself had grown up in a household with many women and a father who travelled a great deal, and yet he was "perfectly secure." Andy suggested that the stereotypy resulting from defining sex roles through sex segregation also created problems, and the topic now shifted to the "bitchy" girl, whose father had wanted a boy. Andy wondered if such a girl, "rebelling against a feminine role," wasn't often swept away by a "very strong older person," although ultimately rejecting him because she wanted someone weaker. David agreed but suggested that it wore off when she in fact discovered that he was weaker than she thought. He felt that such women really preferred a submissive role when it was offered to them, and gave the example of "the hen-pecked husband with a 250-pound wife, and he turns around and snaps at her and suddenly she's on her knees beside him." After some discussion of the conditions under which this pattern might hold, David wondered if a girl who typically picked out "weak" men would really respond to a "strong" one. Andy argued that such a man would never pick the girl in the first place. David disagreed.

DAVID: I know a guy like that, who's very much of a dominating character, and he was going out quite a bit with little girls—you know, girls up to his arm—so high—and suddenly he met this girl—he was about six-foot-seven, I think, and he's thin—he weighs about 235 or 240—and he met a girl who was six-two and almost as built and strong as he was, and she was—she was just murder on wheels. She liked to dance—she liked to dance with little boys. Well, they met each other at a dance, and by George, I think they're married now, and they have a wonderful time. They were just like a couple of large bears—I mean nobody could push them around. She was a big blond—she wasn't terribly attractive, but she was big and very strong, too, and they got along wonderfully.

ANDY: That reminds me of something that happened to me when I walked around a corner at Long Beach one time—I was looking at these two people about right here, and I looked up and here was this blonde, Nordic type, who must have been at least six-three or four, and this guy—I swear he was at least seven feet tall, and they must have weighed 600 pounds between them (laughter). And they were beautifully proportioned people, both of them. They were both beautiful people. It was just astounding. I felt like . . . God, maybe I felt like I was a child again.

There was an immediate return to the interpersonal dynamics of the couple in the case, and after a few minutes Ted again raised the issue of the effect of not having a male model. Andy agreed that the father of the boy in the case was "probably a weak person." Ted qualified this by describing him as "a totally absent person." They discussed the effects of this for a few minutes, and Ted again reiterated the point, recalling that earlier in the year they had joked a lot about Ed's concern with paternal prerogatives "like cutting the meat and that sort of thing," but that perhaps this really was important. Carol then interrupted to ask, "By the way where *is* Ed?" There were several remarks noting his absence and Ted then continued as before, suggesting that the boy's relationship with the dominant girl was perhaps "a search for a model." Andy then suggested that an older woman would be ideal for the boy, but David disagreed, arguing that a very submissive, dependent girl would be better. For several minutes they discussed age differences in marriage, then began wondering if they were going off on too many tangents.

At this point Ted began a prolonged inquisition of David and his relationship to Carol, who sat next to him. Ted noted first that David seemed unable to identify with the boy in the case, to which David heartily agreed, disclaiming any connection other than pity. Ted then asked David what attracted him to Carol and whether it was a mutual decision to take the course, gradually pointing out the many similarities between David's family background and that of the boy in the case, implying obliquely, although never actually stating, that either David had chosen Carol because she was submissive and demure and therefore would not dominate him, or that she actually did dominate him in ways that were hidden from the group. There was some discussion of Southern women (Carol was Southern) and their techniques of control, and David confessed to a relationship in early adolescence in which he had been dominated "in the most horrible way" by a girl a little older.

The following session opened with a mention of Ed's absence, and a question as to whether an effort was being made to set up David in his place. Adam suggested that interest in David and Carol had increased lately since Carol had been disagreeing with him occasionally instead of "just sitting there." Andy conjectured that their preoccupation with "ideal" couples was leading them to try and break David and Carol up, to show that only ideal relationships were acceptable to the group. This led to a discussion of the search for leadership and ultimately to Ed, whose virtues and weaknesses were debated for the rest of the hour. They wondered how they would feel if he returned, and compared their feelings about this to the Epilogue of Shaw's *Saint Joan*.

This series is among other things a good example of the pre-occupations of an early post-revolt group. It is fundamentally concerned with peer relationships, as seen in its somewhat gratuitous introduction of the resolution of sibling conflict as a topic in the first session. But the group is also worried about the stability of its autonomous position, and this is reflected in the discussion of whether early conflicts can ever be entirely resolved, and also in the continuing search for some figure or figures to invest with special status. Indeed, the effort to find a receptacle for the "group deity" (see this volume, pp. 142–145) seems particularly strenuous here. There is a strong desire to confer such sacred power on David and Carol, but David's lack of psychological sophistication and his unwillingness to lead the group seem continually to interfere, as does the group's jealousy of his "protected" position. There is great concern as to whether David is actually "holding his own" in his relationship with Carol, whom they suspect of being wiser, perhaps because she speaks infrequently although with considerable assurance.

The preoccupation with the absence of a male model reflects the difficulty experienced by the males in the group in maintaining an active, aggressive masculine stance with the group leader passive and silent. This problem was exacerbated by the fact that the group's most active peer leaders, Ted and Ed, had each been subjected to a severe group attack following his period of greatest ascendancy, and neither David nor Andy, although active, showed any inclination to initiate or direct discussion. Furthermore, Ed's disappearance seemed greatly to disturb them.[75] While they had handled their guilt over the revolt

[75] It cannot be stressed too often how disturbing the loss of members is to a group which has no mechanism for replacing them. Groups which have a fixed term and do not add to their membership experience not only loss, and the necessity for readjustment around the missing role incumbent, but also panic. In my experience, *repeated* membership loss has tended to decrease group involvement and the ability to resolve the dependency problem.

"If you remove parts of the population of geese, the remainder get something like an anxiety-neurosis. They are afraid, day and night, and hardly eat. . . .

"I have been told by an Army man and by Air Force men that the greatest heroes are thrown into panic by the gradual disappearance of members of the group; the gradual disappearance of members of the group is the thing which human courage finds hardest to stand up against" (Lorenz, 1959, pp. 229–230).

by placing all responsibility for it upon Ed, they now felt guilty and responsible for *his* disappearance and wished very much to shift this burden onto the group leader.

The search for a sacred couple, then, is a search not only for a vehicle for the disembodied group deity, but also for a replacement for a lost hero. Indeed, the messianic fantasy shifts continually back and forth between Ed himself and the new savior to be produced by the Sacred Marriage. Unfortunately, the suitability of David and Carol for this role had been severely called into question some weeks earlier when, during a discussion of sexual mores in college, David had implied, somewhat to the consternation of the group, that he and Carol had taken a vow of chastity until marriage. It is perhaps in response to some awareness of this group need that David offers to them the story of the giant couple.

Note that although the combative, sadomasochistic element is never entirely removed from the "couple" fantasy, save perhaps in Andy's account, the group ever strives toward such purification. They want the couple in the case to be more equal, although they toy with alternative dominance-submission patterns. They want David and Carol to be on a par, suspect they are not, but are not sure who is more dominant. Equality is finally achieved in David's fantasy, but only after the henpecked husband has reversed the balance, and the bearlike couple have relinquished their smaller partners. These shifts reflect the alternating fear of the leader and of the group as a whole.

This should serve to caution us that the distinction made above between the dependency couple and the pairing couple is a conceptual ideal which is only partially realized in actuality. Elements of the more primitive orientation keep creeping back in and must constantly be purified out.

The same is true, of course, of Zeus and Hera, who bicker continually and are engaged in a perpetual power struggle. What is most important is that it *is* a stalemate, and that under certain conditions the conflict element can be purged temporarily.

There is one other function of the sacred couple, in addition to providing a new (albeit inactive) group deity and expressing the group's wish for immortality. This is the function, referred to above (see this volume, p. 55), of acting as a specialized agency for ridding the group of sexual tension. It is perhaps more characteristic of the pairing examples in IIe (see Chapter III) than of those in IId but probably operates to some extent in all groups. The sacred couple of myth and ritual, whose *hieros gamos* is celebrated with such joy and exuberance, may be seen in part as expressing the search for a group genital, "a special pleasure reservoir, . . . whence [the at first free-floating libidinal strivings will be] periodically discharged" (Ferenczi, 1938, p. 98). It seems likely that all groups, insofar as they attempt to solve their problems through specialization, engage in such a search, just as they engage in the search for other specialized organs.[76] This of course varies with the stage of development of the group:

In the child every organ and every organ function subserves gratificatory strivings to an extensive degree. The mouth, the excretory orifices, the surface of the skin, the movements of the eyes, of the musculature, etc., are used by the child as a means of self-gratification, with reference to which no sort of organization is for a long time evident. . . . Later the pleasure strivings become grouped around certain foci. . . .

(Ferenczi, 1938, p. 97)

In the autoerotic stage . . . the sexuality of each separate organ of the body . . . exists in a state of anarchy which is lacking in all regard for the weal or woe of the rest of the organism. [Later, however, the genital] provides for the discharge of sexual tension on behalf of the entire organism.[77]

(Ferenczi, 1938, p. 16)

Thus far we have merely annotated parallels and pointed out analogues, without troubling ourselves as to the significance of these resemblances. Do mythological echoes imply some universal dynamic of structural development in groups of all types and sizes? Do the varied pathways of cultural evolution reveal a similar underlying pattern with any frequency? We will discuss these questions in the final chapter, but for the moment let us turn once again to the nascent group and the fear of group envelopment.

B. Preoccupations of Nascent Groups

We have repeatedly stressed the difficulty in attempting to compare the early stages of group formation with some level of pre-

[76] The question might be raised as to whether noted Hollywood couples have not often served as a group genital for American society in this sense.

[77] It is perhaps thus that we may understand the magic power assigned to the semen ejaculated by a hanged man. This involves a double specialization—the man is a scapegoat, bearing the sins and rages of the community, and his genital is performing its Ferenczian function of discharging surplus tension for the entire organism. Hence there is a high concentration of *mana* or whatever in the semen.

awareness in human development. We have argued that the terrors of the fight-flight group represent not so much a state of boundary confusion from which the group will later emerge, but a state of boundary confusion into which the members fear they will lapse. Certainly a deep fear of regression is prominent in the early meetings of groups. In IIf it was expressed during the third meeting in a discussion of observing nursery school children through a one-way mirror, together with comments about the difficulty in ordering the chaos of interaction among so many people. In the second meeting of IIg it took the form of a prolonged discussion of freshmen, their immaturity, and their separateness.

What we are beginning to construct it seems is a paradigm of cultural evolution. Where we speak of substituting conscious for unconscious bonds we may also speak of substituting cultural for instinctual connections.[78] We can imagine groups in the far distant past in which this process had hardly begun, but no society in the world today can be thought of in these terms. Yet at the same time there is no society in the world today which has come anywhere near completing the process, if indeed such a completion is even imaginable. Every known society has broad areas in which conscious attachment is very ill-developed.

More important for our present purposes is the fact that any new group formation, while not starting from scratch, must retravel this road to some extent. The principal difference between this experience and that of some imaginary primeval group is that members of a group already embedded in a "conscious" culture "know" that they are separate from one another; it is merely that every so often, in the absence (during the early stages of the group) of clear evidence of conscious attachment and differentiations, and in the presence of an imperative inner desire for unity and belonging, the fear strikes them that perhaps they may forget this fact and "lose" themselves.[79]

But note that this is not really so different from our imagined primeval state. In the absence of awareness there is little fear. The fight-flight stage pertains not to a stage in which the individual feels utterly undifferentiated from his social and physical environment, but

[78] ". . . through a continuous process stretching over thousands of years, the conscious system has absorbed more and more unconscious contents and progressively extended its frontiers" (Neumann, 1954, p. xviii).

[79] In one group a member referred to a previous attack on himself by other group members with the phrase "we attacked me," suggesting that even fighting is not always successful in avoiding the dilemma.

to one when he has recently emerged from such a state and fears lapsing back into it. One cannot fear dissolution until one feels un-dissolved: the fish does not fear drowning. As Neumann observes, it is only with "the emancipation of consciousness" that the fear of being "devoured" by the unconscious arises, and he suggests that this fear is experienced only by the ego itself, i.e., by that which has emerged from unconsciousness (Neumann, 1954, p. 299). What is crucial to an understanding of this sensation is the fact that *boundary-awareness begins with an awareness of weakness and vulnerability*—i.e., con-sciousness begins at the point at which it can be least tolerated. The child begins dimly to perceive its separateness at a time when that which it is separate *from* is enormously powerful, while it is itself helpless. This is no coincidence, furthermore, for boundary-awareness occurs only *because* of helplessness. As long as the omnipotence of wishes holds sway in the child's view of the world, such awareness can never occur. It is only in response to the accumulated failures of this approach that boundary-awareness forces itself upon him.[80] The most confirmed teleologist must shrink before the fact that at no time in the subsequent development of the individual is the fact of separateness so overwhelmingly frightening and difficult to sustain. A grown man could accept it with relative calm. Yet unfortunately it is through the tolerance for such unpleasant realities that the child is able to emerge into adulthood.

We may think of the development of the ego, of consciousness, and of culture in similar terms. It is when this conscious aspect is tiny and weak that it seems in greatest danger of being swallowed up, yet it is at just this time that self-awareness first arises. It is this con-junction to which the term "fight-flight group" or "fight-flight stage" should be applied.

Individuals entering a group have long since mastered this stage in most areas of their existence. Nothing really "primitive" happens in such groups, after all—only shades and echoes and humorous associa-

---

[80] This is perhaps the real root of masochism, that is, the use of suffering to reassure the individual of his separateness. This may seem to be the very oppo-site of Fromm's theory, in which masochism is a way of *losing* oneself. Yet there is no reason why both cannot be true: as we suggested with regard to groups which seem "fixated" in a dependency state, this orientation serves not only to protect them from further individuation but also to protect them from total obliteration. Fromm is perfectly correct in stressing the desire for this obliteration, but it is precisely this desire which is also feared. Masochism is thus a compro-mise between two intolerable alternatives, which perhaps explains its durability. "I am being beaten" says not only "I am not alone" but also "there is still a me."

tions to phenomena which are deadly serious and fearfully real in situations in which this mastery is less developed. We see revolt, but it is gamelike and ritualistic; we see religion, but it is metaphorical and facetious; the cannibalism is symbolic, the sexuality is verbal. The situation, in other words, arouses many feelings, but they are well under control with respect to the consequences they have for the individual's life as a whole. They are out of control only in the sense that they may prevent the formation of a meaningful or enjoyable group experience.

Within this limited sphere, however, the process must be renavigated, and hence it is just as appropriate to talk of a group as being in a fight-flight stage when it is anxious over the absence of conscious ties as it is to speak of a group being in revolt when it is merely asking its leader to go away for a day. The anxiety of a group in the fight-flight state is very real, although for most individuals it could be extinguished at any time by walking out of the room. Only in regard to *this specific situation* is conscious awareness so minimal as to arouse these feelings.

Perhaps, then, the fears of envelopment and loss of individuality in nascent groups are more visible than we first imagined. Both of the groups in which we might expect such fears initially to have been especially strong—making the inference from their later prolonged entanglement in a dependency orientation—began with a prolonged silence. Silence, as we noted above, facilitates a definition of the group on the level of unconscious unity and arouses the fear that unconscious fantasies may be shared. In these groups the first discussion was prefaced by a silence of several minutes, and much subsequent behavior seemed to have been influenced by a desire never to repeat this experience. My impression is that an assiduous task-orientation in the early stages tends to fend off this anxiety in most groups until such time as conscious bonds have developed to the point where the fear is less overwhelming.

One of the most mundane and benign forms of the fear of group envelopment is the complaint, heard in all groups, that people are using the word "we" (or the group leader is using the word "you" in the plural sense) illegitimately—that generalizations are being made about the group as a whole which some individual feels are not applicable to himself. Usually this is raised not around a specific statement from which the individual wishes to dissociate himself but as a complaint against a general group tendency (and hence is itself an example of the objectionable practice). A similar complaint was voiced in Jones' group (see this volume p. 19) about being "members of a mass; just female blobs," and in one of my own groups the more committed members were referred to as "the lump."

Another response to this issue is exemplified by the following:

IId. It was shortly after Thanksgiving and the group was discussing Freud's dream theory. The discussion was slow starting and there seemed to be some unwillingness to share ideas (the preceding week a term paper had been announced). Ted was raising topics at a steady rate but each seemed to bog down after a few exchanges. After a pause David asked jokingly if anyone had had any dreams lately and Dick said he had dreamt that he hadn't finished his paper on time. This produced laughter and some tense joking comments. The group leader suggested that the paper might be interfering with the discussion, and Ted voiced some preoccupation with it. They then began talking about dreams again, and continued to do so for the rest of the hour. The central points of Freud's theory and several recent experiments were brought up, and examples were offered from each speaker's own dream life. There was particular stress on the function of dreams, and toward the end they became interested in the role of the self in dreams—getting in and out of the self, seeing oneself as an object. David told of dreams in which "something terrible is going to happen and I say 'I'm dreaming, it doesn't matter, I can't get hurt anyway.' Then I'll start watching myself fall off the dam or whatever." Others recounted similar approaches, such as watching the self from inside someone else. Then they began to talk of techniques for remembering dreams before conscious reality blotted them out. They talked a little about associations and distortions, then about the therapeutic effect of remembering and telling unpleasant dreams. David recounted a vivid example of this effect and when he had finished, Dick said, "While you were saying that, part of a dream I had last night came back to me." There was laughter and a pause. David said "yes?" with humorous inquiry, and there was more laughter and another pause. Andy then asked if anyone had seen a picture of a sculpture in the *New York Times* book review section the preceding day. To those who had not he explained that it was called "Security" and was associated with an article on the "welfare state." "There was this huge mother figure standing out—she wasn't excessively beautiful but she was excessively strong"—with one hand on a child's head and the other on her husband's. Andy said he was "extremely upset" by the picture and went away, and that when he came back later and read the article he was even more upset. "He thought this was the ideal for our country—full dependence on the mother." When asked, as the session ended, why he had brought up the sculpture he said it was dreamlike.

The underlying emotional issue here seems to have been one of sharing. Since what they wish to share is their deeper and not fully understood anxieties, the danger again arises that unconscious impulses will be reinforced from outside and overwhelm the ego. They reassure each other, however, by (1) emphasizing the positive functions of dreams, (2) showing how the ego can retain control even during a dream, thus avoiding disaster, (3) how it is actually *too* easy to return to conscious reality, and (4) how one feels better once the hidden becomes manifest. The anxiety reasserts itself at the end, however, partly, perhaps, because David never actually *tells* his nightmare to the group, but also because after Dick conspicuously fails to tell his there is a tense silence. Andy's story of the sculpture does two things at once: it unveils in a dramatic way the image that is frightening them, but it also points them back on the road to their solution—destroying the ghosts by turning a light on them and so turning their own common hidden fears into conscious bonds. This technique was explicitly verbalized on another occasion:

IId. It was four months later, the last meeting before spring vacation. Many had already left, and less than half of the members were present. The discussion was tense and halting, with lame efforts at a humorous appraisal of their situation. They seemed to focus rather compulsively on individual differences, perhaps in preparation for separation, and the group leader suggested that a fear of "engulfment" by the group was present.[81] David pointed out the ambivalence of this attitude, that the group represented security as well. Ken agreed with the interpretation, saying, "I think there's a fear of being swallowed up, a fear, as in the beginning of the year, that if Dr. Slater wasn't here that things would fall apart, that we couldn't stand on our own, a fear that if we opened up we'd be swallowed up. But actually if we did open up and express feelings we *wouldn't* be swallowed up."

Ken's statement summarizes rather succinctly the dilemma which groups face in dealing with the problem of loss of individuality: the technique for mastering this fear—changing unconscious bonds into conscious ones—involves doing the very thing that the fear most strongly militates against. Note that Ken refers back to the beginning of the year and that the group leader is defined in that context as a protection against both group dissolution and group absorption, much as we have suggested above. We are again reminded of the comparison

---

[81] Usually, pre-separation behavior is highly solidary, as Mills has shown (1964b).

made in IIe between the group leader and the naval officer in *Lord of the Flies.*

IIg. In the sixth session of this group Neil and Roberta began discussing Lorenz' statement that species without intraspecific aggression cannot form personal bonds (1959). This led to the question whether the group leader united them, and if so, if it were in hostility. Julie felt that his separateness was intolerable, that he would have to be either incorporated or "destroyed." There was some joking about his aloofness and some annoyance that they spent so much time talking about him. They wondered if he were the only thing they had in common. They then expressed concern over their anonymity. Several talked of experiences in losing their accents (e.g., Southern, "New York"), they raised the flocking birds again, talked of student-teacher ratios, and of monogamy versus promiscuity. At one point Julie referred to the group being one body and the leader another (cf. the similar remark in Jones' group, this volume, p. 109).

Two sessions later someone commented that all of the males were sitting together. Neil replied that prior to this remark he hadn't noticed that there were two sexes in the room. He and Roberta then began talking about Maslow's concept of the "peak experience," in terms of becoming "one with the world," etc. Elizabeth asked if it would be possible for a group as a whole to have such an experience. After considerable comment on the impossibility of this, they began to talk about how involved in the group they should be, and of how much of themselves they should bring in from outside. Elizabeth and Penny talked of their resentment of the frequent use of "we" in the group, a resentment which for Penny was waning, but for Elizabeth was waxing.

In the following session Julie opened with the observation that among Lorenz' geese a distinguishing sex characteristic disappeared with domestication, and wondered if in the group greater familiarity would lead to greater "distortion." The pertinence of the analogy was rejected by most, especially Neil, but Leila then commented on the dominance of the females in the group, and they discussed sex roles and the blurring thereof for the remainder of the session. Penny, for example, recounted her dislike of situations in high school, such as dances, which stressed sexual differentiation, since she preferred competing in the nonsexual terms that the classroom typically provided. The conversation then switched to Debbie, whom Paul defined, not altogether negatively, as a dominant person. During all of this there were a number of silences, which various members characterized as "lazy" and "comfortable" unlike earlier ones which had seemed "frightening." Debbie suggested after one of these that now their worst fears had been realized, and it "wasn't so bad."

A week later the session began with some discussion of Bettelheim's *Symbolic Wounds.* This was followed by an inquiry into member relations

with outsiders—bringing them in or talking with them about the group—
and the absence of rules of order, which usually served to prevent people
from getting "cut up" or "cut to pieces." Conversation then dragged, and
pauses were interspersed with individual anecdotes and associations (some
of which are described above in the section dealing with experiment
myths). After one silence Debbie said all she could think of was the movie
The Fly, in which a little insect with a man's head was in the middle of a
web crying "help!" in a tiny voice, and a mass of cat-atoms which a scientist
had disassembled and was unable to reassemble was crying "meow!"

Most of a session the following week was devoted to the use of
drugs and its motivation. There was considerable discussion about how
much drugs actually changed one. In answer to the assurance of one
member that they only brought out what was already there, Stuart objected
that since one didn't know all that was there, this was hardly reassuring. Neil talked some about the loss of boundaries under drugs, and the
group leader suggested that their fears about the group were having
some influence on the discussion—that perhaps they were concerned about
having the wrong side of their personalities reinforced by the group. This
was ignored, but Julie then went on to talk about her fear of her own
needs, which she associated with Weakland's paper on Chinese male
conceptions of sexuality (1956)—the finiteness of the *yang* and the
inexhaustibility of the *yin* (i.e., her own needs). Sylvia said that it was
the needs of others that frightened her, and Neil closed with the remark
that, after all, the idea of an autonomous individual whose being stopped
at his skin was nothing but a Western fallacy and that people were born
interconnected.

This series, although selected for its emphasis on the boundary
issue, still shows the close connection between the problem of group
envelopment and that of dependency on the leader. The feeling that
he is the members' only solid bond is strong in these early sessions,
but at the same time they resent his impartiality and the feeling of
anonymity it gives them.[82] Fear of silence in early sessions gives way
to comfortable passivity later, only to reemerge in the *Fly* association
which is at once an experiment myth (the leader will assemble these
atoms—or will he?) and a boundary-loss nightmare. The "help!" expresses the terror of a fractured ego.

Their ambivalence over the boundary question is revealed consistently. Both in the sex role discussions and in the peak experience
and drug sessions they show positive feelings as well as negative ones.

---

[82] Note that were the leader to distribute rewards unequally he would "solve"
both the boundary and dependency problems. Perhaps this is one reason why
social inequality is so general in human collectivities.

But it is in the drug discussion that they begin really to come to grips with the boundary issue (it is not coincidental that more intellectual consensus was achieved in this session than in any previous one) by verbalizing more directly some of their own fears about boundary-control. Neil's closing remark expresses a general feeling that they already have bonds between them which are consciously understood and nonfrightening.

IIg. Several sessions after the above incidents occurred the group went through a rather trying period, apparently associated with writing a paper. On the day before it was due, Sylvia came late, recoiled visibly as she entered the room, and remarked that it was a "terrible group to walk into, it's such a monolith." She said it made her feel "amorphous," that she had no sense of projecting a definite image of herself. In the following session they had many silences, talked of air raids and military assemblies in high school, and of children and lemmings marching into the sea.

An approaching midyear exam and a two-week hiatus over Christmas vacation seemed also to produce some difficulty. The first meeting after the vacation was one of unrelieved apathy and depression. The second session, however, was lively, active, and a little rebellious. When the previous meeting was recalled they spoke of how "contagious" the depression was, although since all those who commented upon it said they had been happy before entering the room, they found it difficult to account for the origin of the "disease."

Note that the more explicit the statements of fear of group absorption become the more easily that fear is overcome. That all of the active group members could be swept up in a depression none of them had felt individually was the most clear and direct threat of all, yet it was an entirely momentary phenomenon. Both incidents seem to arise out of a general regression produced by an external reinforcement of the latent fantasy structure of the traditional atomized classroom situation. Dependency themes thus appear as well, and the members are forced to choose between the equally grim images of the leaderless, collectively possessed, and suicidal lemmings on the one hand, and authoritarian schoolrooms and Pied-Piper-led children on the other. Sylvia's view of the group as a monolith suggests that the frequent equation of the leader with a stone deity (see this volume, pp. 10 ff.) may be a function of his early identification with the group as a whole.

XI. It was the second meeting of the group. Irritation was expressed at the inconclusiveness of the first session, and the group leader was asked if he had really said they could say whatever they wanted. Upon his reaffirming this position one girl brought up a friend who "panics when she loses anything." After some discussion and interpretation of this, they began to focus on the leader, his silence, and his cryptic interpretations. There followed "a long discussion of liquor and its effect on the mind and why people drink. There are references to 'emotions,' 'opening up,' 'letting down barriers,' 'longing to be loved,' 'nightmares,' 'the guilty morning after,' etc."

In the fifth meeting, the following exchange occurred:

G: When I get out of this class my mind is a blank.
G: What makes things in your past that you had forgotten all of a sudden come out?
G: Will things that don't bother us now, or never bothered us before, bother us later because of these meetings?

Two girls then reported dreams of pregnancy and childbirth. One dreamt her sister had had a baby prematurely and put it back. Another reported a prophetic dream of death which her mother had had. The rest of the session was "spent discussing the pros and cons of belonging to a group and the relative merits of 'lonely individuality.'"

(Jones, 1960, pp. 35–6, 38–9)

Leaving aside the clear dependency concerns and the Oedipal fantasies, the predominant theme in these sessions (the third and fourth are not reported) seems to be one of maintaining the integrity of the ego, which is threatened by the leader's explicit permissiveness and by the needs his detached role arouses (like the girl who "panics when she loses anything"). This is revealed in the topics chosen: drunkenness (see the drug discussion above), disinhibition, longing, nightmares; and in the later session forgetting, eruption of forgotten material, anxiety reinforcement by the group, premature birth; and finally the more explicit and deliberate discussion of group involvement. One could hardly find a better summation of the multiple threats to consciousness generated by the training group setting.

Let us now examine some examples of identical fears occurring at other stages in group development.

IVc. In support of a suggestion by one girl that cases were useful in getting to know one another in a less threatening way, a male student gave the following illustration:

"I first tried talking about the case, and it was—I felt pretty good about it. Then as I spoke about Harry [a character in the case] I felt I was talking on one level and yet it seemed as though there was a parallel stream going on—it was becoming more and more turbulent as I summed it up and I thought: 'This is me.' I was defending Harry, and trying to find justification for what he was doing, because associations were going on in my subconscious mind—something a little closer to the surface—the threshold, and I was being affective, and this was disturbing me. I backed off as quickly as possible."

Another girl agreed. "There was a day in this class in which I remember being distinctly uncomfortable—that I remember thinking that there was nothing in this case which possibly could affect me, but I also remember thinking: 'I wish I could be anywhere but here, with any discussion but this one,' and I felt I had to keep moving around in my seat. . . . And when the class was over and I left—and when I tried to think of what it was that we were discussing that day I couldn't remember what it was. What it was that was making me uncomfortable, or even the case that we were discussing. And there have been times when I've walked out of this classroom when my whole day has been terrible, because there were things that started trains of thought I'm sure I'd prefer not to think about."

In the next session, during a discussion of nudist colonies and the stripping away of defenses, there was a considerable amount of self-revelation regarding connections between early family relationships and group experiences. In the course of these exchanges the following remarks were made:

FEMALE: I think you could feel far more naked when these emotions sweep through you; very much more naked than you ever would be in a nudist colony. . . .

FEMALE: . . . I'm afraid to talk ever since I made a slip . . . the more I got so now I think I might make a slip some place. . . . When I stop to think of it I *would* like to marry somebody just like my brother. . . . And it's all right to keep it down to the subconscious level but in this class all of a sudden it erupts to the conscious level. It's a little disconcerting. . . .

FEMALE: I find myself saying things in this class and I don't know why I said them—things I would never dream of saying, and I think it's partly because it's eight o'clock in the morning (laughter).

FEMALE: I think it's because these forces are so elemental that they are so strong.

(T. M. Mills, transcript)

XIII. During the third meeting of the experimental group (see this volume, pp. 127–129) there was considerable expression of shared feelings: hostility, anxiety, and guilt toward the group leader, desire to leave the field and "party" together, fear of finding out about themselves, erotic interest in one another, etc. During one interlude one of the two girls in the group, who had been upset over the group and the interviews associated with the experiment (a fact which gradually emerged, piece-meal, during this session), described getting mildly drunk during the previous evening. This led to a discussion of the quality of food in the various dining halls, and then to the location of the "central kitchen."

BOB: Did you know they have tunnels connecting it to all the Houses?

JACK: Yeah, all the Houses have an underground system.

ALEX (haltingly):   All we ever need is a vast network of tunnels and mazes.

JANE: That would be—

BOB: —a great place for a party.

PATTY: That would be like having—

GEORGE: Do they have these steam tunnels for the food? How does the food pass through the tunnels? Are there little green men that push it?

HENRY: Little men at the controls.

ALEX: You take your life in your hands walking through them.

GEORGE: Do they let you walk through?

PATTY: Man, this must be like the sewers of Paris, and you . . .

JACK (at the same time):   Sometimes they let you walk through them (laughter at Patty's comment).

HENRY: Large sewer rats dragging you through . . . (general laughter, especially Jane).

GEORGE: Do they have people pushing it on wagons, or is it on a conveyor belt, or what?

ALEX: Running and running and pushing, and they smash up and turkey goes flying, and . . . (general laughter).

BOB: Do they have alligators down there like they do in the New York sewers?

GEORGE (excited voice):   What?

BOB: Yeah, they found a 15-foot alligator in the New York sewer.

JANE: Oh God!

HENRY: In the New York sewers?

BOB: Yeah. . . .

PATTY: Yes.

HENRY: Ugh.

JACK: . . . because people bring back baby alligators . . .

JANE: Oh, that's right!

PATTY: They flush them down the toilet. And they *live*. And grow, and spawn! (With happy wonder. Laughter.)

JACK: Seems like . . .

HENRY: Oh God, alligators.

PATTY: Yes sir. That's a line from T. S. Eliot.

HENRY: Well, the next time I want to go for a little walk or stroll through the New York zoo or something (laughing) . . .

PATTY: Just next time you look at a manhole in New York, don't look too hard. [Someone laughs.] Never know.

GEORGE: . . . will come out at you.

HENRY (inaudible): . . . shouldn't bring my . . . watch with me today.

BOB: There's a dead alligator in the room next to us. He died.

JANE: I'm sorry.

BOB: They gave him a fish that was too big, and he wore himself out trying to catch the fish. He caught it a couple of times, but he couldn't swallow it.

JANE: Where did they get it from?

GEORGE: What was it—running around the room?

BOB: From a pet store. No, no. It was not. It was in this little dish with some water in it, and . . .

PATTY: Oh, that's not . . .

BOB: . . . and they threw . . . they had little tiny goldfish they used to give him. This was fine, you know. They were fast, but he was big. [Loud laughter.] And then they gave him a big goldfish that was faster, and he was kind of ruined. He kept trying to catch the goldfish and finally he . . .

JACK: He wore himself out, huh?

BOB: They decided . . . the next day they were going to cut off the goldfish's tail, to give him an advantage, but he died in the night, so . . . [loud laughter] I assume it was peaceful. I don't know, maybe he's . . .

PATTY: What I hate are those man-eating vegetables. What are they?

ART: Venus?

PATTY: Venus' flytraps.

JANE: Oh yeah, they're pretty horrible.

PATTY: People . . . people actually left [starts to say 'left'] keep them in their room (general commentary).

HARRY: They eat insects.

GEORGE: But don't they eat people too?

JACK: I don't think there are such things.

JANE: Do they snap at other things?

PATTY: They're horrible. If you put your finger, they snap at it. Then you have to pull . . .

JANE: Really?

PATTY: I never put my finger in, but that's what I've seen.

HARRY: No, they're not strong enough for that. They're small.

JANE: I wonder if they have minds?

HARRY: They're watching you (general laughter).

ALEX: Psychology is a Venus' flytrap.

HENRY: Actually there aren't people behind that thing: that's what you see (laughing).

JANE: Is it real? (There is loud laughter after Henry's comment.)

PATTY: I associate them with "Oh, Dad, Poor Dad." [Brief silence.] Did anyone else see that?

GEORGE: What is it?

JANE: Mamma's hanging in the closet.

PATTY: Yeah.

JANE: Is it good?

PATTY: Well, it is sort of peculiar.

LARRY: Where'd you see it? In New York?

PATTY: No, no, here.

LARRY: A couple of years ago?

PATTY: It was my freshman year. It was here.

GEORGE: Where was it?

LARRY: Dunster.

PATTY: It was in Agassiz. See, they . . .

GEORGE: Oh, I remember something about that.

JANE: It's on Broadway now.

PATTY: Well, the thing was, these Venus' flytraps kept [hah-hah] spasmodically erecting themselves [laughing] and going like this, and doing everything [hah-hah] . . . plants [slurs this word in a strange way] and all, and they were enormous things. Couldn't have been real, I suppose. They are quite enormous. [Little laugh.] They sort of . . . looked as though they'd eat you all.

BOB: What was the name of the play?

PATTY: "Oh, Dad, Poor Dad, Momma's Hung You in the Closet and I'm Feeling So Sad" (pauses slightly before 'closet').

GEORGE (voice seems to drop):   That was the name of the play?

BOB: That reminds me of a story my roommate tells—that there's this crazy family that lives down next door to him, and the parents are very old. One of the daughters is quite out of it completely, and finally the mother passed away, and—I guess this is true, I don't know— he says that the daughter, when they took her away, stood on the front stoop and yelled "There goes mother!" [Said as if mother was flying away like a bird. Laughter from Jane, Patty, and a boy.] I don't know why this reminded me of it; it's pretty sordid (general murmuring).

PATTY (in undertone):   There goes mother! So there.

(R. D. Mann, transcript)

Here we have a remarkable range of symbols expressing the fear of unconscious bonds and the threat of submersion of the individual ego, fears activated by the general emotional contagion of the meeting and the specific and familiar theme of intoxication. The crucial symbol is the central kitchen linked to individual houses by underground tunnels—a metaphorical description of the unconscious bonds produced by their common fantasies of oral plenty, of a nurturant group leader who would feed everyone copiously. This fantasy is touched off by their common deprivation at the hands of the leader.

Two themes then struggle for the upper hand: the party theme which dominates the entire first half of this meeting and which is expressed in the general hilarity of the above passage as well as in the specific references; and the theme of the devouring monster lurking in the depths (the sewers). While the passage is exceptionally rich in symbolism and subject to a variety of interpretations, it seems clear that the fear of being overwhelmed by unconscious impulses and losing bodily and psychological integrity is pervasive. Only when the maternal spectre of group contagion is exorcised by Jane (in her substitution of "Mamma" for "Dad" in the closet) and at the end by Bob and Patty ("There goes mother!") can they move on to more explicit matters, and this is achieved by extremely concrete conversations about mutual acquaintances, common "gripes," and particular group members. (See this volume, pp. 128–129.)

As noted before, the fear of group envelopment often occurs at this point, when the group leader is being dethroned or secularized, and libidinal bonds between members are becoming stronger without having been made fully conscious. Both the title and content of Kopit's play reflect these concerns: loss of paternal support, fear of maternal envelopment, and the struggle for mature sexuality.

For a similar expression of this triple concern, occurring at a comparable point in another group, let us examine another incident from IIg:

IIg. Early in March a brief discussion of a theatrical performance, which must either hang together or altogether collapse, led Debbie and Neil to make the obvious connection to the group. They wondered whether the group "reached a climax," like a play did, or not. They expressed some satisfaction with their recent progress, although not with the preceding two sessions. They felt they had been "working together" well.

Discussion now turned to a conflict between the student body and the university administration over parietal rules. (Someone had written a slogan on the blackboard which synthesized the name of the university president and the concept of sacrifice. To add to their troubles, furthermore, the group leader had at the beginning of the session refused to give extensions on a paper which was due in two weeks.) Most of the members had attended a student rally on the issue, and expressed considerable ambivalence over the experience—on the one hand stirred by the great unanimity and involvement of the students, on the other hand a little frightened by the mass emotionality, fearful of being swept away by it, and looking down on it as a little "childish." They spoke of the disquieting fascination of "getting excited together as a group," of the mobs of the French Revolution, and of being more comfortable with more intellectually-oriented protest groups, in which the participants were a little older. Occasionally they made rather off-hand comparisons with their own group, but quickly reverted to the more general issue, until Neil asked rather suddenly: "Are we an organism? Maybe we're an animal." He asked what part of the body everyone was, whereupon Penny suggested identifying chemical rather than anatomical components, and asked who the carbon was. Bill, a silent member who had never spoken a word to anyone but the group leader, even when directly addressed, at this point grabbed a magazine and began reading it. Julie suggested that they should do something together as a group, whereupon Penny proposed that they adopt a Cambodian infant.

There is probably no better illustration of the fear of group envelopment than the portrait of Ralph in Golding's *Lord of the Flies* (1955), which is essentially a description of group evolution in reverse—an exchanging of conscious for unconscious bonds. Like the training group, the island group carries into the situation a cultural framework for the maintenance of relational consciousness, but this almost immediately breaks down and the most basic group ties become unconscious ones. The dilemma of the individual in such a situation is exhibited by Ralph, who must constantly fight against the seductive influence of Jack's barbarity. He is confused and has difficulty in concentrating on conscious goals. Jack is reinforcing an aspect of himself which he wishes to keep suppressed, and he feels like people always do when they imagine their unconscious impulses to be shared by others: as if he were being overwhelmed from within and without at the same time, as if the boundaries of his ego were disintegrating. One by one the differentiated individuals in the group are destroyed, and separate identities become merged in what ends as a full-fledged and all too real fight-flight group.

In *Lord of the Flies* the original unconscious impulses which are too overwhelmingly reinforced by others are as usual left unstated, although dependency needs receive considerable early emphasis and one may assume that not all of the oral savagery later exhibited can be accounted for in terms of the "fight modality" (i.e., as defensive). It is interesting, in any case, that these impulses receive externalized expression in the impersonal image of the Beast. Of course this is typically the case with powerful impulses, despite the fact, noted above, that there are almost no beasts with impulses as intense as those of man. Does the Beast really represent the impulses themselves or the loss of conscious control over them? I recall a conversation with a subject undergoing an experiment with LSD, in which he expressed an intense fear of losing control and becoming "bestial." When asked what he pictured himself doing, however, little content emerged beyond an image of senseless and dehumanized laughter. His terror of this seemingly harmless act was nonetheless very real, and seemed to be a clearcut example of the psychoanalytic concept of instinctual anxiety (A. Freud, 1946). This image seems similar to that found frequently in dreams and psychotic fantasies, in which a small, formless, crouching black shape gradually expands until it overwhelms everything in darkness. Both fit extremely well the Jungian paradigm of the conscious ego being swallowed up by the unconscious. It is in this way that the swallowing of the sun by the monster of darkness is usually interpreted (cf. Neumann, 1955, pp. 186 ff.).[83]

It is scarcely coincidental that we find the beast emphasized so strongly in portrayals of primeval chaos: ". . . dark and watery, the habitation of monsters and demons," nor that Tiamat appears against Marduk aided by an entire menagerie of monsters, nor that the great earth-mother, Gaea, never ceases producing them. The monster is whatever overwhelms conscious control and the maintenance of ego boundaries, and this may be anything from hunger and sleep to sexuality, anger, dependency needs, group seduction, or any combination of these.

Yet we should not forget, in emphasizing the fearsome aspect of group envelopment, that it also offers strong attractions. Were this not the case, after all, the fears would be groundless, since it would be easy to avoid what no one wanted. The yearning for ego-dissolution, for union with the world, is as old as the awareness of individuality and separateness. One does not need a group composed of mystics in order to have a desire for effortless communication and biological fusion emerge, as the following example illustrates.

IIh. During the third month of the group there was for a brief period considerable joking about bringing toy animals to the meeting (a dog, an alligator) as a kind of group symbol, and one day a member brought in a little live dog. David opened the meeting by discussing his reactions to having read a paper by the group leader, which had made him feel the latter's inactive role more acutely. He then suggested

[83] There are also, of course, myths which portray the reverse process, such as myths of the bringing of fire. The most dramatic of these is the Tsimshian myth of Raven's theft of the daylight (Boas, 1916, pp. 60–62, 641–650).

that his own role in the group (usually defined as diverter, provocateur, intellectualizer, but always as active) had been that of sacrificial lamb to distract attention from the void left by the group leader. After some elaboration of this point there was a very long silence. Eddie broke it by asking the group what they would think about having the power to read minds—which he compared with a fantasy in which the members had indulged at some length in a previous meeting: being invisible. He suggested that such an ability would facilitate taking the role of the other, and hence reduce neurosis. Sidney related it to Hayakawa's discussions of difficulties in communication, and observed that if everyone could read minds, they would all have exactly the same experiences simultaneously and would react to everything in exactly the same way; so that all the time and energy spent in trying to communicate would be unnecessary. After some discussion over whether experiences would indeed be identical under these conditions, Sidney suggested that there would be "one big brain, of which each of us had a little section. There would no longer be any individuality."

Eddie objected that the original fantasies of invisibility and clairvoyance were egocentric, and assumed a secret and special power of one individual. He suggested that such power comes to some extent from knowing a person well, but Beverly disagreed and there ensued a brief discussion of Simmel's "The Stranger," of feedback, and of parallel experience and thought processes. In defense of his position, Eddie remarked with some asperity that his lack of surprise in seeing David blow some smoke in the dog's face was not due to any parallelism in attitude or experience, but to its compatibility with the other information he had about David.

The group leader marvelled at the complexity of their schemes for finding out what other people were thinking, and wondered if simpler methods were not at hand. Sidney replied that "by becoming this one universal brain with all the same experiences, we'll all know what we're thinking, so we won't have to worry about the silences." The group leader suggested that perhaps the silences were an expression of that fantasy. Eddie said it was a more "pure" form of communication, and that an alternative would be "talking lots," so that all would have enough data to see trends. The rest of the meeting was spent discussing communication in the group.

The group's infatuation with the brain fantasy is partially conveyed by the fact that any interpretation or comment upon it provokes a loving restatement. It is probably important that this fantasy follows a renewal of the group's preoccupation with the role of the leader, although the precipitating factor is obviously the long silence. We would expect David's reference to the "void" and his flattery of the group leader and pleas for rescue to arouse competitive feelings in all the members, at the same time that it made them aware that only by drawing closer together could they fill the vacuum. The silence produces a fantasy of total union, with its attendant joys and fears regarding boundary dissolution.

But what of Sidney's statement that the universal brain would *prevent* "worry about the silence"? Does this not suggest that some fear other than that of boundary dissolution is operative? To resolve this contradiction we need to explore the significance of silence a little further. For while the meanings of silence are manifold, in the present connection it seems clearly to be a have-your-cake-and-eat-it-too type of mechanism, in which the members can fantasy total union and total separateness at the same time. In some instances the second fantasy alternative may be a private union with the leader, just as in a Quaker meeting the fantasy of collective identity is coupled with that of being individually selected by God for divine inspiration.

Like all such syntheses, however, it lends itself to another duality. The joyful fantasy in silence is that one will find mystical union with others without boundary dissolution (cf. Smith, 1965)—in other words, a kind of intrauterine condition. The dark counterpart of this is boundary destruction in a state of utter isolation—the worst of both worlds. This is the terror of silence, aroused by some dim sense of the tenuousness of conscious control and a feeling of aloneness.

The "universal brain" fantasy is a protection against this latter combination since it opts for total union, while at the same time rendering the dissolution of boundaries somewhat harmless by its stress on *cognitive* union, instead of the union of unconscious impulses (and the consequent overthrow of ego-control).

The meeting as a whole illustrates the evolution of conscious bonds from unconscious ones. The fantasy is at first covert, then made explicit and shared, although it is presented as superior to (more "pure" than) realistic unity. The latter is examined more and more, however, as the meeting progresses and the real problems in their communication with one another are confronted. Yet it is interesting that the two members most intensely involved in the brain fantasy substantially withdrew from the group when a higher level of candid communication was achieved.

C. The Evolution of Religion

In the first chapter we argued that the study of small groups throws a great deal of light on certain religious phenomena and essentially endorsed Freud's interpretation of religion as an expression of dependency needs. Freud's position is often rejected, however, on the grounds that while it works rather well for Western religious systems, and in general for the various forms of theism, it seems only mildly relevant to many of the phenomena usually grouped under the broad heading of "primitive religion." We ourselves, in the meantime, have complicated our concept of group development to the point where a reexamination of this view might be appropriate.

The dependency interpretation of religious beliefs would now seem applicable primarily to individuals and collectivities at a stage of boundary-awareness in which the fear of boundary-loss is manageable but the fear of isolation is not. We should also expect to find religious phenomena to which "fight-flight" and "pairing" interpretations were the most pertinent.

Roughly speaking, we do. It should be remembered, however, that boundary-awareness is a continuum, and that it is probably more useful to speak of establishing the position of various religious phenomena along that continuum than to try and equate them with the three specific defensive modalities.

Consider, for example, the enormous amount of energy which has been expended in the attempt to establish a definitional frontier between "magic" and "religion." [84] If we view our problem in terms of a continuum of boundary-awareness, this effort becomes unnecessary. We can accept the fine gradations for exactly what they are.

Classical magic, in which a verbal or motor formula is seen as having an automatic effect on environmental forces without the latter necessarily being personified, properly belongs to a pre-awareness stage, in which the distinction between self and environment is not yet established. This was of course noted long ago. [85] A subtle shift

[84] As a sample: Malinowski, 1948, pp. 37–90; Durkheim, pp. 43 ff.; Frazer, 1900, I, pp. 60 ff. Kluckhohn remarks that "anyone can make a definition that will separate magic from religion; but no one has yet found a definition that all other students accept: the phenomenal contents of the concepts of religion and magic simply intergrade too much" (1953, p. 518). But cf. Ames (1964).

[85] Freud, 1950b, pp. 83 ff. Once again it should be stressed, however, that no simple equation between infancy and a level of cultural development is being made. The most primitive practitioner of magic in the world is far from being unable to distinguish himself from his environment in many spheres. As Malinowski demonstrates so ably in "Magic, Science, and Religion," magic can coexist with the most sober empiricism (1948, pp. 25 ff.), but we need not go so far afield. A man may have an empirical orientation toward the workings of his automobile and still protect himself by attaching icons and amulets to his dash-

in emphasis appears when we come to those practices involving the control and placation of more or less personified forces, spirits, and bogies. There is an element of greater apartness and greater anxiety —a sense that one may be overwhelmed and destroyed unless proper measures are taken. This attitude is analogous to the "tiny ego" phase of development discussed in the preceding section. By imperceptible degrees this in turn shades into practices such as prayer, supplication, and sacrifice, which are appropriate objects for analysis in terms of a dependency orientation.

At the other end of the continuum we may put the concern with immortality, rebirth, and messianic fantasies found in our pairing groups. These are, after all, concerns arising from an awareness of individuality sufficient to generate the fear of personal extinction.

Other religious attitudes may similarly be located at various points along the boundary-awareness continuum. The idea of *mana*, for example, in its most typical form, is a rather beautiful expression of that stage of awareness to which the fight-flight modality is most pertinent. Here a single force unites the universe, yet by its unequal quantitative distribution establishes a primitive differentiation of objects. Some of the concentrations, furthermore, are defined in terms of the social structure. Yet the idea of *mana* contains within itself the implicit fear of being overwhelmed and disintegrated by this generalized force. Its protuberances must be avoided by the average individual lest his puny ego be dissolved in its immenseness. Prominent persons are less subject to this danger by virtue of the greater support given to their individuality by the social structure. As we would expect, the idea of taboo is developed with particular virtuosity under these conditions.

Our scheme also helps to clarify shifting attitudes toward fullfledged deities. Over time we find a change from rituals of placation and sacrifice to those of praise. The former pertain to the fear of being swallowed up and absorbed. The latter involve a more sophisticated conception which presupposes some kind of narcissistic self-awareness on the part of the worshipper. He now views the deity with a certain amount of detachment, as a separate being who has concerns which are independent of the worshipper's fears. He can therefore approach the deity with the same finesse that he would employ with a mortal leader—encouraging him to assume difficult responsibilities by flatter-

board or mirror, and Western medicine is still riddled with magical beliefs and practices. Magic simply pertains to those spheres in which the individual has *not* differentiated himself.

ing his narcissism. The narcissistic deity is of course most highly developed in the Judaeo-Christian and Islamic traditions, in which flattery becomes the principal offering.

But an important caution must be stressed here. Early theories of cultural evolution came to grief primarily because they used inappropriate units. Instead of analyzing empirical entities into components which might show genetic relationships, they accepted these entities themselves as units and tried to show that one was more '"advanced" than another, despite the fact that each was the culmination of thousands of years of development, amalgamation, and compromise.[86] Thus while we can locate segmental and abstracted practices or beliefs on a continuum of boundary-awareness we can by no means do so with the larger complexes in which they are embedded. All of the major world religions, for example, are polyglot agglomerations of fight-flight, dependency, and pairing mechanisms, and it would be folly at this stage of our ignorance to attempt to compare them on any continuum. Does a religion with a strong dependency orientation which seems relatively free of magical ideas but also lacks any stress on immortality or rebirth show more or less boundary-awareness than a messianic religion full of magical notions? Until we can find some way of observing, measuring, and weighting these components such a comparison is as impossible as it is in any case frivolous.

But the problem extends even to more refined entities. If we find a *hieros gamos,* for example, should we consider this to be an expression of a "pairing" orientation in and of itself? Can we ignore the fact that rites of this sort typically occur in the context of homeopathic magic? We must be careful to distinguish, in any concrete practice, that part which exhibits a high degree of boundary-awareness and that which reveals the survival of a more primitive orientation (cf. Ames, 1964; Bellah, 1964, p. 361).

This viewpoint can be extremely fruitful in studying the changes that take place within specific religious contexts. If we examine reform movements within religions in all parts of the world, for example, they all seem to push in the same direction, seeking either to eliminate magical and "fight-flight" elements from the religion or to emphasize immortality and rebirth at the expense of dependency attitudes. Similarly, the decay of these movements involves a reintroduction of the purged elements, so that what we see historically appears less like evo-

---

[86] This is often of a type that psychoanalysts would call "neurotic compromise" because of its rigid, contradictory, and obsessively overelaborated nature.

lution and more like a seesaw movement, or a series of shifting combinations, like cabinet coalitions in a multiparty system.

Thus while the mystic may seek the same kind of boundary-dissolution exhibited by a shaman, he appears among far more sophisticated peoples, and makes a much more *conscious* effort to eliminate the very separateness which consciousness creates. Mysticism springs from a preoccupation with mortality and aloneness, yet often stresses fusion with a particular deity, although its goal is the obliteration of all boundary-awareness. The many forms in which it arises thus involve a considerable segment of the continuum.

Consider also the many forms which may be taken by ancestor worship, which we would on the face of it place squarely at the "dependency" level along with the worship of major deities. Such placement results from an image of the worship itself, of praying and paying homage to ancestors. But when we look at some of the associated beliefs and practices the picture becomes more complicated. In many, if not most societies with ancestor worship, there is an associated fear of the dead returning and a number of rituals and practices designed to ward off ghosts. These ideas pertain to a level at which individuation is minimal, problematic, and terrifyingly precarious. As the society becomes more sophisticated, these ideas should drop out progressively and give way to a focus on personal immortality. At this point the idea that the ancestors are dependent for their survival on the libations and homage of living descendants receives increasing emphasis, usually taking the significant form of an absorbing preoccupation with producing male heirs. It is quite common to find all of these attitudes coexisting. Yet we should nonetheless be able to isolate the separate components—fear of the ego being swallowed up because of its inadequate separation from the dead, desire to perpetuate the nurturance and protection the dead provided while living, and desire to ensure one's own immortality by extending it to one's predecessors—and evaluate their relative importance to the members of the society (cf. Neumann, 1954, p. 228).

Finally, let us examine a phenomenon of special relevance to the present study—the constellation of beliefs and practices usually grouped under the heading of totemism. The reader may have wondered how the revolt of the primal horde could be considered to represent an evolutionary development, since totemism is generally thought of as so much more "primitive" than the dependent orientations supposed to precede it, and which characterize long periods in the great civilizations of history, including our own.

Since we have argued, after Mills, that the primal horde myth portrays a sociological process rather than an historical event, we must reconsider Freud's interpretation of totemism in these terms. If the totemism-exogamy constellation to which Freud refers is no longer a reaction to an event, then to what *is* it a reaction?

Probably the best solution to this problem is that suggested by Kroeber (1952, pp. 306–307) and Lévi-Strauss (1949, pp. 609–610): that the primal horde is a perpetual virtuality. Totemism and exogamy, rather than expressing remorse over an event, express avoidance of a desire—of an alternative social structure and social attitude. This alternative is at once regressive and progressive. On the one hand it embraces collapse into the undifferentiated mob, the dissolution of incest restrictions and all distinctions between people; on the other it involves the abandonment of a fusion with the environment and the acceptance of a greater self-awareness and separateness. The totemism-exogamy constellation may thus be seen as a kind of neurotic mechanism which blocks off, through its obsessive elaboration, successful environmental adaptation along with the dangers it attempts to avoid.

But how should we evaluate totemism in terms of boundary-awareness? Our first problem is to decide precisely what we mean by totemism, before we find ourselves in the dilemma of Lévi-Strauss, who wrote a whole book about it while stoutly maintaining its nonexistence as an entity (1963). Ordinarily, people using the term totemism wish to convey to each other a constellation of four traits (I am here excluding efforts to cram the term into some more logical and abstract system): (1) a division of the society into exogamous clans, (2) designations of these clans by names, most often those of animals, (3) belief in a special relationship with the animal species, usually common descent from a totemic ancestor, (4) taboos associated with the animal, especially a prohibition against killing or eating it.

Lévi-Strauss' objection to this usage, shared with most modern anthropologists, is that all of these components can and often do appear without the others. This is an argument over classificatory convenience and need not concern us.[87] Indeed, we are primarily in-

[87] I cannot help pointing out, however, that the same objection can be made to the constellation "Englishman," which we normally understand to refer to a person (1) of Anglo-Saxon descent, (2) living in England, and (3) a citizen of the English polity. All of these occur frequently in isolation or in pairs, and if we shift to "American" the problem becomes even worse, in spite of which the designation occasions no real difficulty.

One also suspects that some of the intercultural variation dealing with the

terested in the separate components, so as to obtain some understanding of their place in our formulation.

As we examine these four traits using the conceptual scheme we have been discussing, we are struck by the fact that they seem to move in several directions at once (a characteristic which may explain the frequency of their separate appearance). The division into clans, the separate designations, even the use of animal names—insofar as the function of this usage is, as Lévi-Strauss maintains (1963, pp. 87–89), the intellectual one of simultaneously expressing unity and separateness—all represent a striving toward differentiation, conscious bonds, and awareness. The relationship with the animal species, insofar as it is a vague and unspecified identity rather than a clearly conceptualized connection,[88] expresses the undifferentiated unity of the most primitive state.

Interestingly enough, those facets in which Freud was most deeply interested—exogamy, the belief that the totem animal is an ancestor, and the taboos on killing and eating (together with miscellaneous respect and deference patterns)—all seem to pertain to an intermediate stage, one more germane to the dependent orientation. It is perhaps the striking incompatibility of this last subconstellation with the stereotypical idea of the weak ego-boundary of the savage that caught Freud's attention. It is indeed difficult to look at these traits together without their conjuring up the image of a stern patriarch. Yet such patriarchy is totally alien to totemic cultures, hence Freud reasoned he must have existed in the past and been destroyed, although remembered. Generally speaking, looking to the past is a logical approach which served Freud well, but we might ask if it would not be equally reasonable to say that the patriarch for a totemistic society exists not in the past but in the future, not as a memory but as an anticipatory fantasy.

belief system is spurious, being a function of the interaction between individual variability *within* the society and the selective emphasis of the ethnographer on whatever is novel and unique. It seems obvious that within any tribe there will be a vast assortment of beliefs, rationalizations, and metaphors dealing with, let us say, the relation between man and the totem animal, a relation which for most purposes can be left rather vague until an ethnographer starts probing for a rigorous explanation. A good example of what happens when an ethnographer deliberately samples beliefs is found in Minturn and Hitchcock's study of the Rājpūts of Khalapur (Whiting, 1963, p. 276).

[88] For we must admit that such kinship exists, in a purely biological sense. Since Darwin even Western peoples accept a distant relationship with the primates, although no one ever views dogs and cats as cousins.

Let us imagine that individuation and boundary-awareness proceed to a point at which anxiety results. Could not the fantasy of an all-powerful father begin to take shape in response to such a feeling? In this view, totemism in the form with which Freud was most concerned would be a kind of cargo cult for authoritarianism.

The flaw in such a comparison is that cargo cult followers experience some prior stimulus to their fantasy. Where does the notion of an authoritarian leader come from in our scheme? Yet perhaps it is not necessary to have a cultural model. Every child in every culture encounters a stern or angry male at some time or other, and insofar as a tribe is moving in the direction of authoritarianism such encounters will progressively increase.

At the same time, the emergence of a kingdom is dependent on many other variables—social, economic, ecological. Some societies will stop short of this phase or regress to a more primitive level. Others may bypass authoritarian dependence in many respects and develop a form of totemism which combines "pre-dependence" and "post-dependence" attributes in a variety of syntheses. All we can argue from this notion is that a society in which the several "dependent" totemic traits are highly developed and the totem animal receives increasingly personalized treatment is in a proto-authoritarian stage and will develop some sort of monarchy if other conditions lend themselves to it.

But let us now abandon speculation and look briefly at the one existing set of empirical data which might lend support to our theory. This is the cross-cultural study of religious beliefs by Swanson, entitled *The Birth of the Gods* (1960).

Swanson's study of the "origins" of religious beliefs utilizes a set of determinants which are largely orthogonal to ours. Since such beliefs, like all fantasy constructs, are overdetermined this presents no special difficulty, save that we must ask ourselves if there is anything in his analysis which can be related to ours. Swanson's view of the matter is essentially Durkheimian:

"The experiences which seem closest to having the supernatural's characteristics are those connected with the primordial and constitutional structures of social relationships" (Swanson, 1960, p. 28).

Selecting a sample of 50 societies, Swanson proceeds to test a series of predictions involving the relationship between specified social forms and conditions on the one hand and supernatural beliefs on the other. A number of these are borne out.

Now, we noted above that religious phenomena must be cut very finely before we can make discriminations along a continuum of boundary-awareness. Since Swanson utilizes traditional categories in his study there are few points at which we can adapt his material for our own purposes. We would perhaps associate the presence of "high gods" with the "dependency" phase, and possibly witchcraft with the "fight-flight" phase, but we must despair at the absence of anything we can equate with a "pairing" phase.

Most encouraging in Swanson's data is the strong positive association between the presence of high gods, especially *"active"* high gods (which provide the most meaningful expression of the dependent orientation), and a variety of sociological variables reflecting differentiation, specialization, and complexity in the society. (See Swanson, 1960, pp. 55–81, 194–217.) It seems not unreasonable to interpret this relationship as expressing the increased awareness of individual and group boundaries which accompany such social complexity, as well as the erosion of "fight-flight" attitudes brought about by the proliferation of conscious bonds, and the "fear of freedom" (in Fromm's sense) which results from individuation and provokes fantasies of more powerful supernatural beings.[89]

It would also be helpful if we could compare our conception of religious evolution with one derived from a more direct and scholarly cognizance of the relevant data. Such an opportunity is conveniently provided by Bellah's recent paper, "Religious Evolution" (1964). Bellah proposes five stages of religious development reflecting corresponding points on several parallel continua. Particular attention is paid to the symbol systems, the religious action patterns, the type of religious organization, and the social implications of each phase, and it is shown

[89] We assume individuation to be greater in societies with specialization and overlapping groups, even though the individuation in Swanson's sample as a whole is mild relative to industrialized societies.

To make as direct a test as possible of this hypothesis, I combined all variables which seemed like logical individuation or differentiation measures into a single index, predicting that it would correlate positively with "high gods" and negatively with witchcraft (the variable "exuvial magic" would have been much preferable from a theoretical viewpoint, but Swanson found it unreliable). The variables used in the individuation index are: (1) individually owned property, (2) social classes, (3) specialties in noncommunal activities, (4) specialties in communal activities, (5) sovereign organizations, (6) nonsovereign organizations, (7) nonsovereign communal organizations. (For explanations of the derivation of these variables see Swanson, 1960, pp. 42 ff., 199 ff.) Each variable was weighted equally, and the resulting index correlated with the two religion measures. The prediction was nicely borne out with respect to the "high gods" ($\chi^2 = 10.56$, $p < 0.01$) but not with respect to witchcraft, which showed an insignificant positive correlation.

how the limitations of each phase nevertheless contain the seeds of the next.

Bellah's stages, while representing complex empirical amalgams rather than deductively derived segments of a single strand, still reveal a clear relationship with the continuum of boundary-awareness and its associated mechanisms. Thus Bellah's first phase, "primitive religion," is characterized by weak and elastic distinctions between self and world, between mythical and empirical worlds, and between religious and other roles (Bellah, pp. 361–364). "Archaic religion" contains more characterization of mythical beings (essentially their transformation into personified and motivated gods), an elaborated cosmology, priestly roles, and a sharper distinction "between men as subjects and gods as objects," with the consequent emergence of communication systems such as worship and sacrifice and of "a new degree of freedom as well, perhaps, as an increased burden of anxiety" (Bellah, pp. 364–365). "Historic religion" introduces a sharp dualism between the empirical cosmos, which is derogated, and life-after-death. Hierarchical ordering of mythical symbols, which began in the archaic phase, is extended in this one and is reflected in further social differentiations—between religious and political hierarchies as well as in class stratification. Emphasis on salvation or enlightenment appears for the first time, as does a new insistence on submission to divine will or understanding (Bellah, pp. 366–367). "Early modern religion" is essentially equated with the Protestant Reformation and evinces a return to worldly involvement, a collapsing of both symbolic and organizational hierarchies, a reversal of the separation between religious and nonreligious action, and a consequent tendency toward the development of a "voluntaristic and democratic society," despite some extreme initial authoritarianism (Bellah, pp. 368–370). Bellah is a little vague about "modern religion," but stresses its abandonment of dualism for an "infinitely multiplex" structure, the further detachment from religious specialists of religious symbolization and belief, the intensification of awareness of personal responsibility for such symbolization, and the fact that "culture and personality themselves have come to be viewed as endlessly revisable" (Bellah, pp. 371–373).

This is a highly selective and perhaps even misleading summary of Bellah's presentation, since it focuses as much as possible on those aspects most relevant to our own concerns. I have attempted, however, to retain enough of its original flavor to make it necessary from his more general approach to abstract our particular conceptual slices.

Let us take, for example, the variable of increasing separateness or "differentness" between people. In theories of cultural evolution this is typically discussed in terms of "differentiation," as Eisenstadt points out (1964, p. 376). Differentiation is usually particularized in relation to specialized roles, however, and it is always easy to show that role dedifferentiation also occurs with cultural development. This is because role specialization is really an intermediate form of individuation. When the ability to avoid losing oneself in the corpus of the collectivity is still problematic, the formation of specialized roles serves to fix an observably separate point of reference from which an individual can recognize both his connectedness and his separateness from the whole. This mechanism has the obvious disadvantage of rigidity, however, and typically disappears, both at the societal and at the small group level, when it is no longer required. We are often so preoccupied with the hypertrophy of certain kinds of occupational specialization in our own society that we ignore its widespread evaporation in other areas. As formal occupations become an increasingly trivial temporal segment of life, this balance needs to be corrected. We romanticize the nineteenth century Yankee farmer who was possessed of a vast array of practical skills, indifferently executed, but it is well to remember that this lack of specialization was not from choice but from necessity, and that the social roles played by such a man in his small community were often rigidly specialized indeed. When a modern American competes with specialists in religion or transportation, however, it must be attributed to his passion for self-service, since specialists are in fact available. More importantly, much of the uniformity in social behavior of which we complain today reflects an effort to achieve high role flexibility or interchangeability under conditions of geographic mobility and technological change. (Since new mechanisms tend to be crude and exaggerated, this attempt carries with it an intolerance of behaviors and attitudes which, because of their extremeness or for other reasons, are difficult to rotate in and out of.)

In the small group context we saw how members assumed rather calcified roles early in the group's history, taking refuge from boundary-loss by becoming "characters" with a limited set of stereotyped responses. (It is indeed more characteristic of deviant "individualists" than we like to admit that their responses to any situation are predictable.) Later we observed a desire by group members to enrich their behavioral repertoire so that anyone could perform any role.

(See this volume, pp. 162–165.) This represents the emergence of a degree of individuation which permits the abandonment of fixed roles —a crude device no longer necessary once fear of group envelopment has waned. It is as if a set of quintuplets, separated at birth, were suddenly reunited in a jungle and forced to wear brightly decorated and highly particularized masks for a time in order to tell one another apart, before becoming attuned to more subtle differentiating cues.

We are thus faced with a familiar problem in evolutionary theory. At one level of conceptualization (differentiation of roles) we observe a pendular movement, but with another twist of the lens (individuation) we see a straight line. Indeed, it may ultimately come to pass that the most satisfactory analogue of cultural evolution is the locomotive pattern of the inchworm, a thought to which we shall return in the final chapter. In Bellah's exposition this issue emerges quite explicitly. Specialized religious roles, absent in the "primitive" stage, are present in the next two but tend to disappear in the two modern phases. On the other hand individuation itself tends consistently to increase. From the nondiscriminatory aspect of primitive religion we move to the personalization of mythical beings in archaic religion, to the elaboration of hierarchies in historic religion and to the complete individuation of belief in the modern phases, in which there is "increasing acceptance of the notion that each individual must work out his own ultimate solutions."

A concomitant of this process is the increase in independence, which we have seen to be so prominent a theme in group development. In the evolution of religion, Bellah notes similarly that "at each stage the freedom of personality and society has increased relative to the environing conditions. Freedom has increased because at each successive stage the relation of man to the ultimate conditions of his existence has been conceived as more complex, more open and more subject to change and development" (Bellah, p. 374).

Any attempt to relate Bellah's stages to Bion's defensive modalities, however, runs into not unexpected difficulties, since, as noted above, these mechanisms are not tied to but only attracted to specific points on the continuum of boundary-awareness and frequently make their appearance at any point of transition. In Bellah's analysis we find the clearest representations of these mechanisms all clustering about the middle stage, although in ways that do not contradict the evolutionary ordering of them that we suggested. The stage of historical religion encompasses flight in the form of otherworldliness or transcendentalism (there seems to be nothing here equivalent to "fight"); [90] dependency in the form of submission, placation, and reverence toward a detached high god; and pairing in the form of the incipient concern with salvation, enlightenment, and messianic fantasies. Yet the religious rejection of the world ends with this phase, while the submissive orientation continues into the next, and the concern with salvation into the present.

What is striking, furthermore, is that the essential *drama* of each of these last three phases represents a partial working-through of the three defensive modalities. Thus Bellah says of world rejection that: "the world acceptance of the primitive and archaic levels is largely to be explained as the only possible response to a reality that invades the self to such an extent that the symbolizations of self and world are only very partially separate. . . . *Only by withdrawing cathexis from the myriad objects of empirical reality could consciousness of a centered self in relation to an encompassing reality emerge.* Early modern religion made it possible to maintain the centered self without denying the multifold empirical reality and so made world rejection in the classical sense unnecessary" (Bellah, p. 374; italics mine). This is a crucial passage inasmuch as it shows that the flight mechanism, like the other mechanisms, also contains within itself the seeds of self-extinction, although these by no means always reach fruition. Later Bellah makes another familiar distinction, noting that "'the world acceptance of the last two stages [has] . . . a profoundly different significance from that of the first two" (Bellah, p. 374).

Since the central drama of the early modern phase is the resolution of dependency we are not too surprised to see that some of our revolt themes are rather prominent here. We note first that it is preceded by a phase in which religious specialists "store up a fund of grace that could then be shared with the less worthy," and is itself a phase in which salvation (or enlightenment) is potentially available to everyone (Bellah, p. 368). This recalls the process of magnifying and glorifying the group leader so that later, when he is disenthroned and his "enlightenment" dispersed to all, the spoils will be maximized. We also note that the antecedent historical religions are universalistic—the first step toward a truly democratic religious system. When all are "equal before God" it becomes possible collectively to unite in dispensing with God altogether as an authoritarian deity; just as we saw that the primal

---

[90] Bellah suggests, in a personal communication, that "fight" is also present, in the unique stress which historic religions place on "aggressive confrontation with others" (e.g., holy wars, persecution of heretics, and missionary work).

horde was able, in Mills' formulation, to dispense with the despot once he treated them all equally. Also essential, of course, is the total democratization of the system of religious organization, although this seems somewhat less significant in its parallelism to the group than the democratization of belief. Finally we may recall the distinction previously made (see this volume, p. 107) between the "vaginal" orientation sometimes displayed by dependency groups and the "mouth" orientation of the group in revolt. This distinction seems also to be embraced by Bellah's remark about early modern religion that "the fundamentally ritualist interpretation of the sacrament of the Eucharist as a re-enactment of the paradigmatic sacrifice is replaced with the anti-ritualist interpretation of the Eucharist as a commemoration of a once-and-for-all historical event" (Bellah, p. 369).

The central drama of the modern phase is the crisis over the awareness of individual mortality and responsibility. Its working-through is perhaps represented by the abandonment of dualism for "multiplexity," and of messianic hopes for individual enlightenment. Since Bellah denies that this represents secularization, however, and since the modern phase is still in process, it is perhaps unwise to attempt to find further parallels.

More important than such parallels is the way in which religious symbolization is utilized to effect transitions to higher levels of boundary-awareness. Thus Bellah observes that "the identity diffusion characteristic of both primitive and archaic religions is radically challenged by the historic religious symbolization, which leads for the first time to a clearly structured conception of the self. . . . Primitive man can only accept the world in its manifold givenness. Archaic man can through sacrifice fulfill his religious obligations and attain peace with the gods. But the historic religions promise man for the first time that he can understand the fundamental structure of reality and through salvation participate actively in it" (Bellah, p. 367). These transitions, furthermore, involve the same exchange of passivity for activity that we find in group revolt. Bellah quotes a passage from Lienhardt, discussing Dinka religion, in which it is suggested that religious images serve to effect a "differentiation between experience of the self and of the world which acts upon it." Lienhardt points out that an *interpretation* of suffering in terms of such images enables the sufferer to "dominate" it. "With this knowledge, this separation of a subject and an object in experience, there arises for them also the possibility of creating a form of experience they desire, and of freeing themselves symbolically from what they must otherwise passively endure" (quoted in Bellah, 1964, p. 361). Again we are struck by the fact that the active grasping which we have viewed as the essence of the revolt in groups seems to occur in some form at all points of transition, in relation to all modalities, and at every stage of boundary-awareness. It is this that makes the description of developmental processes so difficult, as Piaget observes in the passages previously quoted. (See this volume, p. 177.)

Yet we must remember that the empirical phenomena we observe are confusing not because of the regularity of this revolt peristalsis, but because at each stage the organism or group uses a different clumsy and dangerous tool to help advance it to the next, at which point the tool can be abandoned for another. By the time this next stage is reached the tool has become so cumbersome that its abandonment is retrospectively defined as the "goal" of the advance.

CHAPTER VI

Conclusion

We have come some distance in our perambulations from the limited and mundane context in which we began. It might be objected that the many parallels drawn merely reflect a kind of grandiosity on our part, an attempt to crowd all of life and history into the tiny shell of one particular and even atypical variety of contemporary group experience. It might further be argued that if one can attach so much significance to a few groups of students and patients one could just as well attach it to a tree or a flower or any other evolving entity. What, then, is the value of all these connections? To the effort to facilitate the development of any given kind of group ("therapeutic," "meaningful," "rewarding," "cohesive," "valid," or whatever) I am certain they will add very little. To the attempt to understand the structure and process of such groups they may help to agglutinate an apperceptive mass which could be either useful or distracting. The title of this book, however, betrays a broader interest, as well as a conviction that these resemblances are engendered by some underlying principle of human association.

A training or therapy group is a sophisticated product of a complex civilization. This fact has indeed made possible the establishment of these connections. It takes no great wit to perceive the relevance of religious symbolism when group members regularly utilize such symbolism. What we have observed in our examples is simply a tendency for group members to draw upon a rich cultural heritage in expressing their reactions to the difficulties of establishing and maintaining a complex set of interpersonal relationships.

Yet it seems reasonable to assume that their choices are not random, but reflect patterns of solution often essayed in the past, which are hence relevant even though not always successful. My argument is not that a training group recapitulates cultural evolution

234

but that any group must recapitulate some of it, and that we are therefore under an obligation to make sense out of whatever recapitulations we find. A theory based solely on this experience is of necessity limited, but since this is true of all theories, we can only advance our approximation and make the best of it until something better comes along.

We spoke of an "underlying principle of human association" as a goal toward which this book should be striving. Perhaps even this is too limited a conception: is it really clear that the common elements in the phenomena we have discussed are only to be found at the human level? From time to time we have caught glimpses of ethological parallels, and it might be more profitable to seek biological patterns of organic association. This is, however, far beyond the scope of this book. Let us content ourselves for the moment with briefly considering how the distinction might be applied.

The nearest we have yet come to an underlying dimension is the continuum of boundary-awareness. This is, as we have discussed it, a psychological dimension, with the majority of its variation occurring at the human level. It is obviously a dimension which is central to any kind of group formation, since the latter requires an adjustment of boundaries almost by definition. But is it the *consciousness* of boundaries which is important or the boundary fluctuations themselves? Might we not be observing phenomena which derive from the fundamental patterns by which units of living matter combine, organize, and dissolve? It is quite possible that this is so, but the problem is made rather complex by virtue of the fact that humans, while going further in their combinatorial proclivities than almost any other multicellular organism, do not dissolve and synthesize their physical selves but only their artifacts, symbol systems, and response patterns. This is not intended to minimize human interdependence—the appropriateness of the organic model of human society is indicated by the fact that elimination of all vehicles of transport in the United States would bring about the starvation of the majority of the population within a few months. It simply means that at the biosocial level we cannot really go beyond analogizing, since we have no idea of the processes through which physical mechanisms are translated into symbolic ones. Let us return therefore to the psychological level and consider the question of boundary-awareness in a little more depth.

All of the essentials of the rather eclectic conceptual montage which has been presented in the preceding chapters antedated my acquaintance with Erich Neumann's *The Origins and History of Consciousness* (1954), although I had encountered many of his ideas in related works. The correspondences between the two are in any case so extensive that they may be utilized to recapitulate and summarize our arguments.

Before doing so, however, a comment might be made about the peculiar difficulties one encounters in trying to make use of Jungian theory. While Neumann is perhaps more clear-headed than others of his school, he nevertheless shows the same ardent platonism, the reification of the psychological, the mysticism and obscurantism, and the obstinate anti-reductionism which has made Jungian theory appeal so strongly to the older of the "two cultures."

A more specific problem arises from the rather droll equation of "masculine" with "conscious" and "feminine" with "unconscious," which seems to be an example of the "return of the repressed"—the repressed being in this instance the patriarchal bias of the early Freudians. While it is certainly true that men have often claimed themselves to be more spiritual, intelligent, and generally uplifted than the allegedly earthy, primitive, and instinctual female, one is a little surprised to find this ancient pederastic motto being given the status of a scientific theory. It is a not unusual instance of the inability of Jungian theorists to detach themselves from the symbolic associations they seek to analyze.

Neumann defends his position as follows: "This correlation is self-evident, because the unconscious, alike in its capacity to bring to birth and to destroy through absorption, has feminine affinities" (1954, p. 125). One might assume from this that Neumann is merely reporting a frequent unconscious association between the two dichotomies—a quite reasonable enterprise—and this is supported by his remark that the application of the term "masculine" to the "conscious ego system" is "dictated not by caprice but by mythology." But he then goes on to argue that these associations are veridical and that while man experiences the unconscious as alien, woman is at home in it and "out of her element in consciousness" (Neumann, 1954, p. 125). Male puberty rites are also seen as directed toward "higher masculinity," although he does not venture to say in what way subincision and related eccentricities are spiritual—only that their "content is not, as in many initiations of young girls, sexuality, but its counterpole, spirit" (Neumann, 1954, p. 141).

It is easy to point out such absurdities in Jungian doctrine and to wonder at the ability of its proponents to remain indefinitely suspended from the empirical world, like a cheap dictionary which sends one in synonymic circles. Yet we must not lose sight of the advantages yielded by such specialization. It is this very unconcern with the concrete origin of their symbols that gives them such great skill at establishing symbolic connections. And this skill must certainly be granted, for no group has so thoroughly and illuminatingly explored the network of symbolic connections underlying mythology and religious systems.

In the case of Neumann we must grant more than this, for even if we strip away such stopthoughts as the notion of "archetype," we are left with a rather straightforward explanatory principle, which may ultimately prove to account for more of the variance in fantasy-production than any other. We know that myths are multi-determined, that they utilize the most varied raw materials—personal fantasies, misunderstood rituals and representations, historical events—and pour them through an endless series of molds: the whims and wishes of story tellers, the forms of language, the strains of the culture, the conspiratorial purposes of revisionist priesthoods, the pressures and seductions of the family system, and so on. But the mold stressed by Neumman is the internal structure of the mind itself, specifically, the relation between the conscious and unconscious segments.[91]

According to Neumann, the growth of consciousness proceeds by stages which are identical whether considered ontogenetically or phylogenetically. His clearest description of this evolution is in its mythological manifestations, and we will follow his method and language in describing the steps. As we proceed, however, the reader is asked to think not only of the development of the individual ego, but also of the emergence of awareness of a group *as* a group—a self-conscious and separate entity with differentiated parts and functions.

Neumann first considers creation myths, and the pre-creation state of things. He notes that in the corresponding stage of consciousness, or rather lack of it, there is no distinction between world and psyche, since "there is as yet no reflecting, self-conscious ego that could refer anything to itself." He also observes that creation generally appears as the creation of light, i.e., consciousness (Neumann, 1954, p. 6). This preconsciousness stage is typically symbolized by roundness and circularity (the egg, the *uroboros*, etc.), and by lack of opposition (i.e., bi-

[91] It is worth noting that Ferenczi employed this approach in 1912 without anyone having thought that a revolution had taken place (Ferenczi, 1912). This perspective, furthermore, obviates the necessity of falling back on such absurdities as a hereditary "collective unconscious." A morphological constant need not imply inheritance, any more than should the fact that certain early and universal childhood experiences are awesome and compelling and serve as symbolic vehicles for intrapsychic conflict.

sexuality). We are reminded here of Bennis' description of the "oral" stage of groups. (See this volume, p. 185.) The lack of sexual differentiation in this phase appears in the nonrecognition of sexuality in early meetings of groups (cf., for example, this volume, pp. 207 ff.).

The ego which emerges in this envelope of the unconscious, this "ocean of the unborn" senses itself as embryonic (p. 14):

"The world is experienced as all-embracing, and in it man experiences himself, as a self, sporadically and momentarily only. Just as the infantile ego . . . feebly developed, easily tired, emerges like an island out of the ocean of the unconscious for occasional moments only, and then sinks back again, so early man experiences the world. Small, feeble, and much given to sleep, i.e., for the most part unconscious, he swims about in his instincts like an animal" (p. 15). This helplessness is not yet negatively defined, however, since the ego is not sufficiently aware of itself to perceive itself as separate. There is a strong desire "to be dissolved and absorbed; passively one lets oneself be taken, sinks into the pleroma, melts away in the ocean of pleasure . . ." (p. 17).

"The more unconscious the whole of a man's personality is and the more germinal his ego, the *more his experience of the whole will be projected upon the group.......* The more unindividualized people are, the stronger the projection of the self upon the group, and the *stronger, too, the unconscious participations of group members among themselves.* But, as the group becomes more individualized and the significance of the ego and of the individual increases, the *more these interhuman relations must be made conscious and the unconscious participations broken down*" (p. 275; italics mine).

This is a succinct statement of the essential problem and process of group development. It should make it clear, also, that our references to "unconscious bonds" have nothing to do with the Jungian idea of a "collective unconscious." We are actually dealing with a very simple distinction between a unity that is voluntary and one that is involuntary. As Neumann observes, emotional contagion has "nothing to do with a conscious feeling-relationship or with love" (pp. 271–272). It is simply an accidental confluence based on (1) a communality of ignorance and (2) a projection of identical fears, which, because they are identical, can seem to be communicated by means of cues so minimal as to appear telepathic.

". . . excitation of one part of the group can affect the whole, as a fever seizes upon all parts of the organism. The emotional fusion then

sweeps away the still feebly developed differences of conscious structure in the individuals concerned . . ." (p. 272).

This is also the phase to which magic is most appropriate: "no ego
center [has] as yet developed to relate the world to itself and itself
to the world. Instead, man [is] all things at once. . . . Everything inside [is] outside, that is to say, all his ideas [come] to him from outside, as commands from a spirit or magician or 'medicine bird.' But
also, everything outside [is] inside. Between the hunted animal and
the will of the hunter there [exists] a magical, mystical rapport . . ."
(pp. 105–6). Exuvial magic and the "perils of the soul" also reflect this
stage of development (p. 288), and, as we have already noted, the
identification aspects of totemism (pp. 268, 288 ff.). Man is "buffeted to
and fro" by this constant exchange between the unconscious and the
environment. "Everything was potentially 'holy' or . . . charged with
mana" (p. 106). Yet as we have seen (this volume, pp. 221 ff.), even
these ideas betray the beginnings of differentiation, since (1) *mana* is
not uniformly distributed through the environment, (2) exuvia and the
idea of the soul betray a sense of individuality, and (3) totemism not
only groups together but also draws boundaries. Gradually this oral
and nonsexual phase gives way: "the world becomes ambivalent," and
pain is an object of awareness (p. 39). The part of the self which remains unconscious, and which retains its primitive identification with
the world (and with the group), appears in mythology as the "Great
Mother."

"Over against all this the ego—consciousness, the individual—remains small and impotent. It feels itself a tiny, defenseless speck. . . .
At this stage, consciousness has not yet wrested any firm foothold
from the flood of unconscious being . . ." (p. 40). But enough separateness has been achieved to make possible a negative definition of
the unconscious as something alien and dangerous to this "speck." The
outside world is also seen as separate, frightening, and random (personal malevolence is, as always, an ambivalently comforting alternative to this cosmic indifference), partly because outside and inside
(unconscious) are still confused.

"Whereas, in the beginning, the waking state was sheer exhaustion
for the feeble ego consciousness, and sleep was bliss . . . now this
return . . . is accomplished with increasing repugnance as the demands of its own independent existence grow more insistent" (p. 45).

The gradual strengthening of the ego in relation to the unconscious
Neumann sees reflected in the changing relation between the Great
Mother and her consort in mythology: from hapless child who is slain,

to tragic adolescent lover who is also slain (but with increasing resistance), to adult male who is not slain. For most of this period the
general picture is one of pretty boys fascinated, overpowered, castrated,
and destroyed by the Great Mother: "the seat of the unconscious [is]
still too near, for the ego to resist the surge of the blood" (p. 61). In-
sanity and transformation into beasts are frequent outcomes of this encounter.

Yet the ability to define the non-ego as an identity indicates that
a degree of separation, differentiation, and self-awareness has occurred.
It is perhaps for this reason that the "symbols of the Great Mother reach
their climax in the great Neolithic cultures of the Near and Far East"
(Long, 1963, p. 37). The development of agriculture and its associated
technologies (cf. Gouldner and Peterson's discussion of the importance
of pottery in generating narcissistic self-awareness, pp. 24–26) mark a
sharp upturn in man's actual control over his nonhuman environment
together with the beginning of increasing complexity in his social
world. Realization of one's own real ability to modify the environment
paradoxically leads to realization of one's separateness from it and
hence of one's overall impotence in relation to it. The civilizations
which evolved from the Neolithic revolution saw not the beginning of
the mythology of the Great Mother but its elaboration and the gradual
enlargement of the Great Mother's consort. Little by little an element
of activity and struggle becomes visible in the latter's behavior. Narcissistic withdrawal asserts itself, and even the deaths and castrations
tend to be self-induced. Side by side with this trend is the progressive
derogation of the Great Mother, and her fragmentation into good and
bad parts (Neumann, 1954, pp. 88 ff.).

Neumann's emphasis on the narcissism of the Great Mother's adolescent lovers has particular relevance for our analogue of group development. For this narcissism is not only a way-station in the growth
of ego consciousness but also in the development of patriarchal symbols.
Let us interrupt our résumé briefly to consider this relationship, which
may also help explain an apparent discontinuity in the orderly and
gradual progression of ego and group development.

There is a point, both in the group and in the individual, at which
individuation seems to be enormously facilitated by identification with
some central person. I have discussed elsewhere (as have numerous
authors) the importance of the father in enabling the child to differentiate itself from the mother and form a complex and generalized concept of parental values (Slater, 1961c), and we have seen how in
training groups the leader is at an early stage viewed as heroically

combating the undifferentiated mass of the group. By focusing one's attention and libido on some prominent individual who appears to have achieved a clear separateness from mother, group, unconscious or whatever; by magnifying and glorifying this individual's power and invulnerability, and identifying with him, one feels strengthened in one's own individuation (although the identification itself makes this individuation somewhat illusory). We have described at several points (see especially this volume, p. 83) how a group builds up its leader in order to gain more *mana* for itself, but we might now wonder whether some of this build-up is not in the service of assisting individual members in differentiating themselves from the mass through identification with this magnified leader. As Neumann suggests, the process of ego development from passive recipient to agent "is first accomplished, not in the collective parts of the group, but only in the great, i.e., differentiated, individuals who are the representative bearers of the group's consciousness" (Neumann, 1954, p. 127). The narcissism of Neumann's youthful victims of the Great Mother perhaps represents a similar mental effort. Through emphasizing the beauty and self-centeredness of these figures the ego makes a fumbling effort to establish an object of identification.

Later, of course, when this identification has been achieved, it too must be relinquished. The ego must be separated from the leader or authority which helped to build it, since this also is a part of individuation. At this point, the authority ceases to be a hero (i.e., a representation of the ego) and becomes the same overpowering object as the original representation of the unconscious (world, void, group, mother). It is here, as we have seen, that the revolt typically occurs.

This interlude is what enables us to talk with any clarity of stages, since it provides an element of discontinuity and demarcation. It is an important interlude, also, and one which needs to be better understood, since it seems to be of great importance in cultural evolution. We seem to see authoritarianism most strongly entrenched in societies of an intermediate degree of cultural and social complexity: those roughly embraced by Stephens' definition of "kingdom" (Stephens, 1963, p. 328). Stephens finds that societies which are both more simple and more complex show less authoritarian family patterns, and this is closely related to the political structure of the society as a whole (Stephens, pp. 325–339). We would view this back-and-forth movement as one which masks a more general and continuous expansion of consciousness.

The importance of this intermediate authoritarianism is also stressed by other authors. Unwin, for example, maintains that: "Every energetic society has begun its historical career . . . as a monarchy" (Unwin, 1934, p. 370). In a similar vein Durkheim, in tracing the evolution of societies from total and unconscious collectivism to individualism, places great emphasis on the idea that: "rather than dating the effacement of the individual from the institution of a despotic authority, we must, on the contrary, see in this institution the first step made towards individualism. *Chiefs are, in fact, the first personalities who emerge from the social mass*" (Durkheim, 1933, p. 195; italics mine).

Returning to Neumann, we find now two different mythological "stages" which seem to express the second half of this cycle: the overthrow of the leader, or the revolt against the formerly enabling but now irksome identification. The first Neumann calls the "Separation of the World Parents," the second the "Slaying of the Father." A closer look at the phenomena to which these fantasy elements refer will serve to reinforce our belief that a revolt can mean many different things at different times (and to different members as well, of course).

The "Separation of the World Parents," so common a theme in the mythologies of the world, in which a pair of primordial parental deities, usually associated with earth and sky, are forced apart by a youthful hero, is interpreted by Neumann as an expression of the achievement of cognitive differentiation: ". . . this act of cognition, of conscious discrimination, sunders the world into opposites, for experience of the world is only possible through opposites" (Neumann, 1954, p. 104). From a Freudian viewpoint this event would be interpreted either as the dawning of awareness of sexual differences or as a simple Oedipal fantasy, while role theory would suggest a related familial experience: the transition between the time when the father is simply another mother, to the beginning of parental role differentiation. These are not at all incompatible, of course, and their close association suggests the hypothesis that sexual differentiation is critical in facilitating the ability to discriminate among objects and ultimately to form a separate idea of oneself. That some sort of enlightenment is involved seems clear from the frequent association of the beginning of light with this separation: "The separation of the parents allows light to shine where previously there was darkness" (Long, 1963, p. 75). Long also points out that solar deities usually begin their reign following such separations (Long, p. 76). We might also note that human beginnings are frequently traced to this moment (Long, pp. 93, 105,

106), just as group beginnings are so often traced to the separation of leader and group. The earliest attacks on the leader may be interpreted as directed toward this same achievement of differentiation. Prior to this time the leader is seen as identical with the group as a whole. Now there is a growing awareness that the group as a whole (e.g., as an unconscious collusion of compatible defenses) may have purposes which differ sharply from those of the leader. As we have seen, members may react to this by anxiously denying it, by reveling in the clash, or by attempting to resolve the conflict through revolt and selective identification.

The importance of such conscious agreement, and in particular of conscious and deliberate *action*, is illumined rather sharply, if analogically, by Neumann when he points out that the ego "begins simultaneously to constellate its independence of nature as independence of the body." When no distinction is made between oneself and the environment, body stimuli are experienced as alien—they "happen" to one—and in fact this view of the matter is never entirely lost. But as Neumann points out, the child "gradually begins to recognize that essential portions of this . . . corporeal world are subject to its will. . . ." This crucial discovery of "the voluntariness of muscular movement," is, he feels, at the bottom of both magic and the technological mastery of nature. As long as the distinction between the body and the rest of the environment is blurred, one form of control suggests the other (Neumann, 1954, pp. 109–110).

In the group the analogous discovery is of similar importance. Just as a contagious affect may be terrifying because it threatens to drown consciousness, so a *deliberate* group action enormously strengthens collective confidence, group self-awareness, and internal differentiation. This is one of the reasons why the group revolt so often marks a major advance in group consciousness. The fact that a group can act collectively is the defining character of its existence.[92]

Neumann also notes that each change in the level of consciousness brings about a change in affect. Just as the transition from the "uroboric" to the "adolescent" stage is accompanied by fear, because the

[92] Thus Neumann observes that the "meaning of ritual, irrespective of the useful effects which primitive man expects from it, lies precisely in strengthening the conscious system." Magic plays a similar role, although with equal inefficiency, in helping to destroy the forces which bring it into being. "Life remains chaotic for the germinal ego, dark and impenetrable, so long as no orientation is possible with regard to these forces. But orientation comes through ritual, through the subjugation of the world by magic, which imposes world order" (p. 126).

tiny ego senses the unconscious as not only separate but overwhelming, so the "Separation of the World Parents" brings about a change from fear to guilt. This is a result of its *active* nature, which produces a sense of isolation and loneliness. The "struggle into the light" is experienced as a great loss, a fall from paradisal unconsciousness, belonging, and passivity (Neumann, 1954, pp. 113–115). We have similarly noticed the importance of guilt in connection with the group's expulsion of the leader.

Nor does the transition from passivity to activity assume a random direction. We noted above that the expulsion of the leader is an active recapitulation of what was first passively experienced as abandonment. Similarly, Neumann remarks that "what was done to the youthful lover by the maternal uroboros is at this point done to the uroboros itself." The negativity of this deed is also stressed: "To become conscious of oneself, to be conscious at all, begins with saying 'no' to the uroboros, to the Great Mother, to the unconscious. And when we scrutinize the acts upon which consciousness and the ego are built up, we must admit that to begin with they are all negative acts. To discriminate, to distinguish, to mark off, to isolate oneself from the surrounding context—these are the basic acts of consciousness. . . . As against the tendency of the unconscious to combine and melt down . . . consciousness strikes back with the reply 'I am *not* that' " (Neumann, 1954, p. 121). Aggression is thus once again seen as essential to discrimination (Neumann, 1954, p. 124).

The unity which follows this achievement "is no longer the preegoid unity of uroboric containment, but an alliance in which the ego . . . is preserved intact" (Neumann, 1954, p. 116). In other words, a group which has reached a level of consensual differentiation has substituted conscious bonds for unconscious ones.[93] Frank discussion of similarities and differences between members, of likes and dislikes, attractions and repulsions, has been substituted for the unconscious collusion of silence, of polite superficiality, of avoided topics, of passive dependence on the leader. General complicity in perpetuating some tedious intellectual discussion has given way to examination of the ambivalent feelings it symbolizes. Unconscious "agreements" (i.e., joint actions created by individuals who sense each other's similar fantasies and ways of viewing interpersonal relationships) to try and make of the group a battered troupe of oppressed and victimized children,

---

[93] "Conscious" is used here in a broader and more inclusive sense than the mere "visual" consciousness discussed by McLuhan (1962). It implies synaesthesia and interdependence (*Ibid.*, p. 269).

or a phalanx of brave soldiers, or a mass society in which delicate and sensitive spirits are brutalized or go unrecognized, or a rivalrous family in which the good little (bad little) older (younger) male (female) child finally wins its rightful place to exclusive possession of a parent, give way to an exchange of similar and disparate experiences and the feelings produced by them.

We might wonder whether the "Battle of the Sexes" which frequently occurs in groups is not a manifestation of this process. Often, as we have seen, it is the first indication of any awareness that sexual differentiation exists or is relevant to the group situation. The group described by Taylor and Rey (see this volume, pp. 107–108) exhibits an interesting, if atypical, example of this. The group being all female, excepting the therapist, the debate is somewhat onesided, with the members merely vilifying males. At the same time, the attack is the first recognition of their own sexuality, which has heretofore been kept out of the picture. Prior to this time the members, with one exception, are united into a homogeneous mass through their middle-class respectability and timidity and their collusion of silence. When they attack the therapist, first exaggerating his strength and individuality, they are able through identification with him to differentiate themselves from one another and unite consciously around their mutually recognized transference and jealousy. Their later scapegoating of their working-class colleague essentially repeats this process, for she, too, is a differentiated hero—sexualized and, to them, adventurous.

Neumann's next phase is termed the "dragon fight" and is simply a further extension of the previous one. He observes, with Fontenrose, that the male and the female dragon both must be destroyed in the typical myth. For a group member this means simply that the dangers of (1) envelopment in unconscious group forces and (2) submission to the leader must both be conquered. From this point of view, in fact, we would argue that only in groups or cultures which have achieved a fairly high level of development *is* there a male dragon to slay. We would agree with Neumann in equating this male dragon with authoritarianism but would go on to say not only that "without the murder of the 'father' no development of consciousness . . . is possible" (Neumann, 1954, p. 184), but also that without a minimal development of consciousness, authoritarianism is not possible.

The fruits of the dragon fight for the hero are the dragon's captive and/or treasure. This again presents nothing new to us. This degree of development of consciousness is simply the awareness of the personal characteristics of sexual objects, separated from their fantasy counterparts (whether these are viewed as "transpersonal" in the Jungian sense or simply as parental figures). The treasure is knowledge or understanding itself, and union with the captive the freeing of libido: "the feminine image extricates itself from the grip of the Terrible Mother" (Neumann, 1954, p. 198). Neumann observes that "the captive to be set free is personal and hence a possible partner for the man, while the perils he has to overcome are transpersonal forces which . . . hinder the hero's relation to her." In his struggle with feminine monsters he is often assisted by a friendly female of a "sisterly" kind, the latter quality serving to demonstrate their common humanity and her friendliness to his consciousness (Neumann, 1954, p. 201). The rescue of the captive establishes the hero's freedom from incestuous bondage, and he "advances toward 'exogamy'" (Neumann, 1954, p. 202). Instead of being united with the Great Mother the hero "combines with a feminine partner of his own age and kind, in the *hieros gamos*" (Neumann, 1954, p. 198).

All this is of course very familiar to us. We have seen how the "slaying" of the leader tends to free libido bound up in transference and produce a heightening of sexual interest between members. We have also seen how in the revolt even the most Oedipal females take an active role in throwing off the paternal yoke and directing their erotic interest toward their peers. The helpful sisterly figure in the hero myth provides a partial remedy for the rather onesided male view which Freud preserves in his primal horde theory. What is achieved in the group, then, by their struggle with unconscious forces, is knowledge, awareness, understanding, and the rescuing of themselves *for* themselves.

I have attempted to give some rather casual structure to this process in Table 1, which simply presents the consciousness dimension with various familiar schemata arranged along it in roughly probable ways. Since we are dealing with a temporal continuum which requires something analogous to "sequence dating," however, correspondence between rows should not be taken too literally, and individual entries should be viewed as overlapping and horizontally elastic. Furthermore, no course of development in an empirical situation would assume this appearance unless there were only a single sector in relation to which consciousness could arise. In reality, every person or group has pockets of superstition and others of great rationality, and complicated secondary adjustments are made to this unevenness. Thus an industrialized society may value its backward segments and incorporate them into the rest (e.g., the television western).

The most important question, however, is whether there is any justification at all in arranging schemata of individual cognitive development, group development, religious and mythological stages, and social structural patterns as if they all had some organic relation with one another. What is the point, for example, of all this familial imagery? If we are not to accept the Jungian equation of masculinity and consciousness, why do we talk of mothers and fathers in these contexts? To any attempt to interpret mythological, religious, or social-structural phenomena in terms of concrete experiences in concrete families Neumann applies the Jungian pejorative "personalistic," and after performing a few passes to exorcize the Freudian devil, recedes again to Olympus. If we are to move beyond the mere parallelism of Table 1, however, we must concern ourselves with the possibility that such familial experiences are closely related to the development of consciousness.

Unconsciousness becomes associated with maternity (and thus with femininity) simply because of the early inability of the human infant to distinguish itself from the most important individual in its environment, who is almost always the mother. As consciousness grows so does awareness of the mother as a separate and vitally important being, who is both the source of most drive reduction (and, frequently, the ensuing unconsciousness) and an apparent impediment to the reluctant efforts of the infantile ego to establish an independent existence. From the point of view of the emotional and physical state of the infant, the mother is the world and hence total and overpowering.

One could rest content here and argue that consciousness comes to be symbolized as paternal (and thus "masculine") by extrapolation. There is considerable evidence, however, that conscious development is indeed facilitated by the role of the father in the nuclear family, so that the association is bolstered on both sides by actual experience. First, the father, as an alternative parental force, provides differentiation and contrast for the child and hence an opportunity to master the environment. "Divide and conquer" is most meaningful as a description of cognition: one cannot comprehend an undifferentiated totality, while analysis makes control possible.

It may be objected that in many nonliterate societies the father's role in the family is peripheral at best, and other, unfatherlike persons may even play a more important role.[94] This objection turns in our

[94] We need lose no sleep over individual experiences with missing parents or with parental substitutes such as collateral relatives and servants. "Mother" and "father" are part of any person's cultural heritage, and if he is without a parent he will have a fantasy of what that parent might be like and thus will subtract nothing from the mythology handed down to the next generation.

TABLE 1. STAGES IN THE EVOLUTION OF CONSCIOUSNESS AND ITS CORRELATES

Level	Correlate	Uroboric →	Creation →	Great Mother and infant →	Great Mother and adolescent →	Separation of world parents →	Dragon fight →	Captive and treasure
Psychological level	Neumann's mythological stages	Absence of all consciousness and differentiation	Beginning of consciousness (light), unconsciousness positively defined	Germinal ego, negative definition of unconscious as dark and overwhelming	Beginning of active, although unsuccessful struggle by ego, growing narcissism	Capacity for active mastery begins, generating feelings of guilt and loss, awareness of sexuality and contrast	Liberation from both unconscious and defenses against it (primordial parents)	Possession of own libido, acquisition of knowledge and control
Social psychological level	Piaget's stages		Motor or individual stage		Morality of constraint, rules sacred		Morality of cooperation, rules modifiable	
	Fromm's "stages"	Primary ties		Destructiveness	Authoritarianism		Automaton conformity	
	Principal social fear		Waking	Loss of consciousness	Abandonment	Tyranny	Death, Isolation	Overindividuation, Segmentation, "Meaninglessness"
Group level	Bennis' stages			Oral-inclusion		Anal-responsibility	Phallic-intimacy	
	Bion's "stages"			Fight-flight	Dependency		Pairing	
	Nature of group bonds	Unconscious		Through shared fantasy	Through identification with leader	Through revolt, common action, guilt	Through common experience, intimacy	Conscious
Societal level	Riesman's stages	Tradition-directed			Inner-directed		Other-directed	
	Power structure	Pecking order	Group pecking order		Patriarchy		Democratic control	
	Religious response	Positive magic, Taboo	Apotropaism, Personification	Placation, Supplication	Praise, Morality	Dualism, Messianism	Enlightenment, Mysticism	Secularism
	Bellah's stages	Primitive religion	Archaic religion		Historic religion		Early modern religion	Modern religion

favor, however, since to say that a significant paternal role in socializa-
tion is correlated with literacy is also to say it is correlated with consciousness (cf. McLuhan, 1962).[95] This is not necessarily because of
anything the father does—although, as we noted above, in most societies it is the father rather than the mother who places greatest emphasis on sex role differentiation among children—but derives primarily
from his mere existence as a salient and differentiated social object.

McClelland's (1961) recent discussion of the negative consequences of father absence for "need achievement" throws some tangential light on this problem. He cites, among others, Mischel's study of
father-absent children to support the contention that such absence in
early childhood is associated not only with low need for achievement
but also with a correlated inability to delay gratification and seek
long-range goals (McClelland, pp. 328–9, 374–5). The importance of
the father in what is usually referred to as superego development has
also been frequently stressed (cf. Burton and Whiting, 1961). All of
this, while not directly confirming our theory, clearly suggests that
the presence of the father has some facilitating effect on the development of conscious awareness and control over internal impulses and
the external world.

This is the same role that we suggested as intrinsic to the leader
of a group. Are we then arguing that the group recapitulates the
family situation? This would be a reasonable theory but to derive
everything from familial experiences is somewhat limiting. Would it
not be more useful to say that a group member uses the leader to help
differentiate himself from the group as a whole not simply because the
leader "represents" the father in his unconscious, but because this
general device for maximizing boundary-awareness tends to be first
learned in the family, although it is applicable to a wide variety of
situations? Thus, for example, the deification or at least magnification of
leaders has always been important in achieving higher levels of cultural
development, since it permits people to cooperate with one another
with less anxiety at times when awareness of their separateness from
an overpowering world has begun (perhaps aroused by large increases
in the size of the group, change of locale, contact with other societies,
etc.). Later, when the world becomes more manageable, limited, and
understandable, democratization can occur.

But this is only the negative side of this complex process. We have

[95] Note also that our mythological examples are almost all drawn from written
traditions. Father figures of the type indicated are less conspicuous in primitive
mythology.

also noticed that in order to *increase* consciousness, libido is invested in a leader or other individual (or subgroup) and then taken back. Such a person is not only permitted but encouraged to be narcissistic in ways that normally are negatively sanctioned. There seems to be a feeling, as I have suggested elsewhere (Slater, 1963), that this withdrawal and hoarding of libido on the part of the leader will ultimately confer a boon on the collectivity.

This seems to me to be one of the most essential meanings of the primal horde myth: that it is a colorful metaphor for the "inchworm" model of cultural locomotion discussed in the previous chapter. Libido is concentrated in a leader or other specialist, the remainder of the collectivity resting submissive and deprived (the sexually monopolistic father and the victimized sons). The leader or specialist, thereby freed from the obligation to reciprocate the love of his followers, now undertakes to solve a problem for the collectivity ("some cultural advance . . . some new weapon"). Upon achieving success, the members of the collectivity cash in their libidinal investment, with whatever dividends the leader or specialist has achieved for them (they kill, devour, identify with, mourn, venerate the father). But not all of their libido is freed: some is merely transferred to the collectivity and diffused among its members (the women of the family are renounced and exogamy is enforced).

In one sense this is simply the sociological analogue of the pseudopod or the mutation—the intrinsic propensity of living matter to experiment randomly from time to time (although the occasion and mechanism of this process remain largely unknown). But it also reflects the fact that libido, like money or any other form of energy, is most effective when concentrated. Our use of the investment metaphor was deliberate—by such spasmodic concentrations and diffusions of libidinal energy, wealth, and power, civilization has expanded itself.[96]

Some Implications for Sociological Theory

With this modest degree of enlightenment we must unfortunately content ourselves for the present. To move further would require, I believe, a more radical departure from existing sociological assumptions than we have here been able to make. I cannot shake off the conviction

[96] It is perhaps for this reason that in the several developmental sequences discussed, alternate phases seem to have more in common than adjacent ones. This may, however, result merely from the poverty of our conceptualizations.

that the proximate solution to these problems will come from a consideration of the formal processes of association and nucleation at the cellular level, despite the relative sterility this approach has demonstrated in the past. As both fields become increasingly sophisticated it would perhaps occasionally be useful to reexamine these hoary analogues.

At the very least I would hope this book has suggested, even though it has not altogether escaped from, the imprisoning and blinding effects of the traditional psychological and sociological units of person and role. Sociologists have long been aware that it is impossible to make any headway with the common sense notion that a group is an association of persons, but largely on the grounds that a group is "more" than the sum of its component individuals. It might be more productive to stress the fact that it is also a good deal less. Unless we are to remain utterly fixated on physical bodies, it is apparent that a group is not a collection of individuals at all but only of pieces of them. If all of an individual were bound up in a group we could scarcely talk of an individual at all, nor of fears of or wishes for envelopment, since he would in fact be enveloped. This is indeed a serious bar to boundary-awareness in extremely primitive societies in which such a situation almost obtains. The elaboration of cross-cutting groups—age groups, sex groups, kinship groups, territorial groups—helps to minimize this condition, and this may in fact be one of the major functions of totemism. As a result of such cross-cutting groups an individual's libido is much diffused, and what we see of him in a given group is an arrangement of feelings, needs, and desires which in no respect constitute a representative sample of his personality.

This point has been made often. But I wonder if the favored sociological unit—the disembodied role, divested of the needs, the motives, the feelings which, however group-specific they may be, nonetheless derive from a breathing organism—has not also exhausted its limited fertility. While most progress in the sciences has come from systematically ignoring large portions of the data at any given time, I cannot see how an understanding of groups can proceed beyond its current level unless the unit of analysis in some way embodies that segment of an individual's instinctual life which he commits to a group. Social scientists have too long tried to operate under the implicit assumption that when more than a few people are gathered together their emotionality and animality can somehow be disregarded. To arrive at abstract principles of association we need not limit ourselves to the utilization of purely symbolic units. In practice such a selection springs largely from sociological chauvinism and cannot be justified on strategic grounds. The process of abstraction is most successfully effected when based on an awareness rather than a denial of the complexity of the subject matter. It is to such an awareness that the present work is dedicated.

APPENDIX I

Some Considerations Concerning Leader Goals and Techniques

It would perhaps be appropriate to say a few words about the educational goals of a group leader in situations such as I have described. Members of groups with which I am familiar benefit in inverse proportion to their therapeutic need, although the not uncommon decision to seek psychotherapy during or following a group experience perhaps forms an exception to this rule. Many members strive assiduously to transform the situation into group psychotherapy, sometimes with partial success. A group leader who believes in his noninterfering role cannot very well prevent this if there is any consensus in the group. It may in fact be an expression of revolt—taking the group away from the leader and making it into something *they* want.

It may help to point out, however, some of the ways in which the group leader's emphasis in an educational setting does differ from that of a therapist. Perhaps the principal differences are that (1) he himself exerts no pressure whatever to bring about the revelation to the group of personal experiences outside the group; (2) he less often makes interpretations of individual behavior, concentrating primarily on responses shared by more than one or two people; (3) he is more approving of intellectualization, except insofar as this pertains to immediate feelings and reactions within the group situation; (4) he includes in the category of valued insight observations of an essentially sociological nature about the group.

It may be noted that for some group therapists these differences are major while for others they are not differences at all, since few therapists try to concentrate on everything at once and some proceed much as described above.

I can conceive of four basic kinds of information and hence six kinds of relationships that can be apprehended in a group situation (ignoring for the moment the individual-group distinction which would generate a confusing number of categories): (*a*) the personal history of the individual, (*b*) reactions and experiences in the immediate group situation, (*c*) reactions and interpretations regarding events external to the individual or group (e.g., personal history of others, written case materials, current events, etc.), and (*d*) sociological and psychological theories, concepts, and generalizations. Only an understanding of the complete interrelationship of all of these could be considered total insight, but as far as I know no one attempts to achieve such a thing, nor is there any particular reason why they should. The relation between (*a*) and (*b*) is the most important for therapeutic purposes, since it concerns the understanding of transference reactions. The relation between (*c*) and (*d*) is the traditional academic domain, i.e., the application of theory to data. This is often extended in psychology courses to the theoretical interpretation of personal biographies or dreams [(*a*) and (*d*)], and in academic group process courses to the theoretical interpretation of group experiences [(*b*) and (*d*)], both of which are exercises in intellectualization and essentially nontherapeutic, although they do perhaps facilitate a kind of psychological openness and sensitivity, an awareness and perceptiveness which can be extended to everything except one's fundamental neurotic problems. Group therapists typically (and rightly) avoid (*d*) as much as possible, and hence it is here that there is a real conflict of influence between teacher and therapist, since the former is inadvertently improving the individual's accommodation to what the latter is trying to reform altogether.

The relations between (*a*) and (*c*) and between (*b*) and (*c*) both revolve around identification and displacement (see Slater, 1962). Both are used to some extent by group therapists but far more by training-group leaders, especially in academic settings. The latter tend to use the (*b*) and (*c*) relationship exclusively, while group therapists use both, some schools restricting themselves to one or the other. (The issue here is whether a discussion of, let us say, a political issue, will be interpreted as reflecting the here-and-now group structure or problems in the lives of the individual speakers.)

One aspect of the (*b*) and (*c*) relationship I find to be particularly important in academic settings is quite irrelevant to the therapy situation. This is the necessity of confronting the group from time to time with a problem external to itself, so that certain collective illusions may be more easily dispelled, e.g., that they really share the same facts and perceptions. Groups are much prone to forming "tacit understandings," which are really agreements to pretend to agree or understand in order to preserve certain satisfying group structures. They also become inbred and ethnocentric and try to shrug off the external world, which in an academic setting is intolerable even as a temporary condition.

The diagram below illustrates these distinctions. Solid lines represent the modal academic approach, dotted lines the modal therapeutic approach. The more commonly the connection is stressed the greater the number of lines. Specific schools of course may show a variety of other constellations.

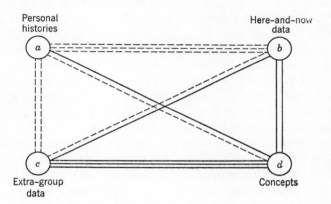

The goal of any educational activity is understanding, a process which is equivalent to innovation (whether invention or borrowing) at the cultural level. Like a cultural innovation a new idea may fit easily into the existing mental structure, or it may require extensive reorganization of that structure. But whether education and psychotherapy are only quantitatively or also qualitatively different, one can at least make a conceptual distinction between understanding what is happening in a group of which one is a member and modifying one's personality structure. One can also make a distinction between such understanding and the development of a more complex and adaptable group structure.

The group leader in an educational setting hopes to bring about an increased understanding by all individuals in the group, including himself, of the psychosocial processes which arise there. Theoretically this could be achieved without significant psychotherapeutic gains for the individual and with little group development. In practice there is some overlap in both directions. While individuals can learn from their failure to develop a group structure worthy of the name, they learn much more from having ultimately succeeded, as well, and from the mere quantity of experience which comes from passing through different kinds of transitions. Similarly, learning anything at all about one's own reactions and contributions to group processes is likely to have some therapeutic effect, even if far less than is usually imagined by the participant.

What we are saying is that when there is no beginning toward the solution of the dependency issue, there will be neither group development, nor understanding, nor therapeutic gain, but that if substantial progress is made in meeting this problem, there will be no further relationship between the three areas. Note, for example, that libidinal cathexis of peers rather than group leader is of not the slightest consequence for the psychological health of the individual. His responses may be just as totally based on transference as before, with parental figures now being represented by other group members (cf. Wolf, 1963, pp. 303 ff.). Yet the group as a whole will be able to function in ways it was unable to before. This will be true, furthermore, even if the transition is not understood by the members.

The distinction between group understanding and group development is perhaps made clearer by considering these in relation to the notion of "acting out." Groups that are never able to verbalize their anger toward the group leader in a sustained and truly collective manner are in my experience generalized failures: they perform poorly in all areas (cf. Wolf, 1963, p. 286). But acting out this anger by expelling the leader or taking his chair adds very little to the process of understanding. Indeed, groups which have never gone beyond verbalizing their collective anger have sometimes impressed me as being superior in understanding to groups which incorporated it in some kind of action. Yet behaviorally and structurally groups which have acted out their revolt are different—more confident, active, flexible, and versatile—regardless of how they appeared prior to it.

A word might also be said about the conditions under which groups are most predisposed to revolt. It is my impression that the larger the group the easier it is to revolt, and that youth and impulsivity are also contributory. Robert Greenway reports in a personal communication that high school students revolt with unusual regularity in a similar setting. Elsewhere (Slater, 1957) I have suggested that group size and impulsivity or aggressiveness are not unrelated.

It is perhaps appropriate to ask here why the leader, who seeks only understanding, agrees to leave the group at all. Why should he not, as in so many other cases, simply probe for feelings and motives associated with the desire to expel him until the issue is "resolved" (i.e., dies down)? The answer lies in the ambiguous word "experiment." At one level the expulsion is just what it initially and superficially purports to be—an attempt to test reality. As Freud pointed out long ago, there comes a time when the agoraphobic patient must simply try walking in the street, and no amount of analysis will make this step either unnecessary or easy. The group leader leaves because he recognizes the need of the group to try its wings and see the effect. There is no question, moreover, but that the "experiment" is often important in consolidating group strength. An amusing symbolic statement of this occurred in IIg when, after a leader absence, a member recited a fairy tale in which the heroes return to their village after an absence of 200 years and find everything changed.

Some group leaders affect to leave because of obedience to majority rule in a group in which they are "just another member." This strikes me as ridiculous for two reasons. First the hypocrisy and sham in this pretense of not having a special role and a special authority in the group have no place in a setting dedicated to enlightenment. Second, if the leader is never to oppose the will of the majority, it is difficult to see what appeal other individuals will have from the vicious fatuities to which unopposed majorities are always subject.

In many academic settings the pretense of having no authority would be especially hollow inasmuch as the group leader maintains his grading function, which, if not the "power of life and death" as one student put it, is at least the power to facilitate or terminate a college career, and many students have in fact been terminated by failure to master traditional requirements in such courses. Even if this is relinquished through some device such as having the members grade each other, one cannot very well pretend that it was not the leader who brought the group together and maintains it as part of an institutionalized program.

Even could this be done I would question its value. Is it not of more significance for a group of individuals to relinquish their dependence on a real authority than to pretend dependency is not a problem by having the leader artificially mute or mask his authority? I suspect that the latter approach solves more problems for the leader than for the other members. Not only can he avoid the dependency issue, he can also be loved as an equal. Finally, when the leader's separateness and authority are more manifest he knows perfectly well that the almost supernatural virtues and abilities sometimes attributed to him are a function of his role, while the masked leader, supposedly divested of his authority, can pretend that they are a response to his personal brilliance and humanity. Regardless of the role he assumes, there is always an expectation that the leader knows a great deal, and interpretations often sound frightfully clever or poignant to the novice no matter how hackneyed they may be in fact.

When the leader maintains his grading function, furthermore, the revolt against him is not simply a gamelike gesture without risks, but requires either courage or trust in the leader's lack of vindictiveness or both.

Finally, I hold no brief for any of the styles of leader behavior and technique which appear, in rather tachistoscopic and unrepresentative fashion, in the examples in this volume. I have indeed always been struck by the minuteness of the differences in group structure brought about by the grossest stylistic contrasts. What seems to me most important in questions of technique is variation itself—that a given approach not be maintained after it has become stale and ossified. By this I do not mean necessarily that the leader must be "authentic" or "genuine." This, too, is a style, and like all styles expresses only some of the needs of both the group and the leader. I am referring rather to a phenomenon which I have observed in ordinary teaching settings: that any educational innovation almost always generates excitement and enthusiasm for a few years and then becomes a dead hand throttling the learning process. At this point another innovation is required, and even if it is nothing more than a sharp reversion to traditional techniques it will tend to generate some of the same responsiveness for a period of time. This is not to say that all innovations are of equal value but only that no change is of permanent value. A leader who never alters his technique has ceased to learn, and he who has ceased to learn can hardly help others to learn.

APPENDIX II

Some Problems Regarding Exemplification

The examples appearing in this book are taken from the author's notes and transcripts or from personal communications with other group leaders unless references are given. Examples with the same Roman numeral are drawn from the same group leader. Examples with the same Roman numeral and the same letter are drawn from the same group.

The use of examples presents many problems. In some instances I have verbatim transcripts to draw upon, while in others I have only notes written immediately following a session—notes which often turn out to refer in broad conceptual terms to what was recalled as a prize example of some process or other, rather than presenting any data which could successfully convey the process to someone else. One also has to make horrendous decisions about lifting material from context. If one takes only the segment of a discussion which deals with the process under consideration one may be distorting the picture enormously and ignoring the very connections that make the process understandable. On the other hand, if one tries to summarize the entire discussion and interpret all of its ramifications and thematic interrelationships and subplots one becomes bogged down in detail, loses sight of the central point, and seems merely to be showing that everything is connected with everything else. As will become evident, I have avoided neither of these pitfalls, zigzagging into the mouths of Scylla and Charybdis alternately. Finally, it may seem absurd that in my own groups (those involving the number II) I have referred to myself always in the third person. This is done not merely to provide homogeneity, but also because the use of the first person is highly distracting in reading reports of this kind: Bion's papers, I feel, suffer from this defect, despite the candor of his reporting. This may, however, be simply a matter of taste. Names of group members are (with one necessary exception) fictitious.

Selection always involves a bias of some kind unless performed with mechanical safeguards, and some consideration of the distortion introduced by the selection of examples here is therefore appropriate. First it should be emphasized that examples can only illustrate, not demonstrate. Hypotheses are being developed rather than tested, and the purpose of the examples is merely to provide an empirical referent for the ideas advanced. For it is from these experiences that the ideas themselves emerged. Indeed, neither the theories nor the empirical studies with which I was most impressed when I began this enterprise have proved particularly useful, while on the other hand those theoretical notions upon which ultimately I relied so heavily were either unknown to me (as in the case of Mills, Bennis, and Neumann) or objects of disinterest (Piaget) or disregard (Freud's *Totem and Taboo*).

This means that the examples chosen should not be viewed as any sort of representative sample of group interaction. They are selected to illustrate the points made and naturally leave out other important preoccupations of groups. They are heavily weighted, for example, on the member-leader as opposed to the member-member relationship and on group rather than individual concerns.

Most of all, they necessarily exaggerate the importance of the dramatic or symbolic event, at the expense of the real day-to-day accomplishments for which these events are merely a kind of metaphorical representation. Unfortunately the human need to reduce gradual change and development to sudden and violent transformations is a powerful one, as instanced by the universal use of ritual and ceremony to mark transition. The sophisticated may recognize that a boy does not change into a man all at once during a puberty rite, or a neurotic individual into a healthy one during a dramatic catharsis-and-insight session in psychotherapy. But "working through" is a profoundly dull and uninteresting process, and the tiny increments derived from it, while of the greatest ultimate importance, tell us nothing essentially new. While we must understand that the individual (or group) is more changed before the event than he thinks (otherwise the event could not take place) and less changed after it than he thinks, some concession must nevertheless be made to the frailty of author and reader: we must first look at what is condensed, direct, and obvious, until it becomes familiar enough to look beyond it.

The examples I have used are therefore not necessarily the "best" ones. They are simply the most crudely condensed ones.

A corollary result is that the groups are portrayed in a somewhat unkindly light, highlighted when blindly acting out and ignored when working and insightful. To construct a functioning group in which all or most members are integrated without the aid of social dishonesty is a painstaking task which proceeds in a block-by-block fashion. Often I have presented a series of scattered meetings which revealed changing attitudes toward the leader but omitted the intervening sessions in which the group was concentrating on building its own solidarity—providing the foundation for such attitudinal change by partial mutual confrontations and so forth. Yet it is these omitted sessions which usually inspire remarks in my notes about how well they are working. They seem to occur in "bursts" of five or six sessions and contain almost nothing in the way of a briefly described incident which might illustrate the phenomenon. Apparently, important things simply happen too gradually to be thus exemplified.

I should also like to consider here the effect produced on group members by their already having read or heard about group revolts or other phenomena of the kind described in this volume. Could it not be argued that much of the material presented is merely a documentation of the effects of our own interpretations and associations, faithfully re-enacted by helpful group members? Can we treat as "evidence" cases which involve so much contamination?

I think I would answer no to both of these questions. Contrary to some versions of the experiment myth, these groups were not designed as experiments and satisfy none of the criteria for hypothesis testing. The examples are, as I have stated, merely illustrative. At the same time, it would be mendacious to pretend that I am not personally convinced of the validity of at least some of the generalizations I have presented, and these are typically distinguishable by the rather larger number of examples I have included in order to seduce the reader into sharing this obstinacy. Thus while I will try to show why I think the regurgitation interpretation of these phenomena is absurd, it is only fair to admit also that where there are several examples of the same phenomenon, a case could easily be made that they are not entirely independent of one another.

There are three related sources of contamination. The first is through hearing about other groups, the second through reading, and the third through the leader's interpretations. They correspond to situations familiar elsewhere in the social sciences such as the problem of secrecy in experiments with student subjects, the problem of diffusion in cross-cultural analyses, and the problem of clinical evidence in psychotherapeutic situations.

Experimental "rigor" in the social sciences is often established by convention rather than logic. One such convention is that one is permitted to treat as independent cases subjects who are sworn to secrecy in the cooling-out period following an experiment in which foreknowledge of the experimental conditions is undesirable, provided that one includes in one's report the phrase that "so far as we know this request was adhered to" or some equivalent. I doubt that many experimenters are so naive as to believe that many of their subjects are so dedicated to social science as to withhold such information from the first person to ask, but since there is no practical alternative to such a procedure, it is accepted as a necessary expedient. Furthermore, although we know that students talk continually about experiments they have been in, it is my impression that those experimenters who have endeavored to discover after the fact how many subjects were actually forewarned have turned up very few cases. Perhaps curiosity is so important a motive for participation in experiments that forewarned prospects drop out altogether, or perhaps those subjects who were forewarned were ashamed to reveal it.

In our groups there is no attempt whatever at such control. Usually a number of the group members have heard a lot about previous groups from friends. I have always been impressed, however, with how little generalization proceeds from this information. In my experience, groups have an exaggerated concept of their own uniqueness, both in pride and in despair, and seem invariably to view their group as vastly different from whatever groups they have heard or read about. Their capacity to distort information about these other groups, furthermore, is impressive (as in the case of experimental subjects), and I often experience difficulty in reconstructing the factual kernel of events alleged to have happened before my eyes. In addition, any group which they read about is usually viewed as having been conducted in an entirely different manner, the other group's leader usually being seen as much more or much less active, or even nonexistent. It is difficult for me to imagine a group imitating the performance of a previous one because I am so used to these assumptions and protestations of group individuality. Nothing could be more of a cliché, for example, than bringing in food or drink or sitting in the leader's chair; yet I doubt that many individuals would be motivated to perform either act, or could muster such self-congratulatory expressions in doing so, if they did not think it was their own inspiration. Despite their dependent longings there is a strong reaction of embarrassment, anger, and futility when a group discovers it has been behaving in accordance with a known formula, and the argument that such would be the case has been enough to smother revolt behavior more than once.

While no effort is made to control intergroup communication, in most of the groups herein described reading bearing directly on these issues is assigned late in the group's career. Some students will already have encountered some of this material, however, so that it cannot be assumed that no "diffusion" of this type has taken place. Initially, of course, readings which discuss or analogically suggest the phenomena in this volume were assigned because we had been made aware of their relevance through events in our groups. Our subject matter thus resembles many primitive societies, which lost their uncontaminated state almost before professional anthropologists could bring sophisticated techniques and theories to bear on them.

An additional problem arises from the fact that our primary goal in the groups is a didactic one. Through interpretations and reading materials we attempt continually to deepen the student's understanding of the experiences he is undergoing. The moment we find reading material which might help the members understand group processes we add it to our repertory, without waiting for any research accumulation. (This does not mean, of course, that we could predict with any accuracy how a reading would be used. We were often surprised and enlightened at the uses to which a given reading was put.) This means our material is hopelessly inadequate for research purposes. Our position is analogous to the one Freud found himself in: as a doctor he felt obligated to apply his knowledge as fast as it was—or seemed to be—acquired, thus becoming vulnerable to the charge that the phenomena he observed had been implanted in his patients by his own interpretations.

There is no way out of these dilemmas, but we can at least strip them of their more absurd assumptions. The foremost of these is the notion that exposure to an idea leads automatically to its adoption. This is the essence of the cultural diffusion explanation of social change, which is a form of contiguity-magic, the spatial version of *post hoc propter hoc* reasoning. An idea, or any item of a given culture, is not adopted by another unless it holds some meaning or value for the latter, and a group that has read *Totem and Taboo* is not under an automatic compulsion to attack the leader. The idea of revolt is not after all an unfamiliar one; it could be suggested by the morning newspaper. Group members are bombarded with information and ideas at all times, yet do not necessarily act them out in the group situation. They read Piaget without suggesting a marble game, they read Bettelheim without enacting mock initiation rites, they read Veblen without engaging in conspicuous consumption, *Street Corner Society* without inaugurating a bowling league, Lillian Smith without instituting segregation, and so forth. They also read Malinowski's *Sex and Repression in Savage Society,* which provides a convenient rationale for ignoring *Totem and Taboo* altogether.

It is indeed difficult to convey how far from automatic is the connection between an idea and its application to the immediate group. As can be seen from some of the examples included in this volume, even after students *have* read the Bennis and Shepard paper the idea of expelling the leader often does not occur to them. Occasionally the relevant passage seems not to have been perceived or remembered. A member will announce to the group what an interesting paper he has found and then give a summary which entirely omits this passage. Sometimes it is mentioned, but in rather abstract terms, so that one could not imagine exactly in what way the Bennis and Shepard groups "got along without" the leader. Sometimes the process is made clear but in the context of a description which assumes (as is usually the case) that the Bennis and Shepard groups were somehow of an entirely different order.

Finally, many things read, perceived, understood, associated to the group, and *told* to the group are not heard when the majority is not ready to deal with them. Bright counterdependent individuals often come up with the idea of group revolt, and if the group as a whole is not more or less "on the verge" it is as if they were speaking an unknown language. The individual who gets credit for the suggestion is usually the third or fourth person to mention it; his predecessors seem even to have forgotten it themselves.

Probably the best example of the way external ideas are utilized in a thoroughly "contaminated" revolt is the discussion from Group IVd in Chapter II. Here the seriousness of the ambivalent striving toward independence seems clear and appears to antedate the playful manipulation of the "primal horde" theme. On the other hand, although the members talk vaguely and lengthily about "getting rid of" the leader, it is not until near the end of the second two-hour meeting that this is discussed in concrete and immediate terms. Even then it arouses some surprise and is ultimately dropped.

What is important and meaningful in the propulsion of the IVd revolt, however, is the group's admiring anger at the leader and the intense and persistent desire to run the group "on their own." All of their exotic imagery expresses these feelings, and if we were to strip it all away they would still be visible. The theatrics and the dramatic incidents change from group to group, but the underlying feelings always appear in one form or another. In my experience, in fact, the "big events" of a group show a conspicuous incapacity for diffusion. It almost seems as if knowledge that a dramatic incident had occurred in a former group establishes a kind of ownership, and if it should be mentioned in a subsequent group it is usually with a gloomy invidiousness. ("They had a really *exciting* group. *Nothing* ever happens here.") It cannot in any case be stated too often that the particular event or metaphor appearing in a group is the product of a great many factors, a large number of which are irrelevant to the issues I have raised.

It would certainly not be difficult to put together a dozen or so examples of deification or revolt which were free from any sort of contamination, and a few of the examples included here can be so regarded. My purpose, however, is not to demonstrate that some bit of behavior (or some specific set of words) can occur in a group (which I regard as long since demonstrated by others) or that it will always occur in groups such as these (which it most clearly will not) but rather to explore the feelings and ideas underlying them and the possible connections between them, and to pass on, for whatever purpose they may be put to, a group of observations which occasioned my surprise when I first came to make them.

Bibliography

Alexander, F., and French, T. M. *Psychoanalytic Therapy* (New York: Ronald, 1946).

Ames, M. M. Buddha and the dancing goblins: a theory of magic and religion. *American Anthropologist*, **66**, 78–82 (1964).

Apollodorus. *The Library*. Loeb Classical Library (1954).

Baruch, Dorothy W. *One Little Boy* (New York: Julian Press, 1952).

Bell, N. W., and Vogel, E. F. (eds.). *A Modern Introduction to the Family* (Glencoe, Ill.: The Free Press, 1960).

Bellah, R. N. Religious evolution. *American Sociological Review*, **29**, 358–374 (1964).

Bennis, W. G. A genetic theory of group development. Unpublished manuscript, Massachusetts Institute of Technology (1957).

Bennis, W. G. Defenses against "depressive anxiety" in groups: the case of the absent leader. *Merrill-Palmer Quarterly*, **7**, 3–30 (1961).

Bennis, W. G. Towards a "truly" scientific management: the concept of organizational health. *Industrial Management Review*, **4**, 1–28 (1962).

Bennis, W. G., and Shepard, H. A. A theory of group development. *Human Relations*, **9**, 415–437 (1956).

Bettelheim, B. *Symbolic Wounds* (London: Thames and Hudson, 1955).

Bion, W. R. Experiences in groups: III. *Human Relations*, **2**, 13–22 (1949).

Bion, W. R. Experiences in groups: IV. *Human Relations*, **2**, 295–303 (1949).

Bion, W. R. Group dynamics: a re-view. In Klein, Melanie, Heimann, Paula, and Money-Kyrle, R. E. (eds.) *New Directions in Psycho-analysis* (New York: Basic Books, 1957, 440–477.

Boas, F. *Tsimshian Mythology*. Thirty-first Annual Report of the U. S. Bureau of Ethnology, 1909–1910 (1916).

Brody, Sylvia. *Patterns of Mothering* (New York: International Universities Press, 1956).

Burton, R. V. and Whiting, J. W. M. The absent father and cross-sex identity. *Merrill-Palmer Quarterly*, **7**, 85–95 (1961).

Campbell, J. *The Hero with a Thousand Faces* (New York: Pantheon, 1949).

Caplan, G. Mental health aspects of social work in public health. School of Social Welfare, Univ. of Calif., Berkeley (1955).

Caplan, G. (ed.). *Emotional Problems of Early Childhood* (New York: Basic Books, 1955).

Cash, W. J. *The Mind of the South* (New York: Knopf, 1941).

Coser, L. A. *Sociology Through Literature* (Englewood Cliffs, N. J.: Prentice-Hall, 1963).

Coulanges, N. D. Fustel de. *The Ancient City* (Garden City, N. Y.: Doubleday, 1956).

Durkheim, E. *The Division of Labor in Society* (Glencoe, Ill.: The Free Press, 1933).

Durkheim, E. *The Elementary Forms of the Religious Life* (Glencoe, Ill.: The Free Press, no date).

Eisenstadt, S. N. Social change, differentiation and evolution. *American Sociological Review,* **29,** 375–386 (1964).

Ezriel, H. A psycho-analytic approach to group treatment. *British J. Medical Psychol.,* **23,** 59–74 (1950).

Fauconnet, M. Mythology of black Africa. In *Larousse Encyclopedia of Mythology* (New York: Prometheus Press, 1959), 480–492.

Ferenczi, S. Symbolism (1912). In *Sex in Psychoanalysis* (New York: Basic Books, 1950), 253–281.

Ferenczi, S. *Thalassa: A Theory of Genitality* (New York: Psychoanalytic Quarterly, 1938).

Festinger, L., Riecken, H. W., Jr., and Schachter, S. *When Prophecy Fails* (Minneapolis: Univ. of Minnesota Press, 1956).

Fontenrose, J. *Python: A Study of Delphic Myth and Its Origins* (Berkeley and Los Angeles: Univ. of California Press, 1959).

Frank, J. D., Margolin, J., Nash, Helen T., Stone, A. R., Varon, Edith, and Ascher, E. Two behavior patterns in therapeutic groups and their apparent motivation. *Human Relations,* **5,** 289–314 (1952).

Frazer, J. G. *The Golden Bough* (London: MacMillan, 1900).

Frazer, J. G. *Adonis, Attis, Osiris* (London: MacMillan, 1906).

Frazer, J. G. *The New Golden Bough.* Edited by T. H. Gaster (New York: Criterion Books, 1959).

Freeman, L. C., and Winch, R. F. Societal complexity: an empirical test of a typology of societies. *American Journal of Sociology,* **62,** 461–466 (1957).

Freud, Anna. *The Ego and the Mechanisms of Defense* (New York: International Universities Press, 1946).

Freud, S. New Introductory Lectures in Psychoanalysis (1933). In *The Standard Edition of the Complete Psychological Works of Sigmund Freud* (London: Hogarth, 1964), Vol. XXII, 7–182.

Freud, S. *Beyond the Pleasure Principle* (New York: Liveright, 1950).

Freud, S. *Totem and Taboo* (London: Kegan Paul, 1950).

Freud, S. *Group Psychology and the Analysis of the Ego* (New York: Liveright, 1951).

Freud, S. *Civilization and Its Discontents* (London: Hogarth, 1953).

Freud, S. *Collected Papers: Vol. II* (London: Hogarth, 1956).

Freud, S. *Moses and Monotheism* (New York: Vintage, 1958).

Fromm, E. *Escape from Freedom* (New York: Rinehart, 1941).

Gloag, J. *Our Mother's House* (New York: Simon and Schuster, 1963).

Golding, W. *Lord of the Flies* (New York: Putnam, 1955).

Gouldner, A. W., and Peterson, R. A. *Notes on Technology and the Moral Order* (New York: Bobbs-Merrill, 1962).

Graves, R. *The Greek Myths* (Baltimore: Penguin Books, 1955).

Harrison, Jane Ellen. *Mythology* (London: Longmans, Green, 1924).

Harrison, Jane Ellen. *Prolegomena to the Study of Greek Religion* (New York: Meridian Books, 1957).

Hesiod. *Theogony* (Loeb Classical Library, 1959).

Homer. *The Iliad* (Modern Library, 1950).

Huizinga, J. *Homo Ludens* (Boston: Beacon Press, 1950).

Jones, R. M. *An Application of Psychoanalysis to Education* (Springfield, Ill.: Charles C Thomas, 1960).

Jung, C. G. *Psyche and Symbol* (New York: Doubleday, 1958).

Kardiner, A. *The Individual and His Society* (New York: Columbia Univ. Press, 1939).

King, L. W. *The Seven Tablets of Creation* (London: Luzac, 1902).

Kluckhohn, C. Universal categories of culture. In A. L. Kroeber (ed.) *Anthropology Today* (Chicago: University of Chicago Press, 1953).

Kroeber, A. L. "Totem and Taboo" in retrospect. In *The Nature of Culture* (Chicago: Univ. of Chicago Press, 1952).

Langdon, S. *The Babylonian Epic of Creation* (London: Oxford Univ. Press, 1923).

Lévi-Strauss, C. *Les Structures Élémentaires de la Parenté* (Paris: Presses Universitaires de France, 1949).

Lévi-Strauss, C. *Totemism* (Boston: Beacon Press, 1963).

Likert, R. *New Patterns of Management* (New York: McGraw-Hill, 1961).

Limentani, D. Symbiotic identification in schizophrenia. *Psychiatry,* **19,** 231–236 (1956).

Linton, R. *The Tree of Culture* (New York: Knopf, 1959).

Long, C. H. *Alpha: The Myths of Creation* (New York: Braziller, 1963).

Lorenz, K. Z. The role of aggression in group formation. In B. Schaffner (ed.), *Group Processes: 1957 Conference* (New York: Macy Foundation, 1959).

Malinowski, B. *Magic, Science and Religion* (Glencoe, Ill.: Free Press, 1948).

Mann, R. D. The development of the member-trainer relationship in self-analytic groups. *Human Relations* (in press).

Maslow, A. H. The need to know and the fear of knowing. *Journal of General Psychology,* **68,** 111–125 (1963).

Maslow, A. H. Synergy in the society and in the individual. *J. Indiv. Psychol.,* **20,** 153–164 (1964).

McClelland, D. C. *The Achieving Society* (Princeton, N. J.: Van Nostrand, 1961).

McLuhan, H. M. *The Gutenberg Galaxy* (Univ. of Toronto Press, 1962).

Miller, N. E. and Dollard, J. *Social Learning and Imitation* (New Haven: Yale Univ. Press, 1941).

Mills, T. M. A sociological interpretation of Freud's "Group Psychology and the Analysis of the Ego." Unpublished manuscript (1959).

Mills, T. M. Authority and group emotion. In Bennis, W. G., Schein, E. H., Berlew, D. E., and Steele, F. I. (eds.) *Interpersonal Dynamics* (Homewood, Ill.: Dorsey, 1964), 94–108.

Mills, T. M. *Group Transformation: An Analysis of a Learning Group* (Englewood Cliffs, N. J.: Prentice-Hall, 1964).

Neumann, E. *The Origins and History of Consciousness* (New York: Pantheon, 1954).

Neumann, E. *The Great Mother* (New York: Pantheon, 1955).

Ogilvie, D. M. An exploration of identification following aggressive acts. Unpublished honors thesis, Harvard University (1961).

Opie, Iona, and Opie, P. *The Lore and Language of Schoolchildren* (London: Oxford University Press, 1960).

Parsons, T. Evolutionary universals in society. *American Sociological Review,* **29,** 339–357 (1964).

Patai, R. *Sex and Family in the Bible and the Middle East* (Garden City, New York: Doubleday, 1959).

Piaget, J. *The Moral Judgment of the Child* (London: Kegan Paul, 1932).

Pruden, D. A. A sociological study of a Texas lynching. In Wilson, L., and Kolb, W. L. (eds.), *Sociological Analysis* (New York: Harcourt, Brace, 1949), 335–343.

Queen, S. A., Habenstein, R. W., and Adams, J. B. *The Family in Various Cultures* (New York: Lippincott, 1961).

Rank, O. *The Myth of the Birth of the Hero* (New York: Brunner, 1952).

Raper, A. F. *The Tragedy of Lynching* (Chapel Hill: Univ. of No. Carolina Press, 1933).

Redl, F. Group emotion and leadership. *Psychiatry,* **5,** 573–596 (1942).

Redl, F. The impact of game-ingredients on children's play behavior. In B. Schaffner (ed.), *Group Processes: 1957 Conference* (New York: Macy Foundation, 1959), 33–81.

Renault, Mary. *The King Must Die* (New York: Pocket Books, 1960).

Riesman, D. *The Lonely Crowd* (Garden City, New York: Doubleday, 1955).

Rodrigué, E. The analysis of a three-year-old mute schizophrenic. In Klein, Melanie, Heimann, Paula, and Money-Kyrle, R. E. (eds.), *New Directions in Psycho-analysis* (New York: Basic Books, 1957), 140–179.

Rosen, J. N. *Direct Analysis* (New York: Grune and Stratton, 1953).

Rougemont, D. de. *Love in the Western World* (Garden City, New York: Doubleday, 1957).

Schachtel, E. G. On memory and childhood amnesia. In Mullahy, P. (ed.), *A Study of Interpersonal Relations* (New York: Hermitage, 1949), 3–49.

Searles, H. F. The evolution of the mother transference in psychotherapy with the schizophrenic patient. In Burton, A. (ed.), *Psychotherapy of the Psychoses* (New York: Basic Books, 1961), 256–284.

Slater, P. E. Contrasting correlates of group size. *Sociometry,* **21,** 129–139 (1958).

Slater, P. E. The Glory of Hera (Unpublished manuscript, 1961).

Slater, P. E. Parental role differentiation. *American Journal of Sociology,* **67,** 296–308 (1961).

Slater, P. E. Toward a dualistic theory of identification. *Merrill-Palmer Quarterly,* **7,** 113–126 (1961).

Slater, P. E. Displacement in groups. In Bennis, W. G., Benne, K. D., and Chin, R. (eds.), *The Planning of Change* (New York: Holt, 1961), 725–736.

Slater, P. E. On social regression. *American Sociological Review,* **28,** 339–364 (1963).

Slater, P. E., and Bennis, W. G. Democracy is inevitable. *Harvard Business Review,* **42,** 51–59 (1964).

Smelser, N. J. *Theory of Collective Behavior* (New York: Free Press, 1963).

Smith, C. W. Social units and collectivities (Unpublished manuscript, Brandeis Univ., 1965).

Spencer, H. *The Principles of Sociology* (New York: Appleton, 1896).

Stephens, W. N. *The Family in Cross-Cultural Perspective* (New York: Holt, 1963).

Stock, Dorothy, and Thelen, H. A. *Emotional Dynamics and Group Culture* (New York: New York University Press, 1958).

Stone, P. J., Bales, R. F., Namenwirth, J. Z., and Ogilvie, D. M. The "General Inquirer": a computer system for content analysis and retrieval based on the sentence as a unit of information. *Behavioral Science*, 7 (1962).

Sturluson, Snorri. *The Prose Edda*, trans. by A. G. Brodeur (New York: American-Scandinavian Foundation, 1916).

Swanson, G. E. *The Birth of the Gods* (Ann Arbor, Mich.: Univ. of Michigan Press, 1960).

Talmon, Yonina. Mate selection in collective settlements. *American Sociological Review*, 29, 491–508 (August 1964).

Taylor, F. K., and Rey, J. H. The scapegoat motif in society and its manifestations in a therapeutic group. *International Journal of Psychoanalysis*, 34, 253–264 (1953).

Unwin, J. D. *Sex and Culture* (London: Oxford University Press, 1934).

Weakland, J. H. Orality in Chinese conceptions of genitality. *Psychiatry*, 19, 237–248 (1956).

Whiting, Beatrice B. (ed.) *Six Cultures: Studies of Child Rearing* (New York: Wiley, 1963).

Whiting, J. W. M. Sorcery, sin, and the superego: a cross-cultural study of some mechanisms of social control. In *Nebraska Symposium on Motivation* (Lincoln, Neb.: Univ. of Nebraska Press, 1959), 174–195.

Whyte, W. H., Jr. The wife problem. In Winch, R. F., McGinnis, R., and Barringer, H. R. (eds.), *Selected Studies in Marriage and the Family* (New York: Holt, 1962), 111–126.

Wolf, A. The psychoanalysis of groups. In Rosenbaum, M., and Berger, M., *Group Psychotherapy and Group Function* (New York: Basic Books, 1963).

Wolfenstein, Martha, and Leites, N. *Movies: a Psychological Study* (Glencoe, Ill.: Free Press, 1950).

Zola, E. *Germinal* (New York: Dutton, 1948).

Zuckerman, S. *The Social Life of Monkeys and Apes* (New York: Harcourt, Brace, 1932).

Index

Abandonment, feeling of, 8 ff, 12–3, 18 ff, 39, 135
Aggression, fluidity of, 151
  and incorporation, 75–6, 76 fn
  and sexuality, 78–9
Alexander, F., 80
aloneness, *see* Abandonment
Ames, M. M., 220 fn, 222
Ancestor worship, 223
Apollodorous, 194
Authoritarianism, 241–2
Autotomy, 56–7, 58–9, 102

Bacon, F., 22
Bales, R. F., 26–7, 51–4, 119, 157
Baruch, D., 137
Battle of the sexes, 94–9, 245
Beckett, S., 17 fn
Bell, N. W., 56
Bellah, R. N., 222, 227–8, 230–3, 231 fn
Bennis, W. G., 3, 4, 9, 29 fn, 49–50, 80–1, 117, 134, 136, 143, 163, 163 fn, 185 fn, 238, 260, 264
Bettelheim, B., 162, 207
Bion, W. R., 112 fn, 120, 123 fn, 131–3, 135, 135 fn, 140, 163 fn, 169, 170, 181–2, 186, 189, 230, 259–60
Boas, F., 10, 217 fn
Boundaries, destruction of, 187, 219
  maintenance, 179–81, 182–3
  and tension, 179–80
  see also Differentiation
Boundary awareness, 135, 173–4, 175–6, 179, 195, 203, 220–3, 226–8, 232, 235, 249, 251, *see* also Differentiation

Brody, Sylvia, 9–10
Burton, R. V., 249

Campbell, J., 76, 91 fn, 192
Cannibalism, 60–75, 147
Caplan, G., 188–9
Cash, W. J., 78
Conformity, 131–2 fn

Darwin, C., 152
Dependency group, 131–2, 135, 182–3, 189–91, 195, 200
Deprivation, 7 ff, 106–7
Differentiation, 179, 187–8, 229–30, 237–41
displacement activity, 78 fn
Dollard, J., 78 fn
Dragon myth, 91 fn
Durkheim, E., 142, 148–9, 220 fn, 226, 242

Eisenstadt, S. N., 229
Envelopment, fear of, 204–5, 209, 215, 216, 217
Equality stage, 156–7, 159
execution of criminals, 81–2 fn
Ezriel, H., 7, 172

Father, 247, 249, 249 fn
Fauconnet, M., 17–8
Feiffer, J., 137
Ferenczi, S., 56, 58, 146, 201, 201 fn, 251 fn
Festinger, L., 74 fn
Fight-flight group, 131–2, 169, 170, 178, 179, 179 fn, 180, 181, 182, 187–8, 203, 204, 221–2

273